# PRIME-TIME BISHOP

# PRIME-TIME BISHOP

## Fulton J. Sheen and Religious Celebrity in America

ALEXANDER NACHAJ

McGill-Queen's University Press
Montreal & Kingston • London • Chicago

ISBN 978-0-2280-2644-0 (paper)
ISBN 978-0-2280-2645-7 (ePDF)
ISBN 978-0-2280-2646-4 (ePUB)

Legal deposit fourth quarter 2025
Bibliothèque et Archives nationales du Québec

Printed in Canada on acid-free paper that is 100% ancient-forest-free, containing 100% sustainable, recycled fibre, and processed chlorine-free.

This book has been published with the help of a grant from the Federation for the Humanities and Social Sciences, through the Awards to Scholarly Publications Program, using funds provided by the Social Sciences and Humanities Research Council of Canada.

Funded by the Government of Canada | Financé par le gouvernement du Canada | Canada

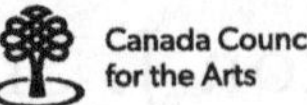

Conseil des arts du Canada

We acknowledge the support of the Canada Council for the Arts.

Nous remercions le Conseil des arts du Canada de son soutien.

McGill-Queen's University Press in Montreal is on land which long served as a site of meeting and exchange amongst Indigenous Peoples, including the Haudenosaunee and Anishinabeg nations. In Kingston it is situated on the territory of the Haudenosaunee and Anishinaabek. We acknowledge and thank the diverse Indigenous Peoples whose footsteps have marked these territories on which peoples of the world now gather.

---

Library and Archives Canada Cataloguing in Publication

Title: Prime-time bishop : Fulton J. Sheen and religious celebrity in America / Alexander Nachaj.

Other titles: Fulton J. Sheen and religious celebrity in America

Names: Nachaj, Alexander, author.

Description: Includes bibliographical references and index.

Identifiers: Canadiana (print) 2025021587X | Canadiana (ebook) 20250215888 | ISBN 9780228026440 (paper) | ISBN 9780228026457 (ePDF) | ISBN 9780228026464 (ePUB)

Subjects: LCSH: Sheen, Fulton J. (Fulton John), 1895-1979. | LCSH: Catholic Church – United States – Bishops – Biography. | LCSH: Fame – Religious aspects – Christianity. | LCGFT: Biographies.

Classification: LCC BX4705.S612 N33 2025 | DDC 282.092 – dc23

---

This book was designed and typeset by Peggy Issenman in 11.5/14 Adobe Garamond Pro. Copyediting by Zubin Meer.

McGill-Queen's University Press
Suite 1720, 1010 Sherbrooke St West, Montreal, QC, H3A 2R7

Authorized safety representative in the EU: Mare Nostrum Group BV, Mauritskade 21D, 1091 GC Amsterdam, the Netherlands, gpsr@mare-nostrum.co.uk

# Contents

# Acknowledgments

Time works differently for the living than it does for the dead.

In the fall of 2014, I was just beginning my doctoral research at Concordia University in Montreal, under the supervision of my long-time mentor Dr Donald Boisvert. I was thirty years old and assumed I knew everything about where the future was going. But then, unexpectedly, and multiple times, things changed.

Over the span of these past ten years, I lost my supervisor, Donald, and then his husband Gaston shortly afterward from the same illness. Dr Hillary Kaell took up the duties of becoming my supervisor and helped push my dissertation across the finish line. I travelled to Peoria to complete my archival research, returning home mere weeks before the COVID-19 pandemic shut down international travel. Outside academia, but not entirely apart from it, I fell in love and married one of my academic peers and closest friends. We bought a house and moved away from the city into the suburbs where I became the father of two girls who are as beautiful as they are curious about the world.

A decade ago, I was young and excited to be working on a figure whom I thought would surely become a saint before the time of my graduation.

However, it was also in late 2014 when I became aware of the first (of many) unexpected delays in Bishop Fulton J. Sheen's ongoing cause. First it was the Archdiocese of New York, having much to say about the matter of a body, and later it would be Rochester. While his cause still fights to move along, it's here that I'm reminded how the most eventful parts of the afterlives of the would-be saints, unlike those of their researchers, rarely unfold across years or even a single decade. In the distant past, it wasn't uncommon for centuries to pass between even the slightest sign of progress as generations of monastics worked tirelessly to promote the cause of their patrons. While we have come a long way from that past, we are not completely detached from it. Its lessons, complications, truths, imaginings, and words long since spoken have a way of staying with us, of affecting the present and those inhabiting it. As much as technologies of access, mass media, and communications have allowed us to expedite our modern world, they, too, hold things back where they once were not.

And so, the transformation from the mundane to the sacred remains a challenge, hoping to be understood by us researchers and those toiling through the years for the cause of the patron they adore. I do hope that Sheen one day finds his name listed among the saints, with this hope not coming from the position of a devotee, or even necessarily as a researcher, but perhaps more generally in the way a fan might want their celebrity idol to be recognized. Time will tell, and fortunately time is something of which those who have departed have no shortage.

For having helped make this work possible, I would like to acknowledge the support I've received along the way. First, I would like to thank Dr Hillary Kaell, Dr Marc Lafrance, and Dr Jane McGaughey for all the guidance and the brainstorming sessions during my doctoral studies that set me on the path toward this project. I'm also thankful to Elyse MacLeod for her keen editor's eye and Joseph E. Brito for all the afternoons at the pub when we should have been researching instead of venting. I would also like to thank Sister Lea Stefancova, FSJB, the archivist and curator for the Archives and Museum of the Diocese of Peoria, for showing me their collection and allowing me to peruse their uncategorized materials when I was there. I am also thankful to Shane MacDonald with the Catholic University Archives in Washington, DC, for having helpfully shared with me their digitized Sheen collections (of which I made great use during the COVID-19 lockdown). I would also like to thank my wife Dr Purna Roy, for having stuck with me throughout the writing of this book, and my daughters Misha and Anya for keeping me in the present.

# PRIME-TIME BISHOP

# INTRODUCTION

## The Busy Life, Many Names, and Numerous Intersections of Fulton J. Sheen

*It's almost 8:00 p.m. on a Tuesday night in America, back in 1952. The dinner table's been cleared, the dishes put away and dried, and the kids have already completed their homework. Like millions of other Americans, the whole family gathers in the living room and tunes their television set to the local station for the DuMont Network. They're just in time as the program cold opens to a brief musical composition along with a hand scrawling the letters JMJ along a blackboard. The camera turns, and gracing the screen is now the smiling, charismatic face not of television legend Milton Berle nor famed American singer-turned-actor Frank Sinatra, but instead a middle-aged Catholic bishop – the Monsignor Fulton J. Sheen, dressed in the full ceremonial regalia befitting his station as an aristocrat of the church. When the rapturous applause from the live studio audience finally dies down, he opens with his traditional greeting, addressing the audience as "friends" before segueing into a thirty-minute monologue on topics ranging from history, philosophy, and even the meaning of love. This staple of early television programming would go on to earn him an Emmy, television's most prestigious award, and cement his status as one of the nation's most well-known and beloved celebrities.*

### In the Beginning

The man who would become Fulton J. Sheen was born in El Paso, Illinois, on 8 May 1895, as Peter John Sheen. His parents, Newton and Delia Sheen, were Irish American Catholics in a predominantly Protestant rural community. Sheen's mother was devout while his father had, by the time of Sheen's birth, fallen away from the church and likely retained little more than a vestigial interest in Catholicism. They ran a modest hardware store in their local commercial strip until it – along with much of the surrounding El Paso business district – was destroyed by a fire, subsequently causing the family to relocate to nearby Peoria.[1] Sheen, the eldest of four boys in the family, was given the name Peter after his paternal grandfather. At some point during his childhood, Sheen either took or was given the name Fulton – his mother's maiden name.[2] Sheen would later make the shift more official when he took the name Fulton as his own during confirmation.[3] From that symbolically poignant moment on, Peter Sheen was no more, and Fulton Sheen would begin his long rise and eventual fall (and rise again) within the institutions of the American Catholic Church.

❍ ❍ ❍

The figure who stands at the centre of this work is Fulton J. Sheen, a twentieth-century American Catholic clergyman, bestselling author, and television personality. Although Sheen's life indeed plays a pivotal role throughout our story, the aim of this book is not biographical in nature, but rather seeks to present Sheen – his body, his identity, his career, and his fame – as a case study on how celebrity studies and masculinity studies both offer important theoretical supplements to the study of mid-century North American religion and specifically Catholicism. It is my conjecture that we cannot begin to properly understand the sanctity nor the religious appeal of major modern religious figures (of whom there are many) without also understanding their celebrity and engagements with wider culture made possible through emergent technologies and media of access. Television, radio, paperback publishing, magazines, and other mass media that became dominant over the past century have transformed the ways in which prominent Catholic figures like Sheen are encountered and understood by fans and devotees alike – as well as how these figures themselves construct, shape, and negotiate the expectations of their own sanctity. In other words, the modern saint is also the modern celebrity, and to understand them as either, we must approach them from both theoretical perspectives.

To a lesser extent, this work also examines how Sheen's religious celebrity continues to influence the lives of his American devotees to this day. While Sheen's earthly life came to an end in 1979, his presence continues to live on through episodes of his television series, in the pages of his books, in the devotional lives of those pushing for his canonization, and in his material remains. The secondary purpose of this work is thus to bring renewed attention to a prominent figure who – despite his own prominence as a mid-twentieth-century figure – remains to some extent on the fringes of academic discussions of American religion and celebrity.[4]

## Introducing Fulton J. Sheen

At the turn of the twentieth century, Sheen and his siblings attended a local parochial school, as was typical for Catholics growing up in rural areas. During his school years, Sheen was recognized as being bright and devout by his peers and teachers and eventually became his high school valedictorian.[5] At graduation, he earned a prestigious scholarship that could have secured his entrance into any university. However, at the urging of a mentor, he went instead to seminary in Saint Paul, Minnesota.[6] Ordained at age twenty-four, he was admitted to the Catholic University of America for his doctoral studies before transferring to the University of Louvain in Belgium.[7] There, he earned his doctorate in philosophy, followed by his post-doctoral *agregé* – a prestigious degree not typically awarded to Americans – which he earned with the highest distinctions.[8] After being temporarily recalled to Peoria to act as a parish priest, and so that his superiors could see whether the rising star was capable of following orders, Sheen received his dream posting as a faculty member at the Catholic University of America (CUA) in Washington, DC. Sheen would spend the next quarter of a century teaching philosophy and theology courses, while spending a significant portion of his time at promotional events for the faculty and away from the classroom, nurturing his already burgeoning celebrity status.[9]

It was during his time as a lecturer when Sheen experienced his first real taste of fame. Between 1930 and 1950, Sheen lent his vocal talents on a weekly basis to *The Catholic Hour* radio program, rapidly becoming their most popular personality where it is estimated that he garnered seven million regular listeners and received about six thousand letters a week. Largely avoiding politics and other matters that contributed to the rise and fall of other radio priests, such as Father Coughlin, Sheen spoke to his audience about everyday concerns and offered spiritual solutions. After his time on radio, from 1950 until 1966, he was made national director for Pontifical Missions Societies, notably helming the fundraising efforts for the national Society for the Propagation of the Faith (hereafter SPOF).

Shortly after having been made national director at the Mission, Sheen was approached by the National Council of Catholic Men to act as a host of a weekly television program they were devising for the ill-fated DuMont Network.[10] That initiative would culminate in *Life Is Worth Living*, a half-hour prime-time television show written and directed by and staring Sheen, where the bishop, with a minimal props and stage dressing, would speak about philosophical and spiritual issues in a manner accessible to the average American. The program was an unexpected success. At its peak, *Life Is Worth Living* reached a weekly national audience of roughly 20–30 million viewers,[11] and brought in so much revenue for his program's sole sponsor, Admiral appliances, that by the second season of his show they were sponsoring him to the tune of $1,000,000 per episode (which he consistently donated to the charitable efforts of the SPOF).[12] He also scored an audience rating of 23.7 by the American Research Bureau, which "was the highest ever recorded for anyone on TV in those pioneering years" among religious programs.[13] Sheen's program was so widely viewed and well received that he won a prime-time Emmy Award for "Most Outstanding Television Personality," pulled audiences away from Milton Berle's popular *Texaco Star Theater* – much to Berle's irritation – and caused Frank Sinatra's upstart *The Frank Sinatra Show* to end after a single season owing to poor ratings in the slot opposite Sheen's.[14]

Sheen's program ran to widespread acclaim on DuMont until the network's closure in 1955. The show was then picked up by ABC where it continued to be broadcast until the end of its run in 1957, when Sheen was arguably at the height of his popularity. Reasons for the sudden ending to the program were never publicly disclosed, yet it was almost certainly owing to a growing behind-the-scenes feud between Sheen and his benefactor, the powerful Cardinal Francis Spellman of New York.[15] Though television would continue to draw Sheen, and he would return to the screen several times in the years after *Life Is Worth Living* was pulled, he never again found the same level as success as during his heyday in the mid-1950s.[16]

Sheen continued to be active within the church after his departure from television. He attended and participated in several Vatican II sessions in Rome before being made Diocesan Bishop at Rochester – again, likely owing to the actions of Spellman. While Sheen arrived in Rochester with much fanfare – in part this was due to his enduring celebrity appeal, but also because he represented the promise of post–Vatican II change – his tenure was widely described as a failure. After three tumultuous years, he abruptly retired his post in 1969. In the final decade of his life, Sheen was made titular Archbishop of Newport in 1969 by Pope Paul VI, a largely symbolic appointment in recognition of his years of service. He spent some time as a mentor to fellow priests during a number of retreats and began composing his autobiography, *Treasure in Clay* (1979), before passing away in 1979 after a series of heart problems.

As is the case of many widely beloved figures within the church, Sheen's story didn't end with his death but continued to develop into his afterlife. While speculation about Sheen's possible canonization began shortly after his death, the first concrete steps were taken in 1998 when the Diocese of Peoria gave permission to the Archbishop Fulton J. Sheen Foundation to begin his formal cause for canonization. By 2008 their materials were submitted to the Vatican, and by 2011, thanks to their work, Sheen was declared a Venerable Servant of God. By 2014 his cause was proceeding steadily toward beatification, however several disruptions put the cause on indefinite hold. As of this writing in early 2025, his cause continues to be on hold with no clear indication as to when it will resume, nor what actions will be taken.[17]

## Theoretical Considerations

### *Mid-Twentieth-Century American Catholicism*

The mid-twentieth century was a time of transition for America and its Catholic citizens. After the conclusion to World War II in the nation's favour, a slew of government initiatives during the Truman and Eisenhower eras helped transform America's economic, social, and political landscapes. Legislation such as the GI Bill helped create unprecedented opportunities for America's young urbanites – including a disproportionate number of Catholics – allowing them to escape their overcrowded inner-city neighbourhoods and multi-family dwellings to attend college or trade school, take up white-collar work or start their own business, and ultimately relocate to the suburbs. While Catholics spent much of the first half of the century occupied with questions of place and identity, by the postwar period Catholics of European descent were rapidly assimilating into the American mainstream. By the 1950s many of the lingering prejudices against Catholics – such as the once-insidious spectre of "popery," the belief in a Catholic "fifth column," and the question of American Catholic allegiances – had largely been settled. Communism became the new catch-all boogeyman to embody America's persistent fear of the incomprehensible other, and Catholic Americans were eager to stand at the vanguard of the nation's ideological war with their geopolitical nemesis – all the while casually reminding Americans that they had been warning of the dangers of communism since the 1920s and 1930s.[18]

Postwar Catholicism is hardly a niche topic in the larger field of American religion, with scholars having produced a veritable canon of literature which has largely (and implicitly) focused on the experiences of Irish American Catholics.[19] Under a certain light, this was unavoidable: since the nineteenth century, the Irish in the United States have historically made up the largest Catholic communities by sheer numbers as well as influence. Irish Americans bishops have wielded enormous power over the development of the tradition in the United States and were largely responsible for building the nation's Catholic educational systems and other communal infrastructure. As such, Irish Americans have largely found themselves entrenched in American Catholic culture, with their own experiences becoming synonymous for the greater whole. This is never more evident than when encountering the oft-repeated trope in of "coming of age" metaphors frequently used in studies of mid-century American Catholicism – whereby Catholics, by virtue of their immigrant heritages, overcame their histories of difference and successfully assimilated into wider American culture.[20] Such narrative tropes are inherently built into the understanding of American Catholicism as immigrant Catholicism – and by extension, Irish American Catholicism. Of course, by virtue of focusing on the life of a particular Irish American Catholic, this work inevitably builds on the tradition of the "coming of age" metaphors.[21] However, my aim here is to problematize this traditional view, as the "coming of age" that interests me is not so much a story of immigrants integrating into society, but rather that of American Catholicism intersecting with American celebrity and media culture.

It should be noted that Sheen, by the 1950s, was by no means the first American Catholic celebrity – the American Irish had largely integrated themselves into Hollywood and the motion picture industry since the 1930s, producing no shortage of film stars such as Pat O'Brien, James Cagney, and Maureen O'Hara – nor was he the first explicitly *clerical* celebrity, as Father Coughlin's radio program entranced the nation earlier than Sheen's had.[22] However, it is my assertion that Sheen stands as the quintessential figure embodying the dual concerns of celebrity and sanctity owing to the progress on his current path toward canonization, the breadth of media he employed – including radio, television, and publishing – and the ways in which his celebrity has both expedited and complicated that very process of canonization. In this regard, the overlap of his celebrity and sanctity has not only transcended the popular appeal that he enjoyed during life his but continues to influence the very institutions of the church taking a part in dictating his afterlife.

## *Sanctity and the American Celebrity*

Methodologically and functionally, celebrities bear much in common with saints – something which numerous scholars continue to comment upon. Celebrities are the focus of adoration, have cults of devoted followers, can have their careers undergo resurrections, and are sometimes even referred to as "gods."[23] While these types of overlaps can be useful for some discussions, scholars should remain wary of directly transposing conceptual categories from one realm to the other and, moreover, avoid discussing celebrity as a possible replacement for religion or the cult of the saints.[24] Rather than argue that celebrities are a modern evolution of the saints or some other facile reading that overlooks the complexities of both concepts, it is more fruitful to remark that what both of these categories of being share is their reliance on charisma, personal magnetism, and the ability for the figures at the centre to influence emotional change in the people around them.[25] In this regard, Sheen's dual identities – as celebrity and would-be saint – intersect with his own charisma and presence, magnified not only by his virtuous life as a bishop but also through the lens of the camera as he was projected onto television screens across America.

Historically, technology was never a decisive factor in shaping and expanding the initial cults of the saints, nor was it necessary for sustaining the complex network of relationships that exist between a saint and their devotees. In the pre-modern era, word of mouth, personal encounters, or clerical authorization were the dominant factors in building up recognition for these figures, with the focus often falling on the miracles that were understood to have taken place in their presence.[26] However, mass media has the capacity to allow figures to become more widely known in a quicker period of time and also more widely accessible. This suggests that the construction of both celebrities and saints is closely related to the technologies of access available in a given society or historical context – whether it be word of mouth, pen and paper, or having one's eyes glued to the television screen on a weekly basis. For example, in a 2017 study, historian Andrea Graus explored several overlaps between celebrity and Catholic sanctity, by examining the cultic following of several female mystics in Europe at the turn of the twentieth century. In the case of these women, many of their devotees initially flocked to them based on the power of their *reputation*, rather than the traditional links of regional proximity, shared community membership, and so on. Graus remarks that the living saints in these cases functioned very closely to celebrities in that popular enthusiasm – rather than interpersonal relationships – built up and constructed their celebrated (and sanctified) identities, effectively allowing them to acquire a level of fame that could entice visitors from distant regions.[27] Discussing the means through which this was made possible, she highlights how the identity and reputation of saints in the modern era comes to be constructed differently than for saints in the pre-modern era, largely owing to the emergent and ongoing prevalence of mass communication.

While the mystics examined by Graus benefited from technology and media in spreading their renown beyond their geographic area, it was a process that was taken up by their devotees – that is to say, out of their hands. For Sheen, however, this was not the case: he was the primary actor in using technology to transmit his person beyond his stationing in Washington, the Archdiocese of New York, and elsewhere, first with radio, then with paperback books, and finally with television. While he was not the first priest to take to the radio (nor was he necessarily the most famous to do so, compared with Fr Coughlin), he nevertheless utilized the medium to great effect, connecting with millions of American listeners and becoming one of the most well-recognized figures in the American Catholic Church even before his television fame would later cement that status. In many respects, Sheen's sanctity is thus a product of the modern world and the media and technology available within it, with his own charisma certainly playing a role, seeing as much about Sheen fits the expectation and criteria for both American celebrity and Catholic sanctity.

The confluence of celebrity and sanctity in the modern world, while certainly novel, is perhaps not unexpected. After all, the word *celebrity* derives from the Latin nouns *celebritas* and *celebratio*, referring to the presence of a multitude or the gathering of a crowd. These words also point to the thing or presence giving rise to said crowds or multitudes – effectively the figure around which they rally. Celebrity is thus that which is out of the ordinary – not unlike sanctity itself, which at its heart refers to an act of demarcation, of being set apart. Where the mundane might go unnoticed, to be a celebrity is to be the focus of the crowd. The status of celebrity conveys on the person a level of visibility – to be suddenly seen by multitudes.[28] In this there is also an element of desire – a craving to encounter, be near, and see that which is being celebrated. Despite often hoping to be seen and acknowledged in return, those who gather nevertheless remain at a certain distance from the celebrated by virtue of being among their audience.[29] While celebrities come into being through the visibility of their actions, much like saints, the individuals who become celebrities are often only one among many agents proposing and sustaining their own star status.[30] In the case of celebrities, it is not cults, but managing agents, marketers, studios and audiences that play a role in the construction and maintenance of their celebrity and stardom.[31] Through their constituent parts, celebrities thus become complex and aggregated texts, the readings of which reveal not just the characteristics of the individual celebrity, but also much about the nature of celebrity as it is understood in a given culture by given audiences.

As such, celebrities can be understood as composite images patched together from carefully managed personas. They are, simultaneously, the person behind the screen, the person unseen by the cameras, and none of the above. The persona that appears on the screen is known to the public to be an act, a performance, about which we readily accept and agree to play along with. Yet, even when they leave their stages behind and appear on screen as themselves, the celebrity offers the audiences a performance of another, more subtle kind, even in their ostensibly private or personal lives. "Performance is a critical component in any public figure's identity," writes celebrity studies scholar P. David Marshall.[32] He goes on to state that "celebrities perform in their primary art form – as actors, musicians, singers, athletes – as well as the extra-textual dimensions of interviews, advertisements/commercial endorsements, award nights and premieres."[33] The celebrity never stops acting so long as they are under the public gaze. As such, their public persona as citizens is always a carefully managed act, one that fits and plays into the expectations of their audiences, providing just enough humanity behind the mask to make themselves relatable. Their public face is one that is highly mediated and refined, with blemishes on their skin or in their personal lives covered up by makeup and marketing. Celebrities do allow certain images from their private lives to be offered for public consumption, but each one is carefully selected in "order to construct and control a complete persona."[34]

Though Sheen held a tenuous relationship with his celebrity, he was not blind to its potential benefits with respect to his sanctified work – his celebrity provided him with certain opportunities with America's elites that might not otherwise have been available to the average priest. His celebrity granted him access to notable public figures such as Henry Ford II, columnist Heywood Broun, and politician Claire Boothe Luce, all of whom would eventually convert to Catholicism after one or more encounters with the bishop. Thanks to his national recognition, he was even able to secure meetings with organizers of the American Communist Party – Louis Budenz and Bella Dodd – who also renounced communism and returned to Catholicism shortly after. In *The Bishop Sheen Story* (1953), biographer James C.G. Conniff notes that Sheen was also a popular companion to Hollywood starlets of the day – notably Loretta Young and Irene Dunne, who both happened to be devout Catholics – with whom he was frequently seen going to brunch in New York.[35] Sheen was so inspiring and influential among fellow American Catholics that Martin Sheen – née Ramón Gerard Antonio Estévez – chose his surname for his acting moniker.[36] Indeed, historian Christopher Lynch has referred to Bishop Sheen as none other than "an aristocrat" in the church and in America itself.[37] Taken as a whole, these encounters demonstrate the ease with which Sheen moved through circles populated by many of the city's, if not the nation's, most affluent and influential.

This discussion reminds us that religion is neither separate nor detached from the cultures and contexts within which it operates. However, the ways in which it intersects and overlaps with concepts of celebrity and fame have often been overlooked by scholars of religion and celebrity studies alike. Nevertheless, celebrity studies, while still an emerging field compared with that of American religion, has been rapidly expanding its reach and scope from its niche origins. In the 2020 volume of *Celebrity Studies*, Lucy Bolton approached the perennial virgin/whore dichotomy of Mary Magdalene not from their usual points of departure but instead from the angle of a celebrity.[38] The intermixing of the spirituality and celebrity of Mother Teresa has also been the topic of several works, notably by Gëzim Alpion, who has also written about the conspicuous absence of spiritual icons being the focus of celebrity studies.[39] Nevertheless, where fame and celebrity studies continue to lag not only concerns religious icons but notably *male* religious celebrities, of which America has produced no shortage of in this past century. While America's Protestant preachers – such as Martin Luther King Jr, Billy Graham, or even Aimee Semple McPherson – may be the first to come to mind where religion and celebrity mingle, Catholics have been equally visible. Charles Coughlin, Tom Dooley, Thomas Merton, and Dorothy Day all stand out as well-known American Catholic celebrities whose fame is intricately bound with and cannot be detached from their religious identities – even if these intersections have drawn comparatively less attention from scholars than the case with Protestant figures.[40] While there is undoubtedly more work to be done on those figures, I would argue that Sheen, by virtue of having been an American television star as well as a famed radio host and bestselling author, granted him a level of visibility and even presence that rises above and beyond the others. That there has been no such study on his fame and its intersections with his sanctity strikes one as a major lacuna in understanding the crossover of religion and celebrity in mid-twentieth-century American culture.

### *Identity and American Masculinity*

In the same vein that Sheen cannot be understood without analyzing his celebrity, it would be impossible to discuss Sheen's career, identity, and body without also addressing his masculinity. As a celibate clergyman from a minority religious tradition, the ways in which his male identity was constructed and his body understood differed greatly from the expectations of mid-twentieth-century celebrities, not to mention the average American male, even if our analysis necessarily adheres to many of the same theoretical concepts.

The foundational canon of men's studies and masculinities is well established, largely rooted with the work of R.W. Connell's 1993 magnum opus *Masculinities*. Here, Connell argues against the wider cultural assumption that there is an immutable, fixed element of "true" masculinity – often rooted in the biological or somewhere deep inside a person's core – instead asserting that gender is primarily performative and not fixed in advance of social interactions.[41] Gender, as such, exist as a means of structuring social practices, which are organized hierarchically at the societal level. Dominating all such patterns of interaction is hegemonic masculinity, "the configuration of gender practice which embodies the currently accepted answer to the problem of the legitimacy of patriarchy, which guarantees (or is taken to guarantee) the dominant position of men and the subordination of women."[42] While some authors, such as Michael Moller and Eric Anderson have sought to either distance themselves from Connell's theoretical models or present new structures for understanding the operative patterns of masculinity at the societal level and in lived experiences, her arguments concerning masculinity as configurations of social practices continues to inform the theoretical underpinnings of virtually all endeavours in this field.[43]

Where studies of American masculinity are concerned, Michael S. Kimmel's 2006 *Manhood in America: A Cultural History* remains a pivotal text that provides a broad framework for understanding currents and patterns in masculinity particular to the United States as it underlined certain archetypal patterns and models of masculinity that have implicitly and explicitly informed American conceptions of manhood.[44] While the concept of "crisis" has been an oft-repeated adage about the state of masculinity in America, Kimmel, along with others such as Kathleen Starck and Russell Luyt, has successfully problematized that notion by pointing to the apparently cyclical nature of anxiety perceived to be manifesting itself in society.[45] Others, such as James Gilbert have further critiqued narratives of American masculinity for focusing on uniformity of experiences and overlooking the inherent diversity of experiences.[46] From the 1990s onward, there have also been several works – such as by Roger Horrocks and Susan Jeffords – which examined the intersection of American masculinities with popular culture.[47] Jeffords, in particular, isolated the ways in which the norms and expectations of *hard* masculinity – that is, patterns of masculinity hinging on demonstrations of strength, valour, and a rigidity of body and emotions – manifest themselves through popular culture at times of national crisis or instability.[48] Using films and popular culture as her primary sources, she demonstrates the overlapping reciprocity between national anxieties and anxieties about male bodies that occurred during the Cold War of the 1980s – a link which holds similarly true for conversations over nation and body in the mid-century setting of this work and which are discussed further in chapter 5.

In recent years, masculinity studies have intersected with studies of religion in the United States, often commenting upon how religious men's lives, bodies, and actions complicate or refigure traditional understandings – both academic and popular – of American manhood. Kristin Kobes Du Mez's *Jesus and John Wayne: How White Evangelicals Corrupted a Faith and Fractured a Nation* (2020), along with Kelly J. Baker's *The Gospel According to the Klan: The KKK's Appeal to Protestant America, 1915–1930* (2011), focus on the intersections of Protestant self-identity and ideals of hardened American masculinity. Twentieth-century American Evangelicalism was often infatuated with toughness, culminating in a mid-century rebranding that sought to prove Christianity was compatible with "red-blooded" American masculinity.[49] Popular figures such as Billy Graham preached for the necessity of maintaining traditional gender roles and patriarchal authority while themselves embodying these ideals as they performed to massive audiences in their live or televised sermons. For her part, Baker has demonstrated how even the KKK positioned itself as a means for white Protestants to become "manly" Americans in contrast to the suspicious others (which included Catholics) in their midst, offering men the tools and means to reclaim the societal dominance they felt entitled to.[50] What these studies both seem to suggest is that shared ideals of hard, patriarchal masculinity between Protestant and secular America and fears of effeminacy have been frequently close to the heart of white, heteronormative, Protestant self-identity and self-construction – often standing in contrast to the identities of Catholic men.

Fortunately, Catholic masculinities have not gone unnoticed in the study of American masculinities. However, as is the case with celebrity studies, American Protestants are more likely to be tied to the larger trends within the field and the nation, while Catholics tend to be read in more inward-looking and devotional focused contexts. We can see this in the recent work of religious studies scholar Alyssa Maldonado-Estrada, *Lifeblood of the Parish: Men and Catholic Devotion in Williamsburg, Brooklyn* (2020). Basing her ethnographic study of the male devotees of the Our Lady of Mount Carmel, she has signalled some of the ways in which traditionally understood "male practices" overlap and are at the same time devotional acts. Notably, going against the usual demarcation of male and female spaces along the public and private, the secular and the religious, she argued for the church as "a vital site for the making of masculinity," whereby men can simultaneously perform masculine behaviour (such as construction, carpentry, etc.) and devotional acts (adornment of icons, wearing costumes, preparations for ritual procession, etc.) in the same space.[51] The Catholic masculinity examined here is largely enacted at the local and intersocial levels by making actions and spaces simultaneously devotional and masculine. In effect, we can witness not only intersections but overlaps of religion and gender as these men embody both their masculinity by performing tasks and engaging in behaviours that align with the Catholic virtues of labour, charity, and physical austerities as well as the ideals of working-class/blue-collar masculinity. While Moldonado-Estrada's work insightfully bridges traditionally understood male actions with Catholic male devotional practices, it nevertheless continues to root Catholic masculinity within Catholic devotional contexts. This isn't to say that Catholic masculinity should be removed from all devotional elements of its enactment – far from it – but rather that there remains work to be done in bringing Catholic patterns of masculinity out of their devotional ghettos and into negotiation with wider patterns in the modern nation.

There has nevertheless been some work in recent years focusing on examining Catholic masculinity outside devotional spaces and activities – albeit focusing on priests, rather than the laity. Franklin Rausch and John C. Seitz highlight the versatility of clerical masculinity in wartimes – in these cases, on the battlefields of World War II and the Korean War.[52] Both authors note the adaptability of traditional clerical masculinity (coalesced as father figures, spiritual leaders, et al.) in these contexts and the ways in which priests can enact modified elements of *hard* masculinity. However, most of the theoretical literature on clerical masculinity continues to be rooted in the medieval period, such as with Andrew Holt and Ruth Mazo Karras.[53] Nevertheless, despite this temporal gap, I would argue that many of the same considerations and challenges of clerical masculinity – such as sexual abstinence versus sexual conquest, spiritual fatherhood versus biological fatherhood, non-violence versus violence, household authority versus spiritual authority – continue to inform the masculinity of priests to this day.

On the surface, the clerical masculinity embodied by Sheen in mid-century America in many ways clashes with the expectations of mid-century celebrity masculinity. Though he could match the television celebrities of his day in front of the cameras where charm and charisma were concerned, as well as living or embodying a certain sort of glamour behind the scenes, Sheen's personal asceticism and chastity put him at odds with the sexual voracity and habits of consumption that marked the private lives of his secular television celebrity peers, such as Milton Berle and fellow Catholic Frank Sinatra.[54] However, as is discussed in more detail in chapter 3, mid-century American celebrity was more diverse than its more hegemonic iterations would suggest, allowing the space for men like Sheen to not only inhabit but prosper. In addition, as is discussed in chapter 5, Sheen's clerical masculinity did not prevent him from negotiating some of the elements of *hard* masculinity that America often demanded either, and as such this study offers a contrasting understanding of hard masculinity in American religion as was proposed in the earlier mentioned studies by Du Mez and Baker.[55]

## Notes on Sources

In preparation for this book, I was able to work with numerous primary sources, many of which Sheen had a hand in creating either in part or entirely. First, I was able to review numerous episodes of Sheen's television show *Life Is Worth Living*, most of which are so widely available now that they can even be streamed through services such as YouTube. The majority of these videos on streaming platforms appear to have been posted from unofficial sources using digitized recordings from reruns on Catholic television in the 1990s, and then uploaded by viewers who could be counted variously (or simultaneously, in some cases) as fans and devotees of Sheen. The sheer volume of episodes uploaded, along with their views (many reaching into the hundreds of thousands), says something not only about the enduring popularity of the bishop among American Catholics, but also that new audiences continue to discover this figure to this very day.[56] While the manner of which he is discovered and the relationship formed between his mediated presence over YouTube and with live viewers would make for a fascinating project, such topics are unfortunately beyond the scope of this current work.

As Sheen was a multifaceted creator, my primary sources from Sheen himself also include several of his written works and bestselling paperbacks, the most extensive of which was Sheen's autobiographical work, *Treasure in Clay*, which features prominently in chapter 1. As a text that relies greatly on hagiographical tropes and skims many of the most important moments of his career, Sheen's autobiography comes across oddly at times, as more of a tall tale than an authoritative biography or even a celebrity tell-all. It should be noted, of course, that I supplemented my biographical research of the figure using secondary sources such as the critical academic biographies by Kathleen L. Riley, Thomas C. Reeves, and Lynch, as well as the two insider biographies published by Sheen's former assistant Daniel P. Noonan during Sheen's own lifetime.[57] Noonan's biographies, while often gossipy and intercut with numerous personal remarks from the author, act as intriguing documents owing to the dates of their composition (before and after he was fired by Sheen) and the discrepancies between the two works concerning their overall and highly subjective evaluations of Sheen's character.[58] Additional then-contemporary biographical sources I consulted include the initially serialized biographies put together by reporters Ken Crotty, C.G. Conniff, and Francis Sugrue.[59]

I also made extensive use of two archives that I was able to access before the start of 2020's global COVID-19 pandemic. The first was the CUA's, which I accessed during 2019 and 2020. Their substantial collection contains items ranging from notes taken by Sheen while at the University of Louvain, press clippings from the 1950s and beyond, documents of his from Vatican II and similar effects, all of which are currently digitized and made available through an online portal the archivist shared with me. The second archive was at the Archbishop Fulton Sheen Museum in Peoria, Illinois, where I spent a week in

January 2020. On site, they have a modest museum with a number of Sheen's personal effects on display along with two uncategorized boxes of clippings. I had also petitioned the Diocese of Rochester in 2019 with the hope of accessing their archives. However, my request was never answered.[60] For my theoretical and methodological considerations, a more detailed list of theoretical works are provided in the introductions of each chapter below.

## Chapter Outlines

Each of the five chapters in this book cover one of the salient aspects of Sheen's identity, output, and body. At the same time, each chapter is also an investigation into the wider implications of these themes and trends in mid-century American Catholicism and one or more intersecting disciplines, including but not limited to celebrity studies, masculinity studies, and Irish studies.

In chapter 1, I focus on Sheen's posthumously published autobiography *Treasure in Clay* as a primary source for investigating intersections of religious hagiography and celebrity biography. Using the conventions of the hagiographical genre, Sheen composed a novel document ostensibly providing readers with a "tell-all" of his life, albeit one that was carefully constructed to emphasize his sanctity and downplay his celebrity. Paradoxically, it was his own celebrity and the need to control his persona and "brand" that likely led him to crafting such a sublimated tale of his life in the first place. As such, a serious examination of this text cannot be adequately undertaken without considering Sheen's celebrity, and by foregrounding celebrity as a category of analysis within the examination of this work, I posit that we can deepen our understanding of the ways in which such texts employ hagiographical tropes and demonstrate potential (auto-)hagiographical intent by their authors.

Chapter 2 revolves around Sheen's still-unfolding afterlife, concentrating on his cause for canonization and the regional rifts in American Catholicism it has helped expose. Using coverage from recent events, I outline how Sheen's eventful and often problematic canonization process reveals a remarkably visible and ongoing divide between urban and rural Catholic interests in America. Notably, I position his canonization process as the latest iteration of a tug of war between centre and periphery that has been ongoing since the first half of the twentieth century. As authors such as Jeffrey Marlett and David S. Bovée observe, rural Catholics have faced separate challenges in terms of visibility and identity than their urban counterparts, often focusing on initiatives that root their spiritual identities to the land.[61] Largely rural, Peoria's efforts to reclaim Sheen's body mirror wider concerns of rural Catholics who have often struggled for visibility in the larger whole. There are subtle yet persistent efforts on their part to reclaim Sheen's identity, rooting him in his Midwestern upbringing as opposed to his career in New York. In doing so, Peoria has also reimagined Sheen's sanctity and their own relationship to it. Such considerations serve as a reminder of the diversity of the Catholic experience in America, as well as its often-hidden rivalries that in this case became exposed owing to the urgency and visibility around his status as a potential celebrity saint.

Chapter 3 hones in on Sheen's celebrity and fame as a television star, placing him in context of the Golden Age of Television that coincided with a so-called religious "revival" in 1950s America.[62] Authors such as Michele Rosenthal and Erin A. Smith comment on how the development of new media and media guidelines enabled a new generation of religious leaders – whom I refer to as "celebrity preachers" – in reaching greater audiences than ever before.[63] I posit that Sheen's celebrity must be understood within the context of the advent of television as a medium of access that hinges on familiarity and the approachability of their message, while connecting this popularity to the rise of fellow celebrity preachers who rose to superstardom in America during this era. Though clerical figures seldom make for celebrities in wider culture, Sheen's made-for-television persona, along with his so-called easy religion that focused on temporal concerns, helped him bridge the gap between religious and secular modes of celebrity. Ultimately, this suggests that when considering mid-century religious celebrity, the rubrics we have for understand both religious figures and celebrity figures are inadequate and call for a blended definition to redefine its possibilities.

Chapter 4 examines the visual history of Irish American priests in American entertainment and how Sheen's television appearances, while novel, were also very much indebted to the visual repertoire and language that was cultivated by Hollywood a generation prior. As demonstrated by Irish and film studies historians such as James T. Fisher and Christopher Shannon, popular films from the 1930s to the 1940s – such as 1944's *Going My Way*, 1938's *Angels with Dirty Faces* and *Boys Town* – not only depicted priests and safe and charismatic figures in an era of Catholic suspicion, but also helped create a framework of expectations for a priestly celebrity persona.[64] Though Hollywood in the 1950s had begun depicting priests in a more complicated, nuanced manner that challenges any linear reading of this history, such as with the character Father Pete Barry in 1954's *On the Waterfront*, the familiarity and friendliness of television as a medium helped prevent Sheen from becoming a complete anachronism, even if his style was very much a throwback. As such, Sheen's celebrity persona can be understood as being part of a larger tradition of Irish American priests in visual media that was then reconfigured to the demands and expectations of the small screen.

In Chapter 5, I shift my focus primarily to the bodies of men and the ways in which those bodies stand in vicariously for ideological and spiritual concerns. Jeffords has demonstrated how the popular and political culture of the Cold War era linked the perceived "hardness" of men's bodies with the strength of the nation and its ideologies, whereas "softness" was seen as dangerous, suspicious and ultimately detrimental to the defence of the nation both physically and ideologically.[65] Though her work is focused on the 1980s, I demonstrate how the same hard/soft dichotomy and fascination for the bodies of the nation's leading men was present in 1950s America and can be seen as a particularly Catholic response to the Cold War. Reading the bodies of two men – Fulton J. Sheen and fellow Midwestern Catholic Joseph R. McCarthy – I reveal how these men were both perceived to embody hardness that could stand up to the nation's geopolitical opponents. Sheen, however, as a sanctified person, further reconfigured traditional understandings of hardness, emphasizing its necessary spiritual component. As such, this examination reveals an overlooked element of Catholic bodily responses to the Cold War and communism whereby the bodies of its celebrities can be read to stand in for the strength of the nation.

Ultimately, what I aim to convey by the end of this work is that not only is Sheen a figure worthy of more attention in the contemporary field of American religion, but also that examinations of figures such as this and the societies which produced them necessitate that we take a cross-disciplinary approach to our studies. As such, a similar lens examining the intersections of religion, celebrity, and gender in the bodies of famous figures, along with their complications, that I am proposing here can readily be applied to other celebrated Catholic (and non-Catholic) religious figures of the twentieth century who have yet to become the subjects of similar undertakings.

# 1

# Auto-Hagiography and Authenticity

## Treasure in Clay *and the Celebrity Biography*

> Let it be said here at the beginning, that this is not my real autobiography. That was written twenty-one centuries ago, published and placarded in three languages, and made available to everyone in Western civilization.
>
> Archbishop Fulton J. Sheen, *Treasure in Clay*, 1

## Celebrity and Sanctity

Celebrity has a way of being cumbersome. Never created nor sustained by the figure in question alone, it has a highly crafted and negotiated status. It is also fickle – the prestige of the celebrated waxes and wanes over the course of their careers, with their bodies, lives, and interests subjected to higher levels of scrutiny than that of their mundane peers. Within the Catholic tradition, celebrity has often functioned as something of a paradox wherever sanctity is concerned. Although fame and charisma are often the very vehicles that drive a candidate for sainthood's popular acclaim – that is, the initial drive from the masses giving fuel to their cause for canonization – scholars such as Nathalie Heinich, Andrea Graus, and Gëzim Alpion point out how fame has the tendency to be viewed with suspicion by the wider institutions of the Catholic Church, with charisma and gravitas often seen as things needing to be reared in, reconfigured, or even disrupted.[1] In this regard, modern sacred figures – particularly owing to developments in telecommunications and mass media – find their lives intersecting more broadly with matters of contemporary fame and celebrity than their ancient peers, a development that, one should add, comes with an added set of complications.

Such complications are well displayed in the story of Fulton J. Sheen and have led to no small shortage of delays in his canonization process.[2] Sheen was certainly aware of the complicating factors of sanctity interwoven with his own celebrity, as is partly evidenced by his long-standing practice of self-deprecation and humility whenever the subject of his fame and celebrity was raised in his presence. This awareness is, however, most prominently negotiated in his 1979 posthumously published autobiography, *Treasure in Clay*.[3] Here, Sheen distances himself from his celebrity in an often direct and purposeful manner, spending only a handful of pages discussing the aspects of career – namely, his television shows and radio programs – which made him a household name in mid-twentieth-century America and gave him a recognizability that continues even to this day. Instead of embracing his celebrated career, he pushes the reader toward his energies spent elsewhere, such as as a missionary and a mentor to fellow priests while also drawing attention to aspects of his work and life within the church that would normally be but footnotes in the context of those aware of his larger persona.[4] This move takes him and his autobiography away from the classic tell-all biography so commonly associated with celebrities in their later years hoping to settle the record or achieve one final shot at relevance, resulting instead in a text that is both implicitly and explicitly indebted to the tropes, structure and expectations of *holy writing* – making it part of a genre of literature better referred to as *auto-hagiography*.[5]

The principal discussion of this chapter therefore sheds light on a hitherto largely undiscussed phenomena in modern Catholic autobiography – the intersection of sanctity and celebrity. First, this chapter explores the usage of hagiographic tropes in autobiographical literature, focusing on Sheen's autobiography, *Treasure in Clay*, as a case study. The structure and methodology of this chapter at times mirrors that of a close reading; however, my aim is to highlight where it differs from other forms of biographical matter. My interest is not to retrace or piece together an "authentic" or "complete" biography of Sheen – such pursuits are the work of biographers and devotees alike.[6] Rather, my purpose here is in examining some of the ways in which Sheen's autobiography can be viewed as a carefully crafted and tightly controlled narrative work of modern auto-hagiography.

Scholar Robert Bartlett remarked that hagiography is a genre built on trope, convention, and expectation.[7] All works of the genre follow a structure first charted out in the Gospels and reproduced faithfully throughout history, from antiquity to the present day, and as narrative works, hagiographies record and recount the stories of lives deemed to be sacred and worth remembering with specific purpose and intent.[8] While Sheen's text contains numerous hagiographical tropes, I will focus on the three in particular that I believe to be illustrative of his intentions, namely: the demarcation of childhood; trials, tribulations, and suffering; and the prophetic calling. I hope to illustrate how Sheen, in implementing these conventions into his biographical narrative, sought to reshape the image of his life as free from blemish and devoid of vanity – the latter being a failing that has been frequently been ascribed to his person by detractors.[9] Additionally – by examining the often apocryphal and contradictory passages from Sheen's autobiography – I argue that he composed a novel document, one that tells not only of his life as he wished it to be viewed, but a tale that necessarily also speaks to the precarious relationship between sanctity and celebrity in modern American Catholicism. For instance, In the opening chapter of *Treasure in Clay*, Sheen seems to comment on the dangers of celebrity, its connection to vanity, and the resulting perception, when he remarks, "Generally, the more we accept popular estimates, the less time we spend on our knees examining conscience. The outer world becomes so full of limelight as to make us forget the light within. Praise often creates in us a false impression that we deserve it."[10] With this in mind, it is my intention to demonstrate that a text such as this adds both a layer of depth and complication to the study of modern American sainthood and the memories of saints' lives, whereby the would-be saint must navigate the dangers of celebrity while also being bound by its constraints.

To be clear, while I am not arguing that Sheen sought to actively promote himself as a living saint, I do assert that his invocation of hagiographic tropes was a conscious and intentional choice. After all, Sheen was an avid and well-documented perfectionist, someone who, throughout his career, actively and selectively controlled which elements of his life would be made public. He seems to have been all too aware of how certain aspects of his fame could complicate his memory – both among church insiders and the wider public. In the same manner that Sheen acted as a gatekeeper of sorts to his public image throughout his career, by composing a definitive "autobiography" he sought to present his life in a manner which was free from controversy and speculation.[11] The end result is that Sheen almost completely avoids the conventions of the modern celebrity autobiography, instead composing a text that selectively details his life in the familiar manner of a classical hagiography. As such, a close reading of Sheen's autobiography reveals his attempts to mitigate the tension between his life as a celebrity and as a role model for fellow Christians.

## Biography, Hagiography, and Auto-Hagiography

Hagiography is not biography. While the modern celebrity biography seeks to illuminate the nature and historical truth of the figure in question – often seeking to communicate openness and authenticity – hagiography is instead concerned with expounding upon truths of a largely spiritual nature, taking the exceptionality of the figure in question as the vehicle for such exploration.[12] In doing so, hagiographies often avoid the wholesale chronicling of the central figure's life from birth to death, instead focusing on the pivotal moments that demonstrate the figure's sanctity, the raison d'être for the text.[13] While both birth and death bookend the story of the saint, it is much more pressing that the stories offered are thematically cohesive and present the image of the saint as they are intended to be conveyed, as well as never forgetting to glorify God's role in having singled out the figure in question.[14]

Auto-hagiography differs from traditional hagiography, and indeed my usage of the term differs slightly from its historical use. Historically, the *vitae* of holy men and women as definitive texts and accounts of figures' sanctity were the products of their communities of devotees, the authors of these works often hailing from the same holy order or composed on commission.[15] In the majority of cases, then, the central hagiographic figure is without any agency when it comes to deciding how the narrative takes shape – they are, in effect, muted by having no hand in the composition. However, this is not to suggest that hagiographical authors are keen to highlight their own role in the production of the text: they often write anonymously, and in cases where their authorship is not anonymous, they also typically debase themselves to avoid overshadowing the saint in question.[16] Auto-hagiography, such as Augustine of Hippo's *Confessions* or Thérèse of Lisieux's *Story of a Soul*, by contrast, reverses the traditional hagiographical model in that the central figure acts as both author and subject. Largely acting alone in the shaping of their image, the auto-hagiographer thus becomes the *authentic* voice of their own narratives, which – given the hagiographical focus on sanctity – is itself very much a departure from the historical composition of *vitae* by third parties.[17]

Additionally, while traditional hagiography is explicit in its intentions and structures about promoting the life of the figure in question, auto-hagiography necessitates a more measured approach, replete with caution and subtlety. For though the pursuit of holiness is intended to be the aim of every God-fearing Catholic, sanctity is something that is recognized from without, a recognition declared by popular acclamation rather than personal admission. Self-promotion is strictly forbidden, and an excess of pride is itself the death knell for any potential cause for canonization. This is even more pressing in the case of modern auto-hagiography than its ancient antecedents, as a figure's fame has the capacity to be far more widely known and received thanks to the diverse possibilities of mass media. And so, in the same vein that a modern celebrity often carefully manages their own brand, so, too, must the auto-hagiographer exert tight control over their narrative and self-representation to avoid aggrandizing their life and deeds or seem to be revelling in their acclaim – in other words, the modern auto-hagiographer must often distance themselves very things which likely made them celebrated figures in the first place. As such, auto-hagiography is highly demonstrative of the complicated relationship and balancing act between modern celebrity and Catholic sanctity.

## Celebrity Ordinariness and Authenticity

Ordinariness along with authenticity are valuable currencies for modern celebrities looking to connect with their audiences, particularly in biographical material and moments of sharing and openness with their fans.[18] The case is as true for secular celebrities as it is for sanctified ones. To take one example, in his study on Tom Dooley, Historian James T. Fisher highlights how questions of authenticity also factored into Dooley's self-figuring as well as his legacy – including competing voices interested in reconstructing the supposedly "real" Dooley behind the celebrity figure. Dooley was hardly ignorant of his own celebrity, nor was he ignorant of the perks and complications it brought about. While engaging in lifelong and "manic self-promotion," Dooley sought, on camera and in writing, to portray himself naturally – as just another American – to his fans and devotees back home, engendering familiarity and curating his "ordinariness."[19] However, his early post-death biographers embellished his life, highlighting elements they found extraordinary, effectively dabbling in what Fisher refers to as nothing less than "hagiography."[20] These glowing works underlined not just his perceived virtues but also his celebrity status, whereby many of his proponents positioned him as being a "wholesome alternative" to other young American figureheads such as Elvis Presley.[21]

*Treasure in Clay* shows Sheen on similar footing where the leveraging of authenticity and ordinariness against his own celebrity and sanctity are concerned, albeit with an added urgency missing from Dooley's own biographical material. Notably, scholar Mark McKenna has remarked how late career stars often seek to reclaim their lost cultural and economic value by either reinventing themselves or remarketing their brand as their "true" or "real" self to their audiences.[22] While the celebrity biographer leverages these concepts to appear relatable and thereby combat their waning relevance, Sheen (writing his biography in the years just before his death) leverages them a bit differently – not in the service of staying relevant, but rather in the service of mitigating the tension between celebrity and sanctity that might otherwise complicate his hagiographical narrative. For instance, Sheen was a meticulous perfectionist who carefully controlled what aspects of his life became public. Aware of how the complications of fame could shape his legacy, both within the Church and beyond, he deliberately sought to distance himself from it.[23]

The result of the above exhortation is that Sheen almost completely avoids the conventions of the modern celebrity biography, along with its conventions for authenticity and ordinariness, instead composing an autobiographical text that largely details his life in the manner of classical hagiography and its manner of approaching the subject. However, the fact that he does employ these hagiographical conventions to control his narrative can be read itself as an act of celebrity performance and brand management. And so, paradoxically, to distance himself from his celebrity, Sheen must rely on the expectations and tools of modern celebrity.

## Auto-Hagiography

### *Trope One – The Demarcated Child*

The demarcation of children from their peers is a common convention in hagiographical literature. Since the episode from the Gospel of Luke showcasing Jesus teaching in the temple, hagiographers have sought to portray the noticeable *difference* inherent in their protagonists from an early age.[24] As Aviad Kleinberg remarks, "'Sanctity' implies separation, demarcation. When a thing is sanctified, it is separated from other things belonging to the same category."[25] In this case, it is a separation of the special from the mundane, where the protagonist's demarcated childhood reveals their chosen nature. In many cases – whether it be Christ himself or a pious early twentieth-century schoolboy – childhood is depicted as proof of God's miraculous presence in this world and often signals the protagonist's future greatness and place in God's larger plans and as role models for believers. To take one example, the nineteenth-century saint, Thérèse of Lisieux, spoke extensively of her childhood calling and obstacles to that calling in her posthumously published autobiography, which Pope Pius X referred to as a model for how *all* Catholics – and not simply the young – should practise their faith.[26] Inversely, just as there are saints with exceptionally pious childhoods, there are an equal number who are portrayed as being in conflict or opposition with the virtuous people they would become. The pre-conversion lives of ancient saints such as St Jerome and St Augustine are well attested in hagiographic literature, while the trope continues to be applied in the modern area.[27] For instance, the Blessed Bartolo Longo (d. 1926) was raised Catholic but turned to Spiritualism and Occultism, ostensibly going as far as becoming something of a Satanic priest, before returning to the faith of his childhood.[28] Hagiographical stories such as these emphasize the transformative powers of the cross and serve to be contrasted with the future ascetic discipline and devoted life these figures later adopt.[29] The trajectory of their personal transformation thus highlights their initial fallen state and hints at their future glorification and perfection available only through Christ and the church.[30]

In the case of *Treasure in Clay*, Sheen makes frequent narrative use of childhood demarcation, deploying it in a number of sometimes contradictory ways in the first half of his autobiography. Right from the first pages, Sheen avows that he was hardly a perfect child and was someone who very much needed refinement to overcome his baser nature and better himself. Calling attention to the title of his book, he metaphorically refers to himself as a lump of clay in need of shaping, emphasizing his parent's conviction that a strong education was to be the "determining mold" of his upbringing.[31] As Sheen recounts it, while all his siblings enrolled at the local parochial school in Illinois, it was he, an unruly and troublesome youth, who was most in need of being moulded into something greater. He remarks that he was once locked in a closet by a teacher as a disciplinary measure, and also that he once stole geraniums from the local grocery store and was harshly reprimanded for it afterward.[32] He further avows to being no stranger to horsing around as a child, having on occasion broken windows on the family home while playing ball in the yard. In another instance he remarks that he never earned one word of praise from his parents, and also that he constantly "struggled" to be a leader in class.[33]

Indeed, in Sheen's telling, he was very much a ball of rough clay in need of refinement, which certainly demarcated him from his peers and even his own siblings who were better grounded than him. However, for every instance where he highlights his unruly behaviour, he follows with either an ambiguous or contradictory story that upends his own self-deprecating recollection. For example, Sheen states that he had difficulty spelling and couldn't figure out how to use the word "which" – however, when discussing his participation in a spelling contest, he avows that he lost *first place* rather than being eliminated in one of the initial rounds.[34] In pointing out how he failed at a mathematics contest later on in high school, he recounts that he only stumbled when it came to a tie-breaking problem for the top marks in the class.[35] In examples such as these, Sheen seems to be attempting to portray his childhood as demarcated in both senses common to hagiographical literature – as the child in need of refinement and as the exceptional child who was chosen for greater things.

In this manner, Sheen's recollections of, and musings about, his childhood appear to be at odds with those of his teachers and peers – recounted by other biographers – who remember the young man as having been particularly bright and pious.[36] Indeed, the historical record (along with details from his own recollection) suggest that Sheen was an avid student and overachiever from the start.[37] Not only was he the valedictorian of his high school class, he also won a national scholarship competition that would have allowed him to enter virtually any university of his choice – examples that point to Sheen's early academic potential. However, on the advice of his debate coach (who also happened to be a local parish priest), Sheen declined his university scholarship to enter the Saint Paul seminary in Saint Paul, Minnesota. In doing so, Sheen effectively eschewed the prestige that entering a secular institution could have afforded his academic career in lieu of a humbler and ultimately more pious education.[38]

Sheen's clumsy attempts to paint himself as an underachieving, undeserving child while also being exceptionally devout may come across as puzzling for the more attentive reader, especially when his work is read as a celebrity autobiography. As noted earlier, celebrity autobiographers often try to relate to their readers by leveraging concepts of authenticity, closeness, and ordinariness against their more exceptional qualities and achievements.[39] As the celebrity's fame hinges upon the creation and sustenance of a highly crafted persona and brand, leveraging such concepts acts to impose "coherence and stability on a fluid and perhaps incoherent identity while engendering a belief in a private 'real' behind the public facade."[40] Taken at face value, then, one might wonder how Sheen's contradictory assertions play toward the coherence and authenticity of his character – especially as he himself is author of this work.

Sheen's childhood recollections nevertheless serve clearer hagiographical purposes. As stated previously, hagiographers have often extended the theme of demarcation beyond emphasizing sanctity, employing it as a wider trope to single out the uniqueness of their protagonist. By following suit, Sheen plays with some obvious symbolism: he emphasizes his rowdy, salt-of-the-earth upbringing as he remembers it while contrasting these themes with his later spiritual education at seminary and beyond.[41] Though he touches upon elements of his burgeoning scholasticism, structurally, Sheen appears to be more focused on depicting a mundane childhood upbringing, one that can be contrasted with his eventual recognition and celebrity. While his efforts are not entirely successful, by attempting to paint his childhood as one that was both unremarkable and ordinary, Sheen is clearly attempting to shape his narrative more closely to this hagiographical trope, foreshadowing the transformative trajectory his own life would take thanks to his devotion to Christ – and, in doing so, avoid sounding like a braggart by lingering too much on his early accomplishments or piety.

In his discussions of his youth, Sheen also recounts one episode that mirrors a gospel story. Recounting his days as a doctoral student, he states that the most brilliant professor he had ever known, a certain Dr Leon Noel, advised him to read the works of, and then meet, a recently published scholar cryptically named Dr Alexander. After being invited for tea, Sheen discovered that Dr Alexander had actually set up a debate between himself and the plucky grad student in a massive auditorium in front of hundreds of students. Though Sheen avows that he was clearly out of his depth compared with the professor – as he states, he "did not yet have [his] doctorate" – he nevertheless accepted the debate and openly challenged the professor's views.[42] When Dr Alexander responds by retorting that Sheen had failed to "read [his work] with any degree of intelligence," Sheen goes on to deconstruct the professor's work point by point and elaborate on the flaws of its arguments in full view of the audience.[43]

While this episode hints at the prowess of Sheen's scholastic mind and builds up to his eventual – and highly decorated – thesis defence and graduation, it is also a clear moment of auto-hagiography, mirroring the gospel episode where Jesus as a youth enters the temple with his parents and astonishes everyone when he sits among teachers listening and asking questions.[44] While Sheen is certainly older than Jesus was during the gospel event, the young scholar is nevertheless contrasted against the brilliant teacher he sought to emulate. Like Christ who revealed an uncanny intellect and awareness and was able to teach the teachers, Sheen not only matches the mind of the professor, but also seems to understand his own works better than the man himself. In this episode, Sheen thus seems to have found a way to envision a novel reimagination of the biblical story in a way that fit seamlessly into his own recollections.

Such stories of his upbringing signal that Sheen was cautiously aware of the weight of his fame and the complications it could have, by seeming too much like an overachiever while playing it up with a wink and a nod to his future success. Notably, in one story that provides a clear contrast with his later expertise in public speaking, he avows that he was unable to properly recite the rosary on stage at school because he was too nervous and uneasy under the public gaze.[45]

In another, he tells us that as a young school boy he utterly lacked the chops to become an actor, even though he had "excellent training in Shakespeare" – ultimately arguing that the fault for inadequacy lay with him.[46] As such, he was only barely able to earn a role in the school play, and this was owing to the financial support his family was giving to the project. He even recounts that three of his more talented (and unnamed) classmates later went on to become famous radio personalities – and perhaps there was a fourth talent at that school, but only "if the reader is charitable."[47]

It goes without saying that anyone reading *Treasure in Clay* would be familiar with the much-celebrated television and radio career of its author.[48] However, by his recollection, he was hardly a man qualified to become a celebrity, but one enabled through happenstance and God's transformative power. Such self-deprecation is of course a common rhetorical strategy, hardly absent from the hagiographic genre, to invite sympathy from the reader and deflect any accusations of pride and vanity on the part of the author.[49] By downplaying any latent talents, training or skills he might have acquired as a youth that would hint at his future success, Sheen is effectively suggesting to his readers that his transformation from performance-shy youth to star adored by millions had little to do with his own agency and was nothing short of miraculous – making himself, as a devout man, the site of God's transformative work in the world. Sheen's self-deprecation thus follows this tradition but also finds itself mandated by the baggage his celebrity entails. In this regard, his self-abasement acts as a form of authenticity, allowing for closeness and a sense of ordinariness to emerge in his manuscript all the while keeping himself at a respectful distance.[50] And so, the performance of ordinariness helps give his readers a sense of his projected "real self" and seeks to obscure the performance of celebrity control and brand management he is in fact enacting.

### *Trope Two – Trials, Tribulations, and Suffering*

Opposition to saints is a benchmark element of hagiographical narratives. In the hagiographical tradition, opposition serves to highlight how the saints have been singled out from their peers for a higher purpose – one that they might not understand but that is ultimately demanded by God.[51] Of these, the most common marks of saintly suffering are those inflicted on the body. Physical illness and injury form a bridge through the flesh to the soul, allowing for more direct identification, emulation, and connection with Jesus as the first and most emblematic of all sufferers, and then with every holy model since.[52]

While discussing his childhood and youth, Sheen claims to have been consistently sickly – and even tuberculotic – without even realizing it. He recounts how some "thirty or forty years" after his youth, he was taken to a hospital after collapsing during his radio show. There, he was informed by a doctor about the true extent of his medical history, something he had apparently been unaware of as he suffered silently throughout the years.[53] On a similar note he also recounts how he developed and suffered from ulcers when he began seminary – one of which was so severe that it required he undergo surgery.[54] Childhood illness like these, and tuberculosis in particular, frequently appear in hagiographical literature.[55] On the one hand, they serve to further the theme of childhood demarcation where the youthful saint is separated from their peers owing to the illness of their body. However, the almost ritual disempowering of the body here, like in other hagiographical material, is in fact a reversal. By placing the body and its ravages front and centre in the narrative qualification of sainthood, suffering and illness point toward self-mortification, of disciplining the flesh to bow to the spirit.[56] By extension, the ongoing fascination with suffering through the bodies of the saints reflects the earlier, ancient suffering of the martyrs and Christ himself.[57] In other words, life-threatening ailments act to collapse the space separating their era from the glorified Christian past, reminding the devout of the ongoing possibilities for elevation and the potential for sanctity that only suffering affords.[58] In the American context, Robert Orsi has remarked on the prominent role illness played for mid-century American Catholics in understanding their own exceptionality, stating that "pain [had] the prominent character of a sacrament," and suffering revealed the almost "thrilling" mark of divine favour.[59] The community of the saints is therefore very much a communion bound by pain and physicality, and Sheen subtly focuses on his own body to align his narrative with these saintly role models.[60]

Suffering doesn't only occur in the physical sense, and Sheen extends it along with the wider theme of demarcation during two notable moments of his adulthood. The first of these is during his tenure as a lecturer at the CUA in Washington, DC. The historical record suggests that, although Sheen was an enduring fixture at the university, he was frequently at odds with his peers and the administration, his willfulness and strong ideas causing him to butt heads more than once. In recounting his tenure, Sheen describes himself as having been branded an "outcast" almost immediately into his posting.[61] He suggests that he faced opposition among his fellow members of the Faculty of Theology after advocating for changes that would reinvigorate the faculty, but which were strongly opposed by his colleagues and the rector.[62] In another incident, the succeeding rector decided that all professors in the Faculty of Theology needed to have a Doctorate of Divinity under their name to continue teaching.[63] One of the popular professors, a certain John A. Ryan, did not have this credential, and a document circulated demanding that he be removed from his post. Sheen refused to sign it, feeling it was "unfair." However, soon after he found himself punished for his stance by having his classes suspended. To make matters worse, while Sheen swears that he stood by Ryan, a "rumour" circulated that Sheen had been the one to oppose Ryan and spoke to the rector about removing him from his post in the first place. The end result saw Sheen feeling ostracized by his peers as well as the colleague he sought to defend.[64]

The second time in his life where he found himself surrounded on all fronts occurred during his largely troubled tenure as the Diocesan Bishop of Rochester. Like many of the chapters in *Treasure in Clay*, the details here are sparse, and the historical record has considerably more to say than our narrator.[65] Rather than closely chronicle his event-filled three years in Rochester, Sheen fills the first half of this chapter with solipsistic musings about the nature of the priesthood, jokes about eating chicken, and praise for seminarians. He makes it seem as if his time there was no more than an afterthought, yet we know from the historical record that he came in with big ideas from Vatican II and sought to implement his transformative vision immediately. He renamed the chancery office the Pastoral Center, formed councils of priests and laypeople to share a voice in diocese governance and priest selection, appointed an urban vicar to address poverty in the city, and opened an ecumenical dialogue with the local Protestant divinity school.[66] He would also give joint talks with rabbis and address crowds and synagogues in effort to inculcate a sense of ecumenism in the community.[67] Although many of his ideas bore fruit, even more did not, and it is only within one of the final pages of that chapter that he cautiously avows he ran into some difficulties in Rochester. He mentions that his plan to reform the local Catholic press – which required months of planning before being summarily declined – failed due to a technicality, and simply states it that "it had to be abandoned."[68] He had also planned to launch an emergency ambulance service for the city's poor, however when no hospital volunteered any medical staff, he states that his idea simply "proved to be more clay than gold" and moved on.[69] As well, in speaking of his plan to rent space in town where he could dedicate a small chapel to Mary, such as at a grocery store, he states that it "it was impossible to find [a place] to rent," signalling that real estate was to blame rather than his handling of the initiative.[70]

While there is a hint of authenticity in admitting his failings, in virtually every case, Sheen would have it seem that the fault for his failures lay elsewhere, owing to chance or circumstance. He does, nevertheless, avow that he personally "failed in the area of housing."[71] However, simply stating that his plan failed obscures the larger story of what happened. According to the historical record, Sheen put together an ambitious plan to expand social housing for the city's poor by donating an older parish and all its structures to a federal program.[72] In total, the donation would have provided several hundred housing units and alleviated the burden already placed on the federal program. While planning, Sheen spoke with Robert C. Weaver, the Secretary of Housing, who gave the plan his enthusiastic blessing.[73] On paper the plan seemed strong, and there had been talks by the priests of closing the parish since the 1950s due to its low attendance. However, while Sheen worked out the logistics and received permission from all the necessary boards and delegations – including from Rome itself – he failed to consult the people who frequented the parish. When he finally presented his plan, he discovered, "to [his] great surprise, there was opposition," coyly adding that protestors even chucked "pebbles" at his car.[74] While Sheen downplays the reaction to his plan, the sense of betrayal felt by the parishioners was palpable. One outspoken critic went so far as to accuse Sheen of hypocrisy and attacked what he saw as markers of Sheen's out-of-touch aristocratic status, by stating that "if the bishop wants to make some grand gesture, he could move in with the poor and live among them. Then maybe he would be selling his books instead of giving away Church property."[75]

It is understandable, however, that Sheen would rather not revisit the pain and failure of Rochester in his memoirs – particularly as the tragedy of his administration may not have painted the most flattering image of himself. Nevertheless, Sheen does find the means of inverting his failures to serve an auto-hagiographical purpose. Regarding the sum of his failures in Rochester, Sheen makes a curious observation, referring to his plans as "clay vessels that broke in my hands as they did in the hands of the potter whom Jeremiah visited."[76] In drawing a comparison between himself and that episode from the book of Jeremiah, it would appear that Sheen is suggesting that in the same manner that the people of Israel were not ready to follow God's plans, neither were the people of Rochester with his. Such a comparison puts Sheen on a similar playing field as the prophets of old, of tireless men sent by God to turn an often-rebellious people around. That the prophets and their work met failure just as often as success is surely how Sheen hopes that this episode will be remembered. In this case, though Sheen was unsuccessful in enacting his plans at Rochester, he was nevertheless successful and obedient in attempting to implement them. After all, if his actions were directly influenced by the church's reform attempts through Vatican II, Sheen was effectively attempting to get his parishioners to follow these same God-ordained reforms – but to no avail.[77]

Sheen, ever the perfectionist, also further absolves himself of his failures at Rochester by remarking that "a wrong impression would be created by dwelling on failures which were generally outside the general practice of episcopal administration."[78] It is an interesting statement, as it at once suggests these failures were outside his control, but also that the initiatives themselves were outside the norm – hinting at his ambition and innovation. It follows that he doesn't want his readers to linger on his failures there or wonder whether he still bore any hard feelings with what happened in Rochester. By dismissing his failures with a quick turn of phrase, it not only tells his readers that he does not wish to cast blame, but also that the whole matter was much more trivial than it was perhaps made out to be.[79] Instead, similarly to how he depicted himself during the chapter discussing his tenure at the CUA, Sheen is eager to linger on the positive and present himself as something of an ambitious, innovative outsider – as a man who wasn't afraid to challenge the existing order if the order could be rearranged for the greater good. Indeed, when considering the historical record, there is no reason to believe that Sheen arrived in Rochester with anything other than optimism and a head filled with good ideas and interesting initiatives he planned to implement. He had, after all, participated in Vatican II and his appointment was at the time considered to be the first diocese in America that would attempt to live up to the reforms of the council. That he came to Rochester with all the promise of Vatican II – of the church's plans to throw open the doors and air out its ancient institutions – and it resulted in failure is telling of the aftermath of that council.

When reviewing Sheen's recollection of events within *Treasure in Clay*, the subtle picture that appears to be painted is that Sheen was not only a prophetic figure fighting to turn the eyes of the people back toward God's plan, but also, by his failure, someone who experienced a certain allegorical martyrdom. Curiously, though suffering is a mark of emulation, and martyrdom is the epitome of suffering – for there is no greater form of emulation than to shed blood for the church – Sheen largely brushes over these events in his book and or refers to them in a cryptic manner.[80] For instance, in the opening chapter he refers to enigmatic "scars" that he received in his later life.[81] Later, in a chapter titled "Things Left Unsaid," Sheen implicitly comments on his experiences at Rochester where he remarks that Christians are shaped through three purifications: crosses, cups, and tensions – each one pointing toward Christ's martyrdom. The crosses are the burdens placed on us that we did not deserve, but that we are forced to carry; the cups are those burdens handed to us that we cannot pass; and the tensions are those that "come within the Church."[82]

That Sheen was at the heart of possible tensions within the American church was hardly a secret. In *American Bishop: The Life and Times of Fulton J. Sheen*, Reeves titles his chapter about Sheen's time at Rochester "Exile," and remarks that while Sheen put on a strong face, after his resignation he seemed to many to be a "broken man."[83] For his part, two-time biographer Noonan notes that "few saw Sheen's appointment as a promotion," and he questions whether Sheen was being "kicked upstate" on Cardinal Spellman's behalf.[84] Further, in his second work on Sheen, Noonan refers to Sheen's posting in Rochester as his personal "Calvary" – again drawing a comparison to Christ's suffering and martyrdom.[85] Considering Sheen's cautious approach to his trials and tribulations – and also how these have been viewed by his biographers – the picture of his later life and career is one that seems to mirror the betrayal and abandonment of Jesus before the cross. Sheen, after all, steadfastly refused to comment on his suffering in any great detail and uses his autobiography to reimagine these episodes, repainting them in a lighter, more accepting light than one might have imagined. Here, Sheen makes it appear that he cheerfully went to Rochester carrying his cross and suffered obediently, and largely in silence.[86]

Sheen's refusal to speak directly about his negative experiences in Rochester and elsewhere may seem odd – especially as speculations about them were rife, and more details of this nature would have been expected in a celebrity biography. However, this very hesitancy highlights the precariousness of Sheen's position and his own need to demonstrate obedience to the institution – and to the memory of Cardinal Spellman, in particular.[87] For instance, rather than seize upon a controversial moment that would be worth more than its weight in gold in any celebrity biographical account, Sheen reminds his reader instead that "any discussion of conflicts within the Church diminishes the content of the Christ … as the hand excessively rubbing the eye diminishes vision."[88] As such, these episodes of trials and tribulations demonstrate that the bishop was devoutly loyal to the church until the very end, carrying his own "cup" as it was handed to him without refutation and avoiding any potential revenge he could have had in exposing his side of the story in his autobiography.[89] Thus, though these chapters of Sheen's autobiography may come across as inauthentic and guarded from a critical standpoint of a celebrity bio, his refusal to address them acts as means of tacitly enacting his own austerity without necessarily having to draw attention to it.

### *Trope Three – The Prophetic Calling*

The third and final element of hagiography that I will be addressing is that of the central figure's prophetic calling. In hagiographical literature, the protagonist's destiny is often made evident to the character and reader alike through moments of anointing and prophecy.[90] In *Treasure in Clay*, Sheen is twice made the focus of such moments. These not only act to single him out from his peers – they also foreshadow the fact that he has been chosen for God's plan. The first occurred while Sheen was still a boy. According to Sheen, one Sunday after Mass while he was serving as an altar boy at the cathedral in Peoria, Bishop Spalding asked him to help carry a wine cruet. Sheen promptly and unceremoniously fumbled and dropped the item on the floor, comparing the apparent catastrophe to "atomic explosion." Although Sheen feared he would be punished, Spalding instead surprised him by coming over and kneeling by his side. In an apparent non sequitur, he asked Sheen, "Young man, where are you going to school when you get big?"[91] Sheen's rather coy answer was that he envisioned attending the Spalding Institute – a local high school the priest had been instrumental in founding.[92] Unperturbed by this sycophantic response, Spalding pushed on and asked Sheen whether he had ever heard of Louvain, to which he replied he had not. In response, Spalding told Sheen – in what he explicitly refers to as a "prophecy" – to "go home and tell your mother that I said when you get big you are to go to Louvain, and someday you will be just as I am," signalling that Sheen would, too, one day become a priest and a bishop of some renown.[93] The "prophecy" was later fulfilled: in 1919 Sheen would be admitted to the University of Louvain to complete his doctorate (and then again in 1921 for his post-doctoral *agregé*), and by 1951 he would be consecrated as a bishop.[94]

The second moment occurred during his troubled tenure at the CUA amid his troubles there. As previously discussed, Sheen felt that he was branded an "outcast" and reprimanded by the rector for proposing reforms that no one viewed favourably and which would have increased the faculty's workload. After this event, Sheen remarks that he spent a week or two feeling insecure before the rector called him to his office. There, rather than receive a fresh series of reprimands, the rector apparently asked Sheen to follow him to his room where he put on his cassock, zucchetto, and other ceremonial regalia. Then, according to Sheen, the rector said to him "'Kneel down, young man.' I knelt before him and he put his hands on my head and said: 'Young man, this university has not received into its ranks in recent years anyone who is destined to shed more light and luster upon it than yourself. God bless you.'"[95] Whether such an event took place or not is debatable and ultimately irrelevant as the placing of the rector's hands on his head can thus be seen as a process of anointing, whereby Sheen the outcast is further demarcated by his superior. In fulfillment of this prophecy, after Sheen's tenure at the CUA, he would go on to achieve national fame with his television series and be recognized across America – further distancing his fame and celebrity from his own desires, and situating them as part of God's plan, invested upon him. Additionally, the story also suggests to the reader that while Sheen was ostracized, the highest authority at the university nevertheless took his side in private, showcasing that Sheen was in the right all along, and would continue to be in the right even when opposed on all sides like saintly heroes of the past.

Taking events like these into consideration, it's worth remembering that prophecy is rarely inconsequential in the lives of saints.[96] As a narrative trope, it foreshadows where the story will go and also places a certain importance on the character receiving the prophecy. In the Gospels, notably that of Matthew, the reader is presented with all the myriad ways in which Jesus fulfilled prophecies, while also being presented with the events that would foreshadow his eventual crucifixion. The same convention continues into the Acts of the Apostles and the larger traditional of hagiographical literature as a whole, where pivotal narrative moments – such as impending martyrdom – are suggested to the reader or broadcast to the saint through a vision, dream, or other revelation. Of course, the importance of prophecy as a hagiographical trope also extends beyond the narrative realm and serves as a means of highlighting the chosen nature of the protagonist and their part in God's master plan. In this case, Sheen's prophecy not only proposes a future career within the church (where he would attain the rank of archbishop, exceeding Spalding's expectations), but also singles him out as a person *chosen* to have their life's trajectory prophesied for him. In doing so, Sheen paints himself as having something in common with both the apostles and saints before him – as someone whom God had a carefully constructed plan for that the world would see come to fruition, and where his own will or desires had no part.

While Sheen is quite keen on incorporating hagiographical tropes and conventions like this into his autobiography, he nevertheless departs from classic hagiographic conventions in a manner that is simultaneously rather subtle yet somewhat blunt. Hagiographical authors generally allow the prophecy to remain implicit, counting on the knowledge and expectations of their reader to fill in the blanks and connect the dots to the biblical parallels. Sheen, however, *explicitly* labels Spalding's speech as "prophecy." That Sheen chooses to bluntly state the trope he is deploying suggests that he did not entirely trust his readers to make this connection without his guidance. Like the celebrity actor who exerts control over their image and brand, Sheen is clearly demonstrating his control over the narrative, leaving little to chance and ensuring that his reader does not deviate from the larger message being imparted – nor fail to notice the hagiographical elements within.

## Conclusion

*Treasure in Clay* is a text that sits uncomfortably at the intersection between celebrity and sanctity, and hagiography and biography, while at the same time demonstrating a complicated link between modern sanctity and celebrity. Ostensibly a celebrity autobiography, its structure and reliance on certain tropes and biblical parallels push the book toward the hagiographical. Yet, as mentioned earlier, hagiographies are seldom composed by their central figure in question. In most cases, the agency of the saint themselves is deflected – though their actions graze the pages of hagiography, as actors they are typically passive in its generation, reception, and spread. Works like *Treasure in Clay* problematize this traditional rubric of holy writing, owing to its autobiographical nature and reliance on the author controlling their own image of sanctity. Rather than see this as a contradiction, I argue instead that such works (along with their composing figures) cannot be properly understood or contextualized without also considering their intersections with modern celebrity.

Modern celebrities are public figures, open to the adoration of their fans but also the scrutiny of the wider public. Scholar Katja Lee remarks that, when writing of themselves, celebrity autobiographers "not only represent but embody in style and content the very terrain they negotiate."[97] Such works don't simply offer insight into the individual celebrity in question; they also offer insight into the way such texts are produced and consumed.[98] The same holds true for hagiography, where each text explores themes that extend beyond the life of the saint and into the larger cultural context surrounding them.[99] The control Sheen exerts over his persona and narrative, shaping it to fit hagiographical conventions, adds to the construction of both his image and reception as a modern celebrity and holy figure. In this case, ordinariness and authenticity are leveraged much differently than by the secular celebrity. Ordinariness for the sacred celebrity is, on the one hand, about demonstrating familiarity with hagiographical tropes and conventions and highlighting how one's life adheres to these standards. At the same time, using self-deprecation to emphasize ordinariness downplays both his celebrity status and any potential claims to sanctity. In tandem, this draws attention to his humility that is itself a virtue of the sacred and a common marker of the hagiographical author.

Sheen's text can be seen as a continuation and adaptation of this historic and religiously significant genre.[100] I might venture as far to suggest that auto-hagiography can be read as a sign of change in the category of modern saint-making, one which allows the long-standing precedent of third-party authorship to be subverted and chronicled by the would-be saint themselves.[101] As *Treasure in Clay* is a decidedly modern work, it is a key textual resource in understanding the broader making of would-be saints in the contemporary era and of this era of American Catholicism in particular. Perhaps then as a logical extension of this, in the following chapter, we shift from the biographical to the post-biographical, moving from the life of the would-be saint to his remarkably eventful afterlife.

# 2

# Locating the Saint

## *Celebrity Remains and the Urban-Rural Divide*

### Cold Weather in Peoria

It's a typical winter morning on 21 January 2020. There's fresh snowfall from the night before, and the sidewalks are already covered in ice. I've just arrived at the local airport in Peoria, Illinois, having flown in from my connecting flight in Chicago. After collecting my bags, I hail an Uber and wait several minutes for "Casey" to arrive and help me load my things in his trunk. As we pull away from the airport and Casey drives me to the city proper, I'm able to survey the area. Peoria is a small city in a mostly rural part of the American Midwest. The homes along the highway are modest and spread out. The downtown core to the city feels similarly open and spacious, its handful of Art Deco and neoclassical buildings separated by wide streets and sidewalks. It's a far cry from New York City – from the dense, urban metropolis where Sheen spent most of his life and made his career. By the time the airport disappears from view, hidden behind small crops of trees and snowed-over farm fields, Casey looks up in the rearview mirror and asks what brings me to Peoria.

"You're here for Caterpillar, right?" he asks, referring to the construction giant whose headquarters are in the city. I gather over the coming days from other local Peorians that most visitors are there on business matters related to the construction industry and little else.

"No," I reply. "I'm here to visit the diocese. It's about Fulton Sheen. Are you familiar with him?"

"Sheen?" He takes a moment to recall the name. "Yeah, Sheen. He's kind of a big deal around here, isn't he?"

"If you're Catholic, he certainly is."

"Right. There was this whole thing about getting his body over here recently. Guess they got it done?"

They certainly did, but not without its challenges.

❍ ❍ ❍

In 2019, the remains of Fulton J. Sheen were removed from the crypt under St Patrick's Cathedral in New York City where they had rested since 1979 and moved to a modest shrine in St Mary's Cathedral in the small city of Peoria, Illinois. As a resting place, the shrine is quiet and modest, largely free of the ostentatiousness that surrounded Sheen during his illustrious life.[1] Encased in a marble tomb beneath a gilded portrait of the Virgin Mother (a figure to whom he was particularly devoted to his whole adult life) Sheen's remains are identified by a small plaque on the tomb bearing his name, the title "Venerable Servant of God" and the initials "JMJ" – standing for "Jesus Mary Joseph" – which he was known for writing on the blackboard at the start of each episode of *Life Is Worth Living*.

The relocation of one's earthly remains is hardly uncommon for candidates on the road toward sainthood – even in modern times, as was the case in the first decades of the twenty-first century for the now Venerable Alphonse Gallegos and more recently for Sister Wilhemina Lancaster.[2] However, unlike most candidates whose remains were either exhumed or moved after their earthly demise, it was hardly a given that Sheen's remains would come home to rest in the rural Midwest. Peoria first petitioned New York to relocate Sheen's remains to their current resting place in 2014. After apparently being given verbal assurances that there would be no issues with the request, the archdiocese abruptly refused the transfer, even as Peoria was in the midst of planning for Sheen's beatification ceremony to be held locally. The resulting disagreement between the two dioceses over Sheen's remains would become a veritable tug-of-war between the big city by the coast and the little one in America's heartland. While there have been moments of contention in the past between competing dioceses over the claims of resting places and relics, the intensity at which these two dioceses allowed their recriminations to spill out in the open, which would be ravenously

Figure 2.1 Sheen's resting place. Photograph taken on 23 January 2020, at the Cathedral of Saint Mary of the Immaculate Conception, Peoria, Illinois. Photo by Alexander Nachaj.

covered by the Catholic press in America and even mainstream media, was largely unprecedented. Of course, rarely has a figure of Sheen's widespread celebrity found themselves on the road toward sainthood.

## Urban and Rural Catholicism in America

The story of Sheen's afterlife is more than the story of a man and the recognition of his sanctity. It is also a story about the complications and urgency celebrity can bring to competing claims over sanctity and which, in this particular case, happens to dovetail into the struggle for visibility and recognition of rural Catholics.

Rural Catholicism is an oft-overlooked area of discussion as well as academic study. While there are scholarly studies focusing on rural Catholicism, the majority of academic works continue to focus on urban parishes and the lived experience of Catholic immigrants and their descendants in America's cities.[3] Classic works such as Ellis's *American Catholicism* (1965) paved the way for approaches like this, while with more recent ones such as McGreevy's *Parish Boundaries* (1996), Orsi's *Madonna of 115th Street* (1985), and even O'Toole's edited collection *The Faithful* (2008) have perhaps inadvertently helped reinforce the perception that American Catholicism is primarily rooted in crowded urban neighbourhoods rather than the remote and often sparsely populated farmlands of the American Midwest and South. One suspects that this lack of scholarly interest in rural Catholicism has much to do with demographics. At their peak, rural Catholics never made up more than a fifth to a third of the Catholic population in the United States, translating to only a small fraction of the total American population at any given time.[4] I would further argue that the prevailing presence and influence of Northern urban centres in the narratives of American Catholicism have themselves contributed to the overshadowing of rural stories, effectively turning small rural dioceses such as Peoria into veritable underdogs in David and Goliath–like struggles for presence, identity, and the negotiations of sanctity.[5]

While it is not my intent to provide anything resembling a definitive history of rural American Catholicism here, I am concerned with how this theme – the urban-rural divide and the influence urban regions hold over rural ones – can be extracted to better understand our investigation into the ongoing afterlife of Fulton J. Sheen. Notably, the competition between New York City and Peoria over Sheen's bodily remains highlights issues related to ongoing regional tensions between centre and periphery, and the extent to which Sheen's celebrated and sanctified status made these matters more pressing. Of particular note is how the Empire State's decision to prominently insert itself into Sheen's canonization narrative has contributed to issues and delays that may ultimately derail the entire process. In response, this has created an opportunity – and perhaps even a necessity – for Peoria to remap Sheen's relationship with his rural upbringing in order to reimagine his body, identity, and sanctity in a novel manner that emphasizes his rural roots, and which might seem at odds with the celebrity lifestyle he often embodied. Ultimately, the tension between these competing pulls underlines the complex and ultimately amorphous nature of the would-be American saint's memory and identity and demonstrates how competing regional factors and interests introduce complications and flux into existing narratives of sanctity and celebrity – all owing to questions about the displacement of a body.

## Sheen's Cause: A Window into American Regionalism and the Urban-Rural Catholic Divide

There have been murmurings about Sheen's potential canonization and sainthood since before his death. However, the first concrete steps toward Sheen's canonization were taken in 1998 when the Archbishop Sheen Foundation was launched by Gregory J. Ladd and Lawrence F. Hickey. That same year, Ladd and Hickey approached Archbishop John O'Connor, a friend of Sheen's who had by then become a cardinal, for permission to begin the steps toward opening the cause for canonization.[6] O'Connor granted the foundation the right to begin amassing data, while his successor, Cardinal Edward Egan, pointed the foundation toward Peoria as a potential home for the cause. Bishop Daniel R. Jenky of Peoria accepted the request, became the principal actor, and then petitioned the Vatican for permission to open the cause toward Sheen's canonization.[7] By 2008, after six years of work, the diocesan phase of the investigation was completed, and twenty-two volumes of testimony and other records were transmitted to the Congregation for the Causes of Saints in Rome.

In September 2010, Sheen's journey toward sainthood took an unexpected and optimistic leap forward. At a hospital in Peoria, a boy was born without a heartbeat. Refusing to accept the inevitable medical diagnosis made by the attending medical staff, the child's mother found herself turning to prayer. She directed her petition toward Sheen, who might seem to have been an unlikely candidate to hear such a prayer, but who was nevertheless a figure she revered and evidently considered to be saintly. Miraculously, before the hour was up, the child's heart began beating and returned to life. The doctors, amazed at what occurred, confirmed that the child was now healthy and would survive without any permanent illnesses or ailments. The boy was promptly given the name James Fulton in honour of his intervening patron.[8] The following year, a Vatican panel of medical experts advising the Congregation ruled that the event at the Peoria hospital with the resuscitated child was satisfactory. The panel closed its investigation into Sheen's miraculous intervention, accepting his role as intercessor and provisionally clearing the cause of one of the greatest hurdles toward beatification and sainthood.[9]

In 2012, Pope Benedict XVI announced that the Congregation had recognized Sheen's life as one of "heroic virtue" and he was proclaimed as a "Venerable Servant of God." Bishop Jenky of Peoria held a mass at the Cathedral of St Mary of the Immaculate Conception in celebration, a fitting choice considering this cathedral was where Sheen received his first communion, was ordained as a priest, celebrated his first Mass, and where his remains would eventually come to rest.[10] However, despite the promising and rapid initial progress of his cause – including meeting the miracle requirement for beatification – all further progress ground to a halt when the cause was suddenly and indefinitely suspended by the diocese in September 2014.

In an official (and notably sombre) news release, the diocese stated that although the cause had been progressing quite well and they had anticipated holding the beatification ceremony in Peoria in 2015, a dispute over Sheen's remains had brought the proceedings to a standstill.[11] Despite the apparently verbal assurances given to Bishop Jenky, the Archdiocese of New York refused to honour the request to transfer Sheen's remains, arguing that it was not necessary to have his remains in Peoria in order to hold the beatification ceremony and that Sheen's remains belonged in New York.[12] Peoria, in turn, categorically refused to hold the beatification ceremony without the transferal of Sheen's remains, arguing that Sheen had no desire to remain buried at St Patrick's Cathedral – least of all, one would suspect, in the same crypt where the remains of his long-time rival Francis Spellman also lay – and that he desired to return to his true home in Peoria.[13] Neither diocese, however, gave any ground, and the issue of the translation of Sheen's remains became a matter for the secular courts to settle.

❍ ❍ ❍

Peoria's decision to suspend the beatification ceremony in 2014 in light of New York's refusal is, in hindsight, hardly surprising. While New York was technically correct in stating that having the remains transferred to the diocese was not a prerequisite for the ceremony to take place, their sudden about-face and refusal points to matters larger than a technicality.[14] It was, after all, the relatively minor and geographically remote Diocese of Peoria that toiled for Sheen's canonization for the better part of a decade. Though Sheen spent decades of his life in New

York, honing the career that would turn him into a national celebrity, including giving recurring sermons at St Patrick's Cathedral where he would later be interred, the city showed little interest or concern for unfolding his afterlife and canonization process until it had sufficiently progressed. Where Sheen's remains had been little more than the bones of a much-adored celebrity, the fast-approaching beatification ceremony signalled that they would soon be undergoing a subtle, yet significant, change as they transformed from mundane objects into holy relics.

Since ancient times, Christianity has largely been focused on bodies – and not simply those of the living. Dead bodies – particularly those of the people proclaimed saints – have played a crucial role in negotiations and interpretations of sanctity, space, sacred authority, and identity.[15] Historically, the tangibility of relics has allowed Christian devotees to locate sanctity in the material as well as the spatial, transforming mere physical geography into a sacred landscape.[16] Such places emanate both spiritual and temporal authority, and, through various associations and interactions with these sacred landscapes, devotees come to shape their identities and understanding of sanctity. Though the power channelled by the saint is understood to come directly from God, in practical matters, their relics have acted as bridges between this world and the unseen, the sacred and the mundane, the normal and the miraculous. While we might often relegate such concerns to the distant past, the relationship between relics, space, and sanctity is not just historical but continues to inform issues of identity and power in American Catholicism even to this day.[17]

Among Catholic circles, it was hardly a secret that the matter – and value – of relics was on the minds of the actors in both dioceses. As James T. Keane, the senior editor of *America*, the Jesuit review, observed in 2017, Bishop Jenky openly petitioned New York explicitly for the "collection of relics."[18] Rather remarkably, however, the Archdiocese of New York issued a public statement that they stood against "the dismemberment of the archbishop's body" implying that Jenky's request was in some way morbid rather than being a fairly routine pursuit in canonization processes.[19] Such a reply suggests that New York was more concerned with preserving the apparent sanctity of the body than the sanctified power of Sheen's remains. Had Peoria chosen to continue with the ceremony in absence of Sheen's remains, the Diocese of New York would have become the custodian of the relics of a beatified American figure.[20] In other words, by refusing to release the body, New

York would have directly benefited from Peoria's efforts – efforts which were on track to make Sheen's remains more spiritually valuable than they had been in the decades before and which would only continue to increase in value should the little diocese attain its goal of making Sheen number among the saints. Peoria's decision to pause the beatification proceedings over their dispute with New York can therefore be read as a means of attempting to regain control, both over the proceedings and the remains of Sheen, their beloved native Peorian.

❍ ❍ ❍

New York's refusal to transfer Sheen's remains and the resulting public spat between the two dioceses is also highly revealing of the power imbalance between these two regions in the American church. New York has historically eclipsed all other dioceses in the influence it wields over the lives of American Catholics and the perception of Catholicism within the wider culture of the nation. As the largest city in the United States and the largest port of entry into the country, New York was the hub through which millions of Catholic immigrants from across the Atlantic entered into the continent, a reality which created large pockets of ethnic parishes and Catholic neighbourhoods in the city.[21] Many of the church leaders who have held the seat of Bishop (and later Archbishop) of New York since the early nineteenth century have been wildly influential, perhaps none more so than Francis Spellman, whose mid-twentieth-century tenure lasted nearly twenty-eight years and oversaw the radical demographic shift that occurred when New York's urban Catholics began moving from the ghettos to the suburbs in droves.[22] It was during Spellman's time that New York solidified its place as the centre of American Catholicism, largely due to his influence among Catholics and wider American society, as well as his active campaigning in the canonization causes for American-born saints.[23] The Archdiocese of New York has also largely dominated the academic discourse of American Catholicism, and this scholarly pre-occupation with themes pertinent to the New York context – immigrant narratives and identities, ethic parishes, and so on – while valid has nevertheless threatened to eclipse the experience of Catholics elsewhere in the nation.[24]

Unlike the dense urban parishes found in America's major metropolises – such as New York City, Chicago, and Boston, which were at times largely composed of immigrant communities – rural Catholics have often found themselves vastly outnumbered by their Protestant peers. Success and survival in rural America often relied on having a dependable family unit and savings to purchase and maintain farming land, both of which were luxuries the majority of America's Catholic newcomers lacked.[25] Despite intermittent attempts at drawing more Catholics to rural living and the heralded spiritual benefits of working off the land, these efforts have largely failed.[26] Rural parishes have also found themselves facing historic shortages of priests, hospitals, schools and other Catholic institutions and resources.[27] Nevertheless, Peoria – once part of the colony of Louisiana – has long had roots as a Catholic centre for the region. After the colony of Louisiana formally became a part of the United States in the early nineteenth century, small communities of Catholic immigrants began to settle in the Great Lakes region of the largely agrarian Midwest.[28] Germans and Poles represented the largest demographic of Catholics settling in America's rural farmlands, with a small but not insignificant number of Irish immigrants also relocating to the Midwest.[29] Today in Illinois – much like the country overall – Catholics make up the single largest Christian denomination, even if their numbers can't compare with the total number of Protestants.[30]

In holding religious convictions that set them apart from their neighbours, rural Catholics in America – like their urban counterparts – have had to contend with the experience of otherness. Like all newcomers, they sought to maintain their traditions while at the same time finding themselves in and identifying with the larger patchwork of American culture. As religious studies scholar Jeffrey Marlett remarked, rural Catholics faced an additional existential challenge by belonging to "a church self-identified with the cities where a largely immigrant, second and sometimes third-generation membership staked a most conspicuous claim."[31] As such, one of the largest challenges was to demarcate their identity from that of their fellow Catholics in urban centres, something largely accomplished by tying their sanctity to the land itself. Catholic clerics and lay leaders alike were strong advocates of the agrarian life, arguing that farm work could suitably instill "whole virtues" through labour.[32] They argued that Catholics would find satisfaction in working the land, and, owing to the communal nature of many rural communities, that Catholics could also hope to foster traditional family values, encourage mutual aid, and keep the population close-knit and focused on "God at all times and in all places."[33]

The attachment these Catholics felt to the land, their spirituality, and bodies was reinforced visually. Rural Catholics freely drew upon biblical imagery and applied it more directly to their situation than their urban counterparts. For instance, several of A. de Bethune's woodcut prints of biblical images – such as "The Sower" and "Christ the Tree of Life" – emphasize the connection between rural living and biblical virtues and were embraced by rural Catholics, while the Liturgical Movement endorsed a wide visual repertoire of explicitly rural Catholic images that specifically rooted their spirituality to the land.[34] The National Catholic Rural Life Conference (NCRLC) – an organization that promoted rural living and values to Catholics in American city centres – also heavily promoted the iconography of St Isidore, the patron saint of farming. In other words, rural Catholics found novel ways and icons with which they could reimagine and reify their identities as Catholics as well as their ties to the lands upon which they toiled.

This Catholic emphasis on rural living can also be read as a backlash against the perceived ills and dangers of the modern world, which were seen to be more prevalent in the cities than the countryside. As Marlett puts it, "Catholic anti-urbanism encompassed both people and the land itself."[35] As such, rural pride would also fuel anti-urbanism among Catholics, a sentiment that would become more prominent in through 1930s with the activism and tacit influence of the NCRLC and its "crusade" against what it saw were the vices of the cities.[36] The NCRLC cultivated a widespread belief that urban Catholics were falling away from the faith, and that the values of the city were incompatible with their spiritual lives. The countryside, in contrast, offered fewer dangers and allowed Catholics to better connect manual labour with their spirituality.[37] Rural leaders such as Christian Winkelman, the bishop of Wichita, were often much blunter, railing against the intrusion of vices he identified as "urban tendencies" attempting to despoil the more purified spiritual existence of rural America.[38] Others also argued that rural life allowed Catholics to more "purely" live their faith than they would in the cities.[39] Ultimately, "rural America offered the nation a comprehensive answer to a plethora of questions raised about modern life. Most significantly, American rural life offered both physical and spiritual security."[40]

Peoria's refusal to give in to New York's obstructions in Sheen's canonization process should therefore be framed within the wider scope of rural Catholicism's ongoing history of rebuke against the urban hegemony.[41] In asserting themselves against New York with their claim for Sheen's remains, Peoria can be read as asserting itself against the Empire State's dominance over American Catholic matters as well as the values and identities associated with the urban metropolitan. After all, the act of reclaiming relics has long been understood as an act of political and cultural self-assertion, and in modern times the repatriation of relics continues to be a frequent feature of struggles for cultural rights and political recognition across the globe.[42] While Sheen's bodily remains certainly figure into the centre of the disagreement between the two dioceses, his body – like the bodies of would-be American saints before – has also become the site where wider tensions and regional imbalances in the American church continue to be played out.

### *Urban Hegemony and American Canonization*

In 2016, Peoria's legal struggles to have Sheen's remains transferred to their diocese took a positive turn when Joan Sheen Cunningham – Sheen's niece and closest surviving relative – became involved and advocated for Peoria's side in the matter. Her petitions as a relative of the deceased appear to have held some weight in the matter, as the Manhattan Supreme Court Justice Arlene Bluth initially granted Cunningham's request to have the body transferred to Peoria. However, as soon as the *translatio* was granted the Archdiocese of York filed an appeal, once again halting any proceedings until the case could reconvene at the appeals court.[43]

The following year, at the New York Court of Appeals, Cunningham testified, reiterating that Sheen had little desire to be buried in the heart of New York City. As an indication of this, she remarked that her uncle had purchased a burial plot not in Manhattan, where he was currently interred, but in Queens.[44] Echoing Peoria's argument from a few years earlier, she argued that the purchase demonstrated that her uncle had no desire to be entombed within St Patrick's Cathedral, and that while he never explicitly stated he desired to be buried in Peoria, it suggested that he would have preferred to have been buried anywhere except where he was currently laid to rest.[45] In other words, as his current burial location went against his earthly wishes, the archdiocese's desire to claim Sheen's body had superseded the man's own desires. Thus, seeing as Sheen's desire was ignored, then at the very least the wishes of the family should be honoured.[46]

While the court ruled that she had provided a "good and substantial reason" for the disinterment and transfer of Sheen's body, attorneys for St Patrick's also had their fair share of ammunition to expend in the battle. Their argument primarily revolved around the technical matter of the canonization process. Though the transfer of Sheen's remains has been called a "key factor in the continuing progress of his sainthood cause" by Peoria, the archdiocese's attorneys made this statement something of a sticking point, arguing that, as there is no guarantee that Sheen's canonization cause will be successful, and the transferal of remains for inspection does not need to occur in the diocese where the process is being championed, any such removal of a body without sufficient cause was, as they had previously implied, tantamount to desecration.[47]

❍ ❍ ❍

While many causes have seen remains successfully relocated or exhumed without issue, the tug-of-war over Sheen's cause was not the first to occur in modern America, nor was it the first to occur between New York and another smaller or more remote diocese.[48] Elizabeth Ann Seton – who in 1975 became the first canonized saint born in what is now the United States – founded several schools and religious congregations in the rural townships in and around what would eventually become the Archdiocese of Baltimore.[49] Yet, during her canonization proceedings in the twentieth century, she became popularly known as "Elizabeth of New York" – a nickname espoused by none other than Cardinal Spellman as he and others from New York City inserted themselves into her cause and sought to lay claim to her legacy.[50] Though New York City ultimately failed to assert complete control over her cause and body beyond a nickname, the metropolitan was more successful in its influencing of the cause of Mother Frances Cabrini, an Italian immigrant who, in 1946, became the first US citizen to attain sainthood. Though Cabrini's charitable work would root her legacy to the Midwest and she would later die in Chicago, New York also sought to claim her legacy, arguing that, since she entered the country through their port, their city represented the doorway for what rendered her "American" in the first place.[51] While her body was initially interred in Chicago after her canonization, her remains were later exhumed, the majority of which were moved to New York City in the 1930s.[52] In Chicago, where her national shrine is still located, a single arm is all that remains of her original relics there.[53]

New York City's claim to the sanctity and resting places of these women raises questions about geographical identifications and the role they can play in shaping and reimagining a saint in their afterlife – particularly in the case of Cabrini. While one has to wonder whether Cabrini would have associated herself with New York City – she spent little time there save for passing through customs, and her charitable work and hospital building in the Midwest seem to have been stronger points of reference in her identity formation as a saint than her immigrant status – New York's claim to her sanctity would suggest that imbuing particular facets of geography can play a major role in the shaping of a saint's afterlife.[54] Similarly to Sheen's case, Mother Cabrini's highlights an imbalance between the East Coast and the Midwest, while also pointing to a secondary layer of competition between the national and universal levels of Catholicism. Where Rome had advocated for Mother Cabrini to be recognized as a universal saint in the church, Americans largely viewed her canonization as a "triumph" of American Catholicism – not only would having a saint of their own put them on equal footing with their European counterparts, they also believed that having an American saint could help ease lingering tensions between Catholics and Protestants, particularly the latter's doubt that the former could ever be considered truly American.[55] Her American devotees and postulators therefore thoroughly emphasize her Americanness and her citizenship, aiming to make her cause an American event and celebration, and not simply a Catholic one. For them, her decision to take on American citizenship not only demonstrated that she was enamoured with the country, but also that she identified with fundamentally with the nation's particular founding values.[56]

As these examples surrounding prominent candidates for sainthood demonstrate, geographical identifications are complex and can generate questions about hierarchies (such as whether which geographical identification should hold precedence) as well as fractures (such as split identifications to various regions). National identities have a tendency to supersede universal or global identities, while regional and local identities can then challenge ongoing or previous national ones. A similar process can be highlighted by the changing geographic relations and spatial identities that occurred in the afterlives of the North American martyrs.[57] Initially, the various actors in the cause rallied around their shared North American identities to differentiate themselves from the wider global community. As historian of religion Emma Anderson remarks, in "the nineteenth century, both French Canadian and, for the first time, American Catholics would utilize the dimly remembered legacy of the small group of seventeenth-century Jesuit martyrs to articulate their own sense of collective identity in their negotiation with more dominant groups within their respective societies."[58] In other words, when Catholics first migrated to North America they developed a temporary and cross-national sense of unity as the result of a shared sense of otherness in a Protestant majority context. However, as time went on, that sense of pan-Catholic unity in the New World grew more divergent and competitive as Canadian and American nationalism strengthened along with their claims to the body and sanctity of the martyrs. Ultimately, the geographic identity of the saints gradually pushed them farther north, whereby the North American martyrs would come to be known more frequently as simply "the Canadian martyrs."[59]

Speaking to the complexity of geographical identifications, Kathleen Sprows Cummings observes that "canonizations and their precursors, beatifications, have special meaning for those who feel particular affinity with the new saint by virtue or a shared profession, state of life, or geographic location."[60] In other words, the geographic factors in a saint's narrative are more than markers, as they contribute not only to the saint's identity but also to the affinity shared between the figure and their devotees. Shared geography thus fosters a shared sense of recognition: though the saint and their devotees may be separated by time and other factors, a shared geography identifies them as coming from the same stock.[61] However, in cases where saintly figures have multiple locations associated with their life and actions, it does raise questions about which locations carry the most importance in their narrative, and which hold the most weight in laying claim to their cause and identification. This leads to competition, as rival causes each hope to lay claim to the powerful presence of the figure and the prestige that comes with it. This becomes even more pressing when the figure holds wide-ranging regional or even national importance and recognition, making these saints something akin to celebrities in their afterlife, even if they enjoyed little such distinction during their lifetimes.

In the case of Sheen, who was a nationally recognized and celebrated figure, fixing him to a single location raises numerous challenges. He was born and raised in the Midwest, was partly schooled in Europe, travelled extensively across the globe, and acquired widespread fame and recognition for his career and charitable work in New York City, before then becoming bishop for the Diocese of Rochester.[62] Sheen's life, like those of many others, reminds us that a body rarely remains rooted in one place, which, in turn, problematizes the notion of fixing one's identity to a single locale or region. For instance, does the place of one's birth or of one's career carry more weight when understanding the root of a figure's celebrity as well as their sanctity? When no simple solution presents itself, the issue then becomes one of imagination and negotiation – albeit not by the figure themselves necessarily, but by actors whose interests, and even very identities, become enmeshed with their afterlives.

## *A Body Imagined and Reimagined*

In February 2018, the ongoing appeal over Sheen's body came to a close. The Appellate Court ruled in a three-two decision that Sheen's body would remain in New York City for the time being. In their statement, the judges declared that there was insufficient evidence to demonstrate that Sheen wanted to avoid being buried at St Patrick's Cathedral. Furthermore, the Appellate Court noted that the previous court ruling had ignored the testimony of one Monsignor Hilary C. Franco, a witness who claimed Sheen had explicitly told him in person of his strong desire to be buried in the crypt of St Patrick's Cathedral. The court therefore ordered a fresh hearing to begin on Sheen's "true" wishes."[63]

After the Appellate Court's ruling, the Archdiocese of New York urged Peoria to resume the canonization process, stating that "there is no impediment to his cause progressing, as the Vatican has told us that there is no requirement that the earthly body of a candidate for sainthood reside in a particular place."[64] Peoria again refused to back down and resume proceedings, continuing on their path to have Sheen's remains legally transferred to their diocese. By June 2018, the courts held another hearing that sought to provide a "full exploration" into the archbishop's desires. This time, they ruled in favour of Cunningham's request only to have the ruling immediately appealed once again by New York. However, on 5 March 2019, the appeals court unanimously ruled that Sheen's remains should be transferred to Peoria based on the wishes of his surviving family.

The Diocese of Peoria welcomed the decision and issued a fairly blunt public statement imploring the Archdiocese of New York "to end their failed contestation which has only resulted in three rulings against them … now is the time to end the legal tug-of-war and begin the final stages of the Cause of beatification of Archbishop Fulton Sheen."[65] A spokesperson for the archdiocese stated the trustees of the cathedral strongly disagreed with the court decision and were "considering their next steps." To no one's surprise, those next steps culminated in the immediate appeal of the ruling. However, on 2 May of that same year their request was rejected. "After almost three years of litigation, the New York Archdiocese' legal arguments have been rejected at all three levels of the New York court system," read a statement issued by the Diocese of Peoria on 6 May 2019.[66] Just two weeks later, the archdiocese filed for a second appeal. "Yet again, the New York Archdiocese is trying to stop Archbishop Fulton J. Sheen's remains from being moved to Peoria," read a news story covering this development.[67] Judging from the tone and word choice, it would seem then that even the media was growing tired of the back-and-forth drama surrounding Sheen's body – like they would for any celebrity caught too long in a news cycle.

❍ ❍ ❍

Throughout the ordeal of his *translatio*, Sheen's body was more than a news piece for the Diocese of Peoria – the way in which it was imagined and remembered is one of the major focuses at the Archbishop

Fulton Sheen Museum. The museum takes up a few small rooms at the diocesan archives and is accessible through a wide doorway right next to the entrance. Though it is not much larger than your average studio apartment, there is no lack of materials both on display and in the handful uncategorized crates of clippings and photographs kept in storage. Numerous photographs, posters, and placards – some of them life-sized – are strategically placed around the space, designed to give the viewer a certain impression of the man whose canonization cause they are championing. When added up, these materials form a visual bricolage that represents the many aspects of Sheen's life and career. They also, unintentionally, point to a tension between Sheen's regional identity that they strongly espouse and his celebrity stature which was crafted back in New York City.

While the diocese and the materials it displays prominently champion Sheen's television and radio careers, a subtle tension seems to surround both these images and the period of his life where they occurred. On the one hand, we might wonder perhaps if this tension echoes Sheen's own awareness of (and general unease) surrounding his celebrity status.[68] More likely, however, is that the tension felt at the diocese and its museum have to do with the locale *where* it was based – especially considering the diocese's recent history with New York City. Although much of the visual media on display inevitably highlights and expounds upon his television career in New York City, one doesn't have to look very far to spot alternative materials that seek to rewrite the nature of his relationship with the city championing his cause by emphasizing to visitors that Sheen was in fact a country boy at heart who never forgot his roots even while he was in the big city.

Take for instance a trio of black-and-white promotional photographs that highlight the aspects of his career for which he is best known (discussed below). In the first image, a young and handsome Sheen stands behind a microphone with the logo of NBC emblazoned on the front. In the photo adjacent, Sheen is dressed like a priest at mass, standing in the control room of a radio station in New York. In the third, an older and greying Sheen, dressed in cassock and zucchetto, works a camera emblazoned with the DuMont Television network logo – also based in New York – where in the background, we can see the slightly blurred presence of the set for *Life Is Worth Living*. When placed alongside one another like this, these three photographs seem to act as a triptych that emphasize his legacy as the self-proclaimed "electric bishop" – as the American cleric who embraced the potential of technology and understood it better than most (and who happened to find this aspect of his career and identity very much rooted in New York).

Despite the prominent placement of images and objects that point to Sheen's celebrity identity and career in New York City, a counter-narrative can also be identified here. Throughout the museum, there are subtle yet deliberate audio-visual cues that seek to characterize Sheen as a salt-of-the-earth Peorian. For instance, in a cozy corner bracketed by several couches and cushioned chairs, a television set played a DVD documentary titled *Archbishop Fulton Sheen: Servant of All* (which ran on continual loop the whole time I was there during my stay in Peoria). In the opening segments, there's a discussion of Sheen's character and upbringing, accompanied by country-folk music that plays gently in the background while Fr Andrew Apostoli, who acted as the vice postulator in Sheen's cause, refers to Sheen as a "country boy" who never forgot his upbringing. Nearby, there's a small but dedicated children's corner, where one can find a table with a handful of colouring books issued by the diocese. One book, in particular, bearing the title *Fulton's Coloring Book* purportedly depicts scenes from Sheen's early life in Illinois (see fig. 2.2 below).[69] The most notable images are a pair in the middle of the book that showcase scene's life on the family farm. There is a caption at the top of the first page, informing the young readers that "during the summers, Fulton and his brothers were sent to work on the farm." In the image below, we see a strapping young man with a square chin and a broad chest behind the wheel of a tractor, looking back with pride as he plows the family field.[70] Sheen has a speech bubble floating above the barn in the background, where he declares, "It is beautiful to see things growing but I think God wants me to be a priest." Like a true Catholic agrarian, the Sheen from the colouring book highlights the beauty of rural Illinois and his attachment to the land while also signalling his faith and dedication to God through his calling. In the image adjacent, we see Sheen again at work, this time pouring feed into a trough for pigs. Once again, he is depicted as a strapping young man with a square jaw and a broad chest. He has a thought bubble over his head that remarks – with a sense of wonder that would seem to contradict his own recollections of this period of his life – "Wow, these pigs never get enough to eat."[71]

Figure 2.2 Children's colouring book. Photograph taken on 21 January 2020, at the Archbishop Fulton Sheen Museum, Peoria, Illinois. Photo by Alexander Nachaj.

While little details such as these might appear to the casual visitor as innocuous or trivial, they nevertheless point toward a subtle tension in the ways Sheen has been remembered, along with a somewhat improbable reimagination of Sheen's identity by prioritizing his rural connections. Notably, the images of the physically fit young Sheen in the colouring book can be contrasted with the older, softer looking man in the photographs from New York. In the colouring book, Sheen visually embodied rural masculinity as he dominates the land with his tractor and provides for the animals by pouring a massive bucket of feed for the pigs.[72] By association, by connecting his body to the land these images also root his spirituality in that same geography. And so, in both the ever-present documentary and the available materials for children, Sheen's Peorian devotees have created material that speaks to the rural, agrarian life and an upbringing which reflects their own rural identity and reconfigures their relationship with him. In other words, Peoria subtly refutes the importance of New York City in generating Sheen's fame and recognition, along with the role it played in charting out his sanctity and character, staking a claim instead to Sheen's "true" identity – that underneath all the fame and the glamour, he was bodily and spiritually one of them.

Peoria's reimagining of Sheen's person along with his identity and relationship with the land is, however, imperfect. After all, it would have been impossible to present any sort of recognizable image of Sheen that didn't also highlight elements or episodes from his life, fame, and career that were defined in and very much by his attachment to New York City. Though the diocese goes to some length to paint him as being a rural man at heart even when living it up in America's largest metropolis, they cannot avoid visually showcasing and emphasizing his radio and television career in New York that established him to the level of fame and widespread acclaim that has helped push him toward sainthood in the first place.

Curiously, Peoria's attempts to re-emphasize (or perhaps re-inject) Sheen's rural "ordinariness" amid the celebrity in some ways mirrors Sheen's own apprehensions toward his celebrity, along with his own attempts to downplay them in *Treasure in Clay* as discussed in the previous chapter. As such, the image we receive of Sheen as it is being promoted in Peoria is both an aggregate of many parts and one replete with contradictions. He was at once the New York City television star, auxiliary bishop at St Patrick's Cathedral, and urban gentleman, while also being the country kid who served as an altar boy at little old St Patrick's in Peoria and who just happened to be destined for greater things. Of course, it would be incorrect to say that Peoria's imaginative rendering of Sheen wasn't based on something that was already there. Sheen himself was a man who one might say lived many lives, in many places. With so much ambiguity at the core of his identity, it seems little wonder that multiple dioceses would stake claims to his memory and the control of his afterlife.

## *Expediency and Embarrassment*

On 27 June 2019, after roughly five years of legal proceedings, Sheen's remains arrived in Peoria, at long last putting the dispute between the two dioceses to rest.[73] Bishop Jenky wrote to the Vatican, informing them that the civil litigations had come to an end and there would be no further appeals from either end. On 8 July of the same year, Pope

Francis officially confirmed the miracle that took place at the hospital nearly nine years earlier and encouraged the Diocese of Peoria to begin formally planning for the beatification of their patron.[74] The diocese was unofficially hoping to secure 20 September 2019 as the date of the ceremony, which would have aligned with the hundredth anniversary of Sheen's ordination as a priest, but a more realistic date was scheduled for 21 December later that same year. However, just as everything finally seemed to be lining up for Sheen and the actors championing his cause, a fresh roadblock would again put his cause on indefinite delay.

Where New York City had acted as Peoria's foil during the years long process of *translatio*, this time it would be another diocese – Rochester, where Sheen had briefly been stationed – that interjected itself into Sheen's cause not once but twice over a period of a few months. Salvatore Matano, the bishop of Rochester, petitioned the Vatican over the summer of 2019 to postpone Sheen's possible September beatification date owing to Sheen's handling of two predatory priests who operated in the diocese during his tenure. Lest there be any confusion or possibility of smearing Sheen, Rochester was also careful to note that "in our current climate it is important for the faithful to know that there has never been, nor is there now, any allegation against (Archbishop) Sheen involving the abuse of a minor."[75] The diocese's grievance with Sheen, which they sent first to Peoria where it was cleared and deemed unsubstantial before being also sent to the Vatican, however, seems to have been more opaquely administrative in nature and was enough to cast yet another delay on the long anticipated ceremony.[76]

Peoria's response to Rochester's intervention into the process has been blunt. Spokesperson Monsignor James Kruse accused the Diocese of Rochester of attempting to "sabotage" the beatification ceremony.[77] Peoria's own previous investigation into the matter found no wrongdoing by Sheen, yet Rochester has requested additional time to conduct and conclude an investigation of their own. To Peoria's fiery remarks, Rochester has replied with an equally blunt statement, declaring that "this is absolutely a false statement and lacks an appreciation for our diocese's genuine concern for Archbishop Sheen's cause."[78] However, while Rochester strives to suggest that they are being genuine and thorough in their investigation, it bears repeating that the Diocese of Rochester has gone through several tumultuous years before their derailing of Sheen's cause, notably as the diocese was among those in the

United States which had recently become the focus in the larger church's ongoing sexual abuse crisis, investigation, and aftermath. In September 2019, the diocese filed for bankruptcy protection after New York passed a law granting victims of sexual abuse a year in which to come forward with claims that may have previously been too old to file.[79]

❍ ❍ ❍

In bringing fresh delays to the cause, Rochester has become the second diocese in the state of New York to obstruct the proceedings. Like New York City, it appears that Peoria is again faced with overcoming what will likely amount to little more than a technicality delaying the beatification. If one were feeling generous, it is entirely possible that Rochester is taking the route of caution, as any mark on Sheen's record during his tenure may well translate into another mark on the already battered diocese. However, the current lack of any credible evidence of wrongdoing on Sheen's behalf and the vague nature of their concerns that Sheen in some way could have been aware of issues in his diocese suggests that their hesitancy may lie with the beatification of Sheen itself rather than any potential misconduct. After all, Sheen's record at Rochester is hardly a matter worth celebrating. While he approached his posting there with optimism and energy, he made numerous missteps which earned him an equal number of enemies within the diocese during his tenure and, by the time of his departure, he left as one of the least popular bishops to have ever held the position.[80] Perhaps the diocese sees little worth celebrating their troubled alumni while it continues to wallow in a legal and ethical quagmire of their own.

The delays brought about by Rochester, while certainly unusual, are perhaps emblematic of changes made to the canonization process in the modern world that have radically altered the ways in which the process unfolds. The days of tireless monks and other religious travelling across continents to gather documents or seek witnesses are far behind us. Where previously every element of a candidate's life had to be meticulously documented and archived by hand, technologies of communication, travel, and transportation have opened up and better connected the world, allowing for innumerable clerical matters to be resolved in weeks rather than lifetimes. However, as the recent string of sexual abuse allegations has shown, modernity has very much become a double-edged sword for the American church. It is no longer taken for granted that dioceses where scandals occurred nor churchmen with skeletons in their closets will be kept under wraps and pushed into the shadows, leading to the very real possibility of embarrassment and anxiety whenever they will inevitably be made public. After all, with rapid canonization comes the risk of rapid embarrassment. In a way, there seems to be a fear rooted in discovery, in the act of airing out old rooms, which becomes a reluctant clamp of sorts in the proceedings for canonization, preventing them from progressing too quickly. Still, the recent string of popes seated in the Vatican have themselves endeavoured to expedite the more than a few causes for canonization. Pope John Paul II, in particular, sought to reaffirm the necessity of saints in the modern world as role models and beacons of hope by initiating what some inside commentators have called a "fast-track" process.[81] Commenting on the extraordinarily rapid sanctification of Pope John Paul II, John L. Allen Jr, editor of *Crux*, remarks "at the time, some critics warned that an accelerated sainthood process risked embarrassment, depending on what a later review might unearth about the way abuse cases were handled on the late pope's watch."[82] The surfacing of long-dormant sexual abuse allegations within the church can in part be attributed to modernity, to the difficulties of keeping things hidden in an era of access to information. What might have once been kept private has a tendency now to be made public, and while those both celebrated and on the road to canonization are very much public figures, there's an increasing stress on and desire to uncover what occurred within their private lives. While promoters of candidates tend to stress the "ordinariness" of their figure's sanctity and devotional acts, there is also the risk of discovering just how mired in the ordinary world they truly were.

As it stands, the desire to avoid controversy has been a recurring theme over the course of Sheen's canonization. As previously discussed in the first chapter of this book, Sheen's desire to take hold of his narrative and refashion it while drafting *Treasure in Clay* was certainly intentional, as was his conscious and stated intention not to get into any of the details involving the feud between himself and Spellman, nor into any other potentially unflattering events or quarrels that could have taken place behind the scenes and hidden from the public's gaze. Should

Sheen have voiced any opinions against his superiors, or the wider hierarchy of the church and its actions in the world, it would certainly have the potential to be just as damaging if not more so to his cause if uncovered during the proceedings, even if it aired afterward. This very possibility that there as something potentially dangerous in Sheen's past appears to have been a concern of the interviewer collecting witness testaments in a massive tome prepared by the cause to be shipped to Rome with the proceedings, as the questions asked to those who knew Sheen frequently turned to Spellman and whether the witnesses had ever heard Sheen make disparaging remarks against the man in private.[83] Whether any potentially embarrassing material related to Sheen does exist is a question beyond the scope of this chapter, but it would seem that all those involved in the canonization process do, to some extent, fear the *possibility* of such material existing. That nothing unsavoury has been uncovered is itself quite remarkable, and even more so when we consider the dual scrutiny the man bore during his life and continues to be subject to in his afterlife as both celebrity and would-be saint.

## Conclusion

In the making of saints, popular piety, personal industry, and structures of power are all negotiated – often across vast reaches of space and time. To paraphrase Emma Anderson, the recognition of sanctity is an interpretive process and not a summation of historical fact.[84] Sanctity relies on the perceptions and recognition of others to be understood, accepted, and approved throughout the process of canonization. Kathleen Sprows Cummings similarly remarks that saints are not recognized as saints simply because they were holy people who lived holy lives; saints are canonized "because a dedicated group in and subsequently beyond their inner circles wanted them to be *remembered* as holy people – and were willing to expend a considerable amount of time, effort, and resources to ensure that they would be."[85] She adds that "all causes for canonization begin when a group of ordinary people lift up the holy heroes who populate their everyday lives; successful ones end when the holiness of the candidate is validated, first by local church authorities and finally by the Vatican."[86] As such, the process of making saints unfolds is indetermined, involving large blocks of time, with numerous actors contributing toward and pulling back against its progress until the candidate climbs the ladder all the way to the top or hangs indefinitely on the nearest rung until further developments, or never proceeds further.

While the exhumation of a would-be saint's remains is a standard part of this lengthy procedure, should the candidate reach the requisite stage, the translocation of said remains to their final resting place, as we have seen, is not without the possibility for challenge and contention. While many saints have had their earthy remains relocated without issues, such as the Venerable Alphonse Gallegos and Sister Wilhelmina Lancaster whom we referred to earlier in this chapter, others such as Sheen may involve lengthy tug-of-wars between competing dioceses and interests. While it could be argued that for Gallegos and Lancaster, though modern candidates for sainthood, their remains were relocated without issue due to the proximity of their initial burial place and subsequent shrine, in both cases being within the same city or monastic compounds, the challenges, as were made clear by both parties struggling over Sheen's cause, had little to do with mere proximity or the lack thereof. In this regard the geographic contestation over Sheen's remains, and association reminds us more of other more prominent cases like those of Elizabeth Ann Seton and Mother Cabrini, who, though relegated to the more distant past, demonstrated several parallels in which a smaller, more remote diocese had their interests pinned against the more powerful New York. Sheen, too, is a renowned figure who, like these past examples that were each promoted in highly visible ways, has the potential to be a highly recognizable and widely adored modern saint, should his cause proceed to that much anticipated conclusion.

Details like these from Sheen's canonization process also remind us that the story of Catholics in America, and the promotion of their saints, isn't solely relegated to its urban metropolitans but is also being undertaken by the smaller minority pockets in rural regions whose identities are tied to and shaped by their connection to the land beneath their feet. In the myriads of legal and bureaucratic struggles that occupied the two dioceses in the courts and newspapers, we have seen how smaller, more isolated locales such as that of Peoria face a constant uphill battle against the voices, resources, and presence of larger dioceses from more populated and predominantly urban states like New York. Despite their underdog position, Peoria has worked tirelessly in their drive to not only bring Sheen home, as it were, but also to propel his cause forward. By calling attention to and highlighting his rural upbringing and salt-of-the-earth Americanness at the museum, Peoria is advocating for a vision of Sheen that retains his celebrity, but which also embodies the more ordinary values of rural American piety. Of course, the success of Peoria's endeavours and the extent to which they have been willing to emphasize Sheen's rural connection in their pursuits have also been mixed. In the same tenacious manner that New York refuses to retract its foot from the door of Sheen's canonization, the same could be said of the inability or unwillingness to fully separate him from his celebrity career in that same state. The best they can do is to suggest that his rural roots lay at the core of his being all along.

Sheen's ongoing canonization process also has a way of drawing attention to numerous facets of modern American saint-making that normally remain unspoken. Notably, Sheen's celebrity appears to have added an additional layer of complication and flux to this matter as his prolific public life and recognition continue to make him a figure at the centre of attention. Due to Sheen's highly visible profile, his cause is not one that can be handled by a handful of actors toiling in the background in the way things may have unfolded in pre-modern times. Rather, the ongoing details of Sheen's cause are very much like the life and afterlife of a typical celebrity where the public craves details and rival claimants fight over their legacy and remains. Whether it be record labels fighting with rights holders for a musician's catalogue or an author's estate guarding their famed creations, more likely than not, we can expect the causes for would-be saints whose wide-reaching fame has pushed their recognition into the public space to become recurring forms of contentious celebrity afterlives. As such, the care taken to ensure the causes of the celebrated proceed may need to rely on a wider pool of resources and materials than previously expected.

In this regard, when promoting the causes for figures who inhabit these dual spaces, historian Anna Stadick remarks that, "although diocesan archives and those of religious communities play an essential role in the process of canonization for ordained candidates and members of religious and secular institutions, a broader range of archives is necessary for thorough proof of biographical details, historical milieu and, possibly, reputation of sanctity."[87] As New York City and Rochester's interventions have shown, the more public a figure, the more care is needed to navigate the exhumation, not only of their body but of their wider careers. In this, I would steer us back to a remark made by Cummings, whereby competing regional claims to a saint have the capacity to generate competing narratives of their lives, posing what could become a "dangerous encumbrance" to their cause.[88] As much as Sheen is adored by many, he is also a troubling figure as his adoration is rooted in his sanctity as much as his fame, each one interwoven to a certain extent and neither detachable from the other. Nevertheless, it is this very twined essence of his sacred celebrity, along with its balance, that elevated him to such widespread appeal and which is the focus of the following chapter.

# 3

# Celebrating the Sacred

## *Watching Television's Celebrity Preachers*

### Our Mystery Guest

In a 1956 episode of the popular and long-running game show *What's My Line?*, host John Charles Daly turned to the star-studded four-member panel. The composition of panellists was typical for the series, made up from recognizable celebrities and several show regulars. Included among them this particular night were Hollywood actor David Niven, radio personality Arlene Francis, journalist Dorothy Kilgallen, and publisher Bennett Cerf. Daly informed them that it was time for the special feature of the program and asked his panellists to blindfold themselves to keep secret the identity of the soon-to-enter "mystery celebrity." After the blindfolds were set, the camera turned to a blackboard as a familiar hand used the chalk to spell out the name of the guest. Applause erupted as the mystery celebrity was revealed to be none other than Bishop Fulton J. Sheen. As Sheen settled himself down alongside Daly, long-time panellist Cerf – still blindfolded – remarked that he'd just witnessed "the most solid round of applause I have ever heard at one time" on the program.[1] Even without knowing the identity of the mystery celebrity, it was evident to the panellists that a persona of some magnitude had entered the stage. That the celebrity happened to be a Catholic bishop, recognizable to American television audiences, was never questioned.

◌ ◌ ◌

In the 1950s, television offered a complex and crowded arena where celebrity was formed, and identities were negotiated in surprising ways as Americans familiarized themselves with the increasingly culturally dominant visual media. While it was once assumed that only "dethroned film stars" and celebrities past their prime appeared prominently on television, a medium that many referred to as the lower form of entertainment compared with the silver screen, the new visual format facilitated the creation of a new kind of celebrity that differed from earlier visual archetypes – notably, the often elevated and unattainable figures of stardom previously established in Hollywood and promoted through the nation's movie halls.[2] Television, instead, offered Americans a more approachable and even familial form of celebrity, one which could be encountered within the privacy of their own homes and which found its place amid a growing need for comfort, reassurance, and spiritual advice across the nation.

As discussed earlier in the introduction of this book, postwar America was a transitional time in the nation's history. With hundreds of thousands of soldiers returning from overseas after having faced the horrors of the war and now thrust into society-wide economic and social changes as result of the GI Bill, America was widely reported to have experienced both a sense of malaise about its present state along with a rising demand for spiritual guidance, tranquility, and hope.[3] While figures such as Aimee Semple McPherson and Harry Emerson Fosdick received widespread recognition for their sermons as well as offering answers to pressing societal questions in pre-war America, emergent postwar technologies of access – of which television would become the most prominent – allowed America's religious leaders to meet this growing demand and encounter wider audiences than were ever before possible. More importantly, by engaging Americans on desirable television slots, many of the nation's religious leaders rose to fill a new category of highly *visible* and nationwide recognition that was not necessarily demarcated according to previously established denominational lines or ecumenical boundaries.

While many of these figures in the postwar era were themselves ministers or clerics by training, profession, and identity, the content of their programs on television and the expression of their personality and character fell far from the tree of traditional religious modes of sermonizing found in the nation's places of worship. As such, this newfound category of fame that came to prominence during the 1950s, which I will refer to as the "celebrity preacher," was a novel development in both spiritual guidance and celebrity, and examining figures from this era will better allow us to better understand and unpack an intersection of American religion and celebrity culture.

Though Sheen stands as a quintessential example of this rubric of celebrity, to bolster our discussion of this category and better understand its wider application, I will draw into our discussion two of Sheen's contemporaries who were also prolific on early television. The first among them is the mainline pastor Vincent Norman Peale. Out of the slew of Protestant contemporaries of the era, Peale's style and the substance of his talks echoed many of the elements of Sheen's approach to television and closely mirrored the accrual of the celebrity associated with it. The second figure of focus is none other than famed American Evangelical Billy Graham, who became a fixture of American television from the 1950s onward.[4] While Graham is more commonly referred to as an early televangelist, the celebrity character he cultivated along with his wider reputation in American society makes him in many ways the most emblematic and widely known celebrity preacher of television's formative years during the postwar era.

❍ ❍ ❍

Before proceeding further into our discussion, I would like to take a moment to qualify the term "celebrity preacher" along with where the nature of its celebrity approaches and diverges from other expressions. First, I use the term "preacher" here intentionally but also differently from how one might expect. While a preacher is typically a pastor, cleric, minister, or other religious figure who sermonized from the pulpit on decidedly religious matters, the religious leaders who appeared on early television were also preachers but delivering a different kind of message. Rather than focus on dogmatic or soteriological concepts, which did emerge in their talks, the main crux of their messages, as we shall see, was a focus on the here and now and how religion could bring comfort, contribute to personal growth, and provide a foundation for the American identity.[5] In this regard, what they were preaching was both a broadly accessibly Christian message, regardless of denomination or tradition, and what was rapidly coming to be perceived as shared American values based out of the nation's believed Judeo-Christian underpinning.

Second, referring to these men as "celebrity preachers" avoids any conflation with the far broader term "religious celebrity." While Sheen and any of his ilk can certainly be said to have been religious celebrities, a religious celebrity is more typically understood in common parlance to be a secular-facing celebrity who happens to hold religious views in their public or private lives. In this vein, 1950s comedian Danny Thomas could be comfortably referred to as a religious celebrity owing to his lifelong Catholic devotion and active parish life, and the same could be said for actor Loretta Young, a friend of Sheen's who was actively involved in Catholic charitable work.[6] However, the nature of celebrity embodied, performed, and displayed by these two personalities and others like them differed greatly from that of Sheen's as their public-facing fame was rooted in their mainstream, secular-facing celebrity activities – namely, their film and television presence – and did not emerge from their religious character, calling, or practices. For instance, if one detached both Thomas and Young from their religious sensibilities, their celebrity would have largely remained intact. Not so for Sheen, whose celebrity differs significantly in that it was simultaneously drawn from and inhabited by his dual role as an ordained spiritual leader and celebrated television personality – the latter of which he earned while publicly and very visibly representing himself as an ecclesiastical aristocrat of the church. In other words, while Young and Thomas were celebrities who held private religious views, which may not have even been widely known by their audiences, Sheen was unabashedly both a public celebrity and religious authority, albeit not entirely one because of the other.

Lastly, "celebrity preacher" should not be conflated with that other category of celebrity standing at the intersection of television and religion: the "televangelist." While Sheen has been referred to as a televangelist, and even as the *first* televangelist by his contemporaries, this term has evolved since the 1950s and is now largely used to identify those television personalities whose primary purpose is to evangelize and win converts.[7] Principally, this niche has been occupied from the late 1950s onward by Protestant Evangelicals, among them Oral Roberts, Rex Humbard, Jerry Fallwell, and Jim Bakker, to name a few. Billy

Graham can also be counted among this category, particularly due to his live or recorded broadcasts of his crusades beginning in 1957. However, the characteristics and persona of the celebrity preacher that I am examining extend beyond – and to a certain extent, apart from – their ability to proselytize. As such, there is a danger in drawing the televangelist, a predominantly Protestant mode of evangelizing celebrity, too close into our discussion as it would risk obfuscating one primary point of departure: namely, that while Sheen and those like him during were concerned with making converts, it was not necessarily a central quality of their television appearances and celebrity character during this era.[8] These early broadcasts (both radio and television, as well as the paperback output out these men) were more focused on discussing the problems and questions of daily life and the American identity in a non-denominational, largely ecumenical manner suited for a public service broadcast, while being able to offer reasonably informed and trustworthy answers from their position as religious authorities and made-for-television personas. As scholar Timothy H. Sherwood rather succinctly put it, "Sheen did not try to convert Americans to Catholicism" with his program.[9] From this angle, referring to Sheen as a televangelist suggests that his viewers and commentators alike didn't yet distinguish his talks promoting America's values from sermons focused on dogma or evangelizing efforts, suggesting that his audience very much saw Sheen and his contemporaries as simply as preachers using a novel medium. And so, as we shall see, the celebrity preachers of the 1950 were very much products and composers in this formative period of television's inception and identity making of its stars.

## New Media, New Possibilities

In 1948, *Texaco Star Theater* made its commercial debut as a television program in the United States.[10] Broadcast live – as were the majority of the programs during that era, and following the precedent set by radio and nightclub routines – the program was the first to offer viewers an hour of television in a consistent format repeated at prime time every Tuesday night from 8:00 p.m. to 9:00 p.m.[11] The first four episodes of the program were hosted by Milton Berle, who was originally envisioned as being one among a rotating cast of hosts. However, Berle's success and made-for-television charisma helped him become the permanent face of the program after only a few months, and – given that *Texaco Star Theater* was the most popular show on television at the time – the de facto face of television itself, something that earned him the nickname of "Mr Television." Inspired by the success of this program and its format, other networks scrambled to launch similar shows dominated by similarly charismatic leads.[12] In the following years, dozens of competing programs replete with their own celebrity hosts and guests fought for time slots and ratings.[13] These early variety shows – and the charismatic personalities of their hosts – would become a staple of early 1950s American visual media, and they established as well as influenced many of the conventions that would be adapted by rival forms of programming offered by celebrity preachers – including Sheen's own soon-to-air *Life Is Worth Living*.

Unlike the variety shows, Sheen's program was one among a wider slate of programs originally envisioned to would fulfill a government-mandated public service broadcast requirement. To give a bit of context, at roughly the same time when variety shows and their hosts were transitioning from radio and vaudeville to television, the Federal Communications Commission (FCC) mandated that all stations in America air at least a minimum amount of programming that catered to the public interest.[14] While religious programs were selectively among the first television offerings in the early 1940s, by the following decade certain forms of religious broadcasting were deemed to be in the public interest and mandated to be available free of charge for viewers on both public and private broadcasting channels.[15] Though the commission did not require a specific number of programs be aired each week, they nevertheless required that each station submit a list of their public programming for consideration every three years (coinciding with their licence renewal forms), tacitly suggesting that the quantity of religious programming could be a factor in staying on the air.[16] In many cases, stations were able to fill their government assigned slots with help from local mainline Protestant churches who were eager to make use of the new medium free of charge.[17] In this regard, the DuMont Network became something an outlier and early innovator of sorts, by promoting a wide variety of religious programming, beginning in 1948 with their choice to broadcast African American Evangelical minister Solomon Michaux, accompanied by his Happy-Am-I gospel choir. By 1951, one of the first public service programs of to attract an audience was *Morning*

*Chapel*, which offered viewers a daily a cross-denominational program that featured a rotating list of Jewish, Catholic and Protestant clergymen who performed religious services and held discussions detailing how "spiritual values could be applied to practical everyday living" while avoiding any outright evangelism or dogmatic quarrels.[18]

Sheen's *Life Is Worth Living* hit the air the following year, emerging out of this same broadcasting requirement. While his show quickly became the most successful of the nation's initial run of public service religious programming, there was apparently little initial belief that it would amount to anything more than a slot filler owing to the fact Berle's program played elsewhere at the same time. However, the format and presentation of Sheen's program was at once novel and familiar for viewing audiences – familiar as a low-budget piece of religious programming, it also borrowed from the variety show format by centring around its charismatic host in a way that was generally unfamiliar for religious programming at the time. Staged in New York's Adelphi Theatre in a carefully decorated studio set designed to look like the office of either a professor or a university rector, Sheen relied only on a piece of chalk, a large blackboard, and his own persona to hold his audience's attention. Shot in intimate proximity with Sheen using the personality-centred focus of variety show programming – albeit, without the extravagant routines, guests, or manic energy for which those shows were known – the setup for Sheen's show would have been an easy watch for audiences still getting accustomed to the possibilities of what television could offer.

Sheen approached every episode the way he might have approached a lecture back at the CUA in Washington, DC, or during some of his more general audience radio broadcasts, breaking down complex ideas into bite-sized and highly digestible morsels for his audience on topics ranging from communism to morality to history and philosophy, all the while finding ways to relate them to the present moment. Sheen's presence in full ceremonial dress may have been startling for some, especially as he was lecturing in English, rather than the Latin which would still have been the norm in pre–Vatican II sermons. Moreover, rather than speaking to his audience as an authority figure at the pulpit – someone to be revered but not necessarily relatable – Sheen spoke in a manner that suggested he was addressing close acquaintances, family, or even a room full of students were seated just out of view behind the cameras filming him.[19] Cementing this sentiment, he began virtually every episode with the welcoming incantation toward his audience by addressing them simply as "friends," signalling both the tenor of the program and the open spirit of ecumenism a move which communicated to his viewers that they were all equal regardless of their faith. In doing so, Sheen helped inculcate a shared sense of humanity between himself and the viewer. He also often relied on jokes or silly anecdotes to break the ice at the start of episodes before diving into more serious content.[20] In this manner, there was an immediacy to his program that was achieved by never forgetting the presence of the audience where many of the variety show presenters – notably Berle – would seem to be more focused on their own antics and the resulting adulation.[21] With his natural good looks and the well-trained voice of a radio host, Sheen might have passed for another American vaudeville entertainer making the transition to television were it not for his obvious and accented Catholic dress, associated visual imagery, and the tenor of his talks.

The initial run of *Life Is Worth Living* lasted for five seasons (three on DuMont and then two on ABC) before being taken off the air, likely at the behest of Cardinal Francis Spellman.[22] Long after Sheen's departure from mainstream entertainment media, commentators continued to refer favourably to the celebrity that he accrued – and was continuing to enjoy – thanks to that program. For example, in 1969 Rochester's *Democrat and Chronicle* ran a piece on Sheen recounting his many achievements and accomplishments – including highlighting his television celebrity[23] – and a 1977 newspaper clipping preserved and affixed to the wall at the Archbishop Fulton Sheen Museum in Peoria remarks that "everywhere he goes, Archbishop Sheen is immediately recognized."[24] Even after death, Sheen's television fame remained a focal point of discussion. The *Washington Star*'s obituary of Sheen, for example, reminds readers that "many industry experts predicted a short run when Archbishop Fulton J. Sheen first decided to go on television in 1952."[25] In fact, in virtually every obituary and later retrospective looking back at his life, the authors either opened with or were careful to include a reminder of the bishop's celebrity and television fame.[26] Such praise heaped on Sheen in the mainstream press, while to be expected for a celebrity, was perhaps uncommon for a Catholic priest.

Sheen's fame was also underscored in Catholic publications, where Sheen's television stardom was highlighted alongside his spiritual qualities. An obituary in the *Twin Circle*, for example, exclaimed that his show was a "Nielsen Hit" and "one of the highest rated shows on TV," reminding readers that his program even outranked those of secular stars such as Frank Sinatra.[27] *The Wanderer* also commented on his television fame in their remark that it "won him great popularity," and the Jesuit review *America* published a piece in their *Vantage Point* series twenty years after his death, referring to Sheen's television and radio broadcasting career as a "triumph."[28] *The Catholic Post* – in a 2009 piece commemorating the thirty-year anniversary of Sheen's death – remarked that he was a man "whose radio and television programs drew audiences in the millions."[29] That similar references to Sheen's celebrity can be found in virtually every publication or piece pertaining to Sheen showcases the excitement and intrigue his figure generated, not just among Catholics but among wider American audiences as well. As well, if the audience's reaction to Sheen on *What's My Line?* – referenced at the beginning of this chapter – is anything to go by, his persona was immediately recognizable to large swaths of the American public, both Catholic and non-Catholic alike.[30]

## Catholic and Non-Confrontational

Like the other early religious programs on American television and particularly the DuMont Network, Sheen's program shied away from evangelism or dogmatism and leaned toward a pre–Vatican II sense of ecumenism. However, there was no mistaking that Sheen's program was not only religious but *Catholic*. On screen, Sheen did nothing to hide his denominational difference from America's majority, and in fact did as much as he could to accentuate it. Every episode he appeared before the cameras not in a tuxedo or dinner jacket – as was common for most television hosts at the time – but, as mentioned earlier, in the full ceremonial regalia of a Catholic bishop, replete with cape, cummerbund, massive pectoral cross, and a red zucchetto atop his silvering head. At the start of every episode, he inscribed the initials JMJ for "Jesus Mary Joseph" in the corner of his blackboard, as if to consecrate it along with the contents of his lectures to the Holy Family. Nestled in an alcove on the wall near the doorway also happened to be a statue of the Virgin Mother, which Sheen humorously referred to as "Our Lady of Television" and who was generally visible in the background while he lectured.[31] When his blackboard became overfull from his scrawls, he would carefully pace away and allow the camera to pan after him, thus giving his little "guardian angel" – as he dubbed the off-camera stage hand – enough time to miraculously clear the board. Though Sheen made no mention of any homilies, encyclicals, or any other explicitly dogmatic proclamations from the church he represented, any casual viewer tuning in to his station while his show was on the air would have no illusions about the religious affiliation of this figure. Those that weren't turned off by his overtly Catholic presentation would soon discover that the tenor of his show was a far stretch from the pulpit in that it contained no rituals, no mysterious sermonizing in foreign languages, and no other markers that might have fed into the stereotypes and superstitions many Americans still harboured about Catholics.[32]

Although Sheen's program was obviously Catholic, he approached the public service intentions of the program gregariously. His main concern was diving into the mundane, on topics and issues that Americans might be facing and wondering about regardless of class, race, or creed – and there lies one of the secrets for its broad appeal. As Catholic historian and Jesuit Mark S. Massa has remarked, Sheen gave speeches that though they were religious in nature were "essentially ecumenical and nondogmatic."[33] Biographer Christopher Lynch also notes that, although Sheen was the national director for the SPOF in America at the time, he nevertheless consciously deployed a rhetoric of inclusion and pluralism over any overt preaching or sermonizing about the superiority of his tradition over that of others.[34] For example, in an episode titled "Signs of Our Time," Sheen optimistically approaches America's own lingering nativism by remarking that "there are not one hundred people in the United States who hate the Catholic Church, but there are millions who hate what they wrongly perceive the Catholic Church to be."[35] To Sheen, the issue wasn't that America's religious traditions were at odds with one another, but rather that some were simply misunderstood. Elsewhere, he goes further in reminding viewers of their shared similarities and heritage. In the episode "Angels," Sheen opines that the modern world as a whole was at risk of turning away from the spiritual as a whole toward the material – a concern which would have resonated with broader Christian audiences, even if it wasn't necessarily backed up by the data.[36] The Soviet Union, he avows, rather than some internal denominational other, is the prime offender, as the Soviets aimed to scrub all need for the spiritual in their culture. Such folly, he argues, lies in atheism, whereas *all religions* present in America – grouped together as Jews and Christians, regardless of denomination – know better.

He elaborates on this vein of thought in the episode titled "How to Compare World Religion." After stating that "there are lots of ways for man to become in tune with God," he goes on to discuss practices of self-mortification and other religious practices and philosophies that appear across the world, indicating that all religions have good practices in them and that we can find commonalities everywhere if we bother looking.[37] The uniqueness of Christianity, rather than specifically Catholicism, he avows, is that "we brought to the world the only religion that began with defeat … we have a God who stumbled to his throne."[38] Thus Sheen's program, though visibly Catholic, didn't seek to necessarily emphasize difference or stark hierarchies through the content of his lectures but instead spoke to the shared Hebraic-Christian religious heritage of his audience and sought to draw attention the shared religious foundations that grounded the nation.[39] That Sheen didn't shy away from discussing the theological – and that audiences didn't turn away either – is itself telling, not only of Sheen's capacity to endear audiences with topics that might not necessarily come up at the dinner table, but also of the American appetite for such content.

## New and Familiar: Celebrity Reconfigured

Owing to its novelty, television didn't carry the cultural or historical gravitas associated with cinema, which, as historian Christine Becker remarks, was very much seen as the higher form of visual media in America at the time.[40] If cinema was the high society of visual entertainment, a medium of artistic craft and lofty ideals of stardom, then television was its earthy, plebian cousin – or as historian James Hudnut-Beulmer put it, primarily a middle-class medium that transmitted middle-class values to the American middle class.[41]

Unsurprisingly, celebrities who had made their name on the silver screen had decidedly mixed feelings about the new medium. At its inception, some of Hollywood's biggest names, including Clark Gable,

Cary Grant, and Katherine Hepburn, chose to shun the medium, believing it was "well beneath the stature of a true film star" to appear on a television program.[42] To Hollywood insiders and agents – figures who exercised firm control over the presence, visibility, and career opportunities of the stars they represented – the regular weekly screening of television shows was a dangerous affront to the model of celebrity they had spent so long building up and carefully measuring out.[43] As Becker remarks, "Overexposure was especially viewed as a potential blow to a star's status, in terms of both rarity value and economic value. In fact, it was common for the major studies to forbid their contract stars from appearing on the small screen in the early 1950s based on the assumption that television viewers would not show up at the box office if they could regularly see stars at home for free."[44] See, for example, the following statement issued during this period by an MGM agent, who argued that top-billed Hollywood stars "shouldn't appear on television. They are too big and important. Such exposure would only dilute [their stardom]."[45] Celebrity was thus almost viewed as resource or material substance; something that risked drying up if left out in the light for too long. If audiences grew accustomed to seeing their celebrities on a regular basis, then some of their magic and mystique would be lost or forgotten. A celebrity, in this sense, was understood to be one to whom the public could only enjoy the occasional, fleeting glimpse, leaving them hungering for more.

While Hollywood celebrities often held the status of remote and untouchable gods and goddesses, the first television stars threw many of these conventions out the window, coming across as approachable, fellow humans.[46] A large part of this had to do with how people encountered the medium. In discussing the act of watching television during this era, historian Tony Wilson argues that viewing television, unlike going to the cinema, was understood to be a social and even familial process.[47] Viewing television typically took part as a family gathering, one that reaffirmed the patriarchal and nuclear bent of families as they gathered around the single set, as the father was the one who generally decided the viewing activities.[48] When viewing television, it was not uncommon for participants to talk among themselves, come or go from the room where the show was on, and engage in other similar behaviours that would not have been socially permissible at the cinema.[49] In addition, unlike cinema – which qualified as an activity or even a special event – television was defined by its comfort, its simplicity, and its familiarity as a pastime. As such, the first television hosts were viewed as familiar, friendly faces that the whole family could come to trust and recognize, like relatives coming to visit.[50]

As Wilson puts it, television watching in this era was "uneventful," and the draw of television lay in its "affirmation of the ordinary."[51] Television thus offered the viewer a recognizable horizon, a "normative background" grounded in the familiar.[52] While audience members might have enjoyed elements of novelty or surprise in their programming, the structures and fundamental offerings of their favourite programs nevertheless remained unchanged and appealed to people craving stability and the familiar.[53] Television programs, even to this day, sustain their audience through the audience's recognition of the program, the repetition of its themes and tropes, and its ability to meet the expectations and needs of their audience. For example, when fans of Sheen's television show tuned in every week, they came with certain expectations of how it would proceed and were generally met with few if any surprises. While the topic of discussion indeed changed from week to week – jumping from classical philosophy to Cold War politics to angels – the format and character of the show, including the personality and character of the host, remained unchanged. And so, just as television relied on notions of the ordinary and expectations of the familiar to build audiences, television itself was also symbiotically responsible for helping to construct these very same expectations.

As a means of mass communication, television rapidly became the default visual medium for conveying *information* to the American populace. While some information could be overt and intentional, much of what was passed on was far more implicit and subtle. Watching the figures who lit up the screens and by consuming their presence on a regular basis inculcated and reinforced numerous ideas into the American mindset that many may have taken for granted. In this period, the normalization of television as a medium and the "ordinariness" of the television celebrity can thus be understood as catalysts for helping to institute and familiarize audiences with changing societal norms – the acceptance of Catholics, yes, but equally the need for shared spiritual guidance, and also (albeit more implicitly) changing narratives about identity, race, gender, sexuality, and wealth and poverty on a far grandeur scale than any medium that came before it. While some scholars, such as Jesuit Mark S. Massa, argue that Sheen, Peale, Graham, and their ilk created the demand for this content in the 1950s, it is more likely that these celebrities responded to this need and their success further fuelled its demand.[54]

## The Age of Reassurance

America's appetite for paternal voices, reassuring content, and the celebrities it produced, was certainly a reflection of the times. As previously discussed, by the conclusion of World War II, America as a society and as a people had fundamentally changed. Over the span of little more than two decades, the nation went from a society struggling to pull itself through the calamity that was the Great Depression to becoming the world's foremost military and industrial power leading the rebuilding and refinancing of a shattered continent overseas.[55] While the nation's military and economy emerged stronger than ever before, by the mid-century it wasn't without cost. The horrors of the conflict left its marks on the bodies and minds of America's servicemen and their families. Scores of postwar Americans came home or went about their day carrying scars – both physical and emotional.[56] The revelations of the Holocaust had exposed the true extent of Nazi depravity to the world, while the atomic bombs dropped over Hiroshima and Nagasaki revealed the extent to which human life could be extinguished instantaneously. Countless others were filled with grief over lost loves ones. Moreover, rather than leaving the horrors and trauma of the conflict behind and settling into a postwar world of peace and stability, rising tensions between America and the Soviet Union found a way of inserting themselves into the everyday lives and mindsets of Americans. During the so-called Red Scare and McCarthy's associated crusades within the State Department, Americans were either persecuted for their potential communist sympathies or made to fear the hidden presence of social and sexual subversives who had infiltrated society.[57] And atop of all other concerns loomed the very real threat of total worldwide nuclear Armageddon should the Cold War ever become overheated.

Americans were, in other words, a people understandably in need of comfort and reassurance. Religion – in whatever form it took – appears to have been the avenue to which large swaths of the population turned in search of guidance and identity. In polls from the decade after the war, the number of Americans who stated that they believed in God hovered around 96 per cent or above.[58] In 1950, nearly half the books on the *New York Times* and the *New York Herald Tribune* bestseller lists were "religious books," and newspapers and magazines effectively "battled each other for ministers who could write advice columns in language accessible to ordinary laypeople."[59] As historian Robert S. Ellwood writes, "Religion was, and was perceived to be, in a profound upswing. The market was good. Religious institutions were growing substantially year by year in numbers, wealth, and real estate; seminaries and novitiates were full; the influence of religion in people's thoughts and lives was considered to be increasing."[60] Kathleen L. Riley, one of Sheen's biographers, also referred to the era as one of religious "revival."[61] Religion, it seems, had become highly visible and normalized, in both the public and private spheres.

While claims that the nation was in the early stages of another "Great Awakening" in the 1950s are debatable, what is certain is that Americans were intimately aware of the of the nation's interest in religious materials and content, and even took pride in it.[62] In tandem with the nation's increasingly visible consumption of the religious was also the intertwining of American patriotism with spirituality. Historian James M. Patterson commented on the growing perception of a shared "ecclesial foundation" that defined American citizenship according to the nation's membership in various religious congregations.[63] One of Sheen's biographers, Thomas Reeves, echoes this in his remark that both Protestants and Catholics at the time held on to a perceived *sacrality* of the rights and liberties enshrined into the nation by the founding fathers.[64] Similarly, Mark S. Massa observes that Americans at large sought a "return to the cultural values" that were believed to precede the rise of modernism, liberalism, and the dreaded atheism – suggesting that a spiritual and religious core grounded in Christianity was at the heart of the American way of life.[65] In other words, not only was religion and its consumption becoming highly visible, but so, too, in a growing ecumenical sense was the belief that to be American was also to be religious.

While America's leaders – both religious and political – have in the past frequently sought to highlight God's intended plans or purposes for the nation, aligning America with Christian values became more pressing in the postwar years as a means of distancing Americans from their ideological opponents on the world stage – namely, the Soviet

Union – all the while effectively creating the conditions for a binding strand that had the potential to tie all Americans together regardless of denominational differences.[66] Though there continued to be significant anti-Catholic sentiments in America during this period, it became more possible for Protestants to push aside feelings of dread or ill will toward Catholics by focusing on their shared patriotism and identity as Christians. As Christopher Lynch remarks of Sheen's audiences, "What bound [them] together was that they were Americans, claiming a shared moral heritage."[67] In other word, despite the doctrinal, ethnic and denominational differences that could divide Americans, the belief in a common ethical foundation rooted in Judeo-Christian teachings had the capacity (at times) to overshadow difference and lend itself to the formation of a common, shared identity as God-fearing Americans – an identity that would find new ways of being reinforced by celebrity preachers speaking to this ideal, all the while taking advantage of this era's emerging technologies of access.

## A Thriving Marketplace

While Sheen is one of the best remembered of the era's celebrity preachers, he wasn't the only one to become part of the mid-century cultural and religious phenomenon taking place in America. Following Sheen to the studio not long after his own show was launched to acclaim was Protestant pastor Vincent Norman Peale. Peale who, along with his wife Ruth Stafford Peale, hosted the television series *What's Your Trouble?* Peale, like Sheen, hailed from the Midwest, and was very much an innovator and early adopter when it came to new technologies, quickly adapting to new media as they became available, all the while building up an expansive audience.[68] Previously, he had been the host of a religious radio program, called *The Art of Living*, of which much of the content and format was then adapted to television. Speaking in his often halting yet measured cadence, and always replete with anecdotes, the program contained elements of Christian sermonizing that were more focused on do-it-yourself self-help messaging than salvation that made it extremely accessible and popular for a generation of viewers feeling bewildered by the changing world. God came into his talks in a broad sense, true, but largely in relation to a person's need for tranquility, peace, and self-assurance.

At the height of his popularity, Peale was reaching an audience of millions through his television program and output across various media.[69] In 1952 – a time when Sheen's three-year-old bestselling book, *Peace of Soul*, continued to be discussed and rabidly consumed – Peale's own *The Power of Positive Thinking* was published and remained on the *New York Times* bestseller list for 186 consecutive weeks and sold several million copies.[70] In commenting on Peale's success, executive editor Sarah Forbes Orwig refers to several distinguishing qualities of his genre of presentation and lecturing that could just as readily apply to Sheen: "Peale's genius – and the key to his success – was in grasping themes that were alive in the culture and then offering them in a practical, entertaining form that helped people achieve results *for themselves*."[71] Orwig adds that Peale sought to help "the individual navigate through the often-lonely byways of modern life. His sermons were peppered with lively anecdotes of people who overcame obstacles and achieved success – and Peale insisted that such success could be had by anyone."[72] In other words, though he was a pastor by trade, his true claim to fame was in the way he could cut to the core of everyday life and demonstrate how spirituality or spiritually adjacent ideas could empower his readers without relying on dogmatism. It should be noted that Sheen has received similar comments in academia. "Sheen promised that religion could bring practitioners personal *fulfillment and happiness*," writes historian David Weinstein.[73] Sheen's bestselling book *Peace of Soul* did just this, arguing how true inner peace, happiness – and to a lesser extent, personal accomplishment – can only come by turning one's conscience toward God rather than human solutions such as psychoanalysis. While salvation was likely never far from Sheen's mind, the goal he was discussing was also more focused on addressing the troubles and worries of the here and now, rather than focusing on the next life per se.

The same thing about salvation cannot necessarily be said for Billy Graham, of course, who was among Sheen and Peale's earliest and most visible contemporaries. As one of the nation's most popular television preachers, much of Graham's celebrity was intrinsically rooted in his success at sermonizing and winning converts. Born on a dairy farm in North Carolina, after graduating from Florida Bible College he got involved as a preacher with the Youth for Christ organization where he spoke at numerous rallies in the early 1940s.[74] His preaching would expand, coagulating into his well-known "crusades" rally format that he would take out of the South and into New York in the following decade. Like many of his rising celebrity peers, he saw plenty of potential in emerging media, making his debut on radio in 1944, as an author in 1947, and on television that same year. His 1953 book, *Peace of God* (not to be confused with Sheen's *Peace of Soul*, released four years earlier), focused on similar messaging that Sheen and Peale provided, going into the ways that connecting with God can help the reader achieve spiritual calmness to counteract life's burdens and worries – it instantly became a bestseller.[75] Concurrently, his television broadcasts would fast become a fixture in the 1950s, so much that by 1957, the same year that Sheen's show would be pulled from broadcast, Graham's widespread popularity and television dominance had effectively made him the most prominent celebrity pastor in America.[76] Moreover, like his peers, his celebrity wasn't simply relegated to religious circles but also among the wider public. In 1958, a Gallup poll revealed that he was the second most well-known man in America – second only to President Eisenhower.[77]

In terms of character and presentation, Graham shared many of the qualities that made Sheen and Peale popular. As an experienced speaker at rallies and on radio, he owed much of his stage persona and presence to the earlier tent revival–style preachers, but he also learned how to tone it down and come across as an approachable everyman.[78] Speaking in a pronounced Carolina accent, he typically began his talk with icebreakers in the form of jokes or anecdotes, often recycling the same ones over and over again – and which his fans came to expect and cherish, in the way a kind relative might tell the same story at every family gathering.[79] Pronounced elements of his messaging also mirrored themes and motifs espoused by Sheen and Peale. Rather than merely arguing for the superiority of his message or how literal answers to history or science could be found in the Bible, as would become a mainstay among television's biblical fundamentalists, he often came across as more interested in expressing how mere faith in Christ could provide answers to public concerns and personal issues – whether it be geopolitical unease, despair over a partner's infidelity or a child's illness, or even loneliness.[80] Only God, as he argued extensively in *Peace of God* and was prone to reiterate in his talks, could truly lead us toward peace, stability, and personal enrichment. He presented his facts in simple language, and often in very short phrases, hardly requiring the viewer or reader to be familiar with Christian exegesis, much less step outside their comfort zone, to appreciate and understand the gist of his talks.[81]

Graham also approached ecumenism under similar simple terms. He tended to identify himself simply as a "Christian," rather than any denominational label. Biographer Grant Wacker suggests this choice wasn't to create boundaries – such as to infer that he was a Christian while others were not – but rather to break them down, pointing to the shared fundamentals of the tradition that grouped his peers together regardless of denominational or institutional divisions.[82] Additionally, notably lacking in Graham's talks was any of the overt or tacit hostility frequently expressed by Evangelicals and later televangelists like Oral Roberts and Jimmy Swaggart toward Catholicism and mainline denominations. Graham wasn't concerned with creating division, as his 1950s output saw him periodically co-operating across denominational lines, much to the derision of many of his Evangelical peers.[83] Such apparent ecumenism and willingness to affirm the validity of other faiths would also seem to parallel the approaches taken by other celebrity preachers of this era, who became part of a large, shared pool of spiritual leaders for Americans of all stripes, even as it made him something of an outlier with most Protestant "televangelists" – especially the ones who would follow in his footsteps.[84]

In considering Graham's approach to the medium, one notable departure between other figures is that while Peale and Sheen were beneficiaries of the early government-mandated public service television slots, Graham's forays into television took a different route. While most mainline Protestants groups, along with Catholics, were more than happy to receive token airtime with the public service broadcasting mandates, American Evangelicals were typically far more concerned with securing favourable slots that would maximize their reach and exposure. Though Catholics and mainlines had little interest in petitioning donations on air as well as overt proselytizing, which would have overstepped the ecumenical nature of broadcasting for the good of the general public, these matters were nevertheless of primary concern to Evangelicals like Graham.[85] First, the purpose of appearing on television for most Protestant evangelists was to win converts and save the maximum souls through their messages, and being relegated to graveyard slots would have done little to advance this agenda (even if other programs, like

Sheen's, had managed to overcome this hindrance). Intrinsically tied to this desire for audiences, however, was also that many Evangelicals were not tied to institutional or traditional churches that could fundraise for their programs. As such, men like Graham and the later televangelists had to rely on these very same souls they sought to save for the donations which would allow them to purchase the airtime in the first place. And so, paradoxically, without large audiences and aggressive pushes for donations, the Evangelicals wouldn't be able to sustain their programs in the first place.[86] As time would go on, this relationship would become more competitive, with televangelists each spending tens of millions of dollars yearly to outbid one another for the top television slots.[87] The ensuing ostentatiousness that came with large-scale fundraising, along with its scandals, would further demarcate, and in many ways, define televangelists from the early celebrity preachers operating in public service capacities and who practised more austere lifestyles.[88]

## Criticism

As popular as the early celebrity preachers were among the American public, neither Sheen nor Peale nor Graham, nor any of their contemporaries, were immune to criticism – both concerning the shape of their message and the medium of its delivery.

First, the same elements that made them widely popular among mass audiences seeking lowbrow and middlebrow programming made them the targets of more highbrow audiences, among them academics and theologians. Sheen, for instance, due to his focus on the here and now rather than the thereafter, along with his Sunday School approach to certain theological topics, was derided as offering little more than some "easy religion" that lacked the substance and ardour due the tradition from which it sprang.[89] It's not difficult to see how his talks could have caused consternation. Here was one of the chief representatives of the church, a man in charge of the national branch for the Society for the Propagation of the Faith, given a platform to reach millions, and his most pressing concern at times was discussing how people can ease their suburban anxieties through jokes and anecdotes. Not that Sheen ever discussed anything inappropriate for a man of his position or proposed a view that was in contradiction to the institution he represented, but coming from a man who not only completed a doctorate in the subject but earned himself a prestigious *agregé*, his approach was certainly a stark departure from his earlier output and academic potential.

While Sheen remained firmly rooted in the orthodoxy of his tradition and sought to carefully balance its teachings as they could be applied to the human experience and its challenges, the same cannot necessarily be said for all his peers.[90] In the case of Peale, in particular, commentators criticized how his message of self-fulfillment was subsumed by America's ultra-elite, effectively finding within his brand of Christianity justification for their financial endeavours and status.[91] As Smith remarks, "the particular offense committed by Peale and his ilk was that they distorted Christian doctrine into an apology for pursuing self-interest."[92] In other words, all of Peale's focus on the power and strength of the individual – that is, positive thinking and one's ability to pull oneself up by the bootstraps – didn't leave very much room or necessity for God in the equation, and all but negated the primary soteriological beliefs of Christianity. If the only thing a person needs to overcome their inadequacies is a bit more belief in oneself, then one begins to wonder what the purpose of prayer is, and whether one even need be dependent on the Almighty.[93] In this manner, one could say that the celebrity preachers were not necessarily repackaging Christianity for the American context, but rather repacking America's *faith in the individual* using theological language with a Christian backdrop.[94]

In this regard, Peale's Protestantism appeared to give him a certain leeway that Sheen as a Catholic was either uninterested in pursuing or unable. In *The Power of Positive Thinking* and in his televised talks, Peale often focused on helping people achieve their personal goals – whether they be tied to career, finance, or other elements of their livelihoods. In what one could argue was a precursor to the Protestant prosperity gospel, Peale argued that, to become successful, individuals had to unlock their God-given drive from within, rather than give and expect more in return the way one might make a charitable donation.[95] For all his success in promoting a gospel of success, Peale would also describe himself in public as a salesman, and would even go on to win a Distinguished Salesman Award in New York City in 1957, no less.[96] It is no wonder that among all the celebrity preachers, Peale became the favourite pastor of America's businessmen and other self-starters, included among them none other than Donald Trump and his father Fred.[97]

Graham, too, endured his fair share of criticism, with the most severe arguing that his televised talks were theologically light at best or factually vacant at worst.[98] Graham's loose and "off the cuff" style of approaching his topics made him a perennial target of ire among the more learned and high-brow circles, many of whom felt who he was treating religion as "show business," as entertainment, rather than the mores serious approach it deserved.[99] While its possible Graham simply operated on more theologically shaky footing than either Sheen or Peale, without the nuance that either demonstrated in their talks, more likely it was a result of his desire to promote "big tent" Evangelical ideas that could gather as many folks together as possible. As such, his lack of denominational restrictions, as well as his indebtedness to an earlier style of country revivalist preaching, facilitated or even encouraged a looser approach than either of his peers. That said, there were also cracks in Graham's down-to-earth "country boy" persona that were hard to ignore, notably with regards to the circles in which he moved. While both Sheen and Peale found themselves the darlings of various societal elites, whether movie stars or millionaires, neither's reach could compare with the ways in which Graham's fame granted him remarkable proximity to America's leadership and government. From the early 1950s onward, Graham was a regular fixture of the White House, acting as close confidant and spiritual adviser to virtually every president he encountered during his lifetime, particularly with the more conservative-leaning ones, such as Richard Nixon whom Graham considered a good Christian gentleman and friend even after the scandals hit.[100]

Second, we can see that much of the criticism levelled against the celebrity preachers was also not unlike the criticism that was levelled against the medium of television itself. Just as television was initially viewed as a "lower" form of visual media than cinema, the accessibility of the talks given by Sheen, Peale, and Graham was viewed as a "lower form" of religion than what was offered at the pulpit.[101] Put differently, just as the medium of television was thought to lower the prestige of a celebrity by making it too near, too accessible, too ordinary, so, too, was the power of television thought to debase religion. While it was certainly intentional on the part of the celebrity preachers to focus on accessibly, much of this has to do with how the medium was received by audiences. Television, after all, was hardly the medium for esoteric discussions of soteriology or difficult-to-grasp philosophical conundrums. It was instead the medium for consuming comfortable entertainment that could be uncritically consumed without even requiring the need for traditional forms of engagement that a local parish or church organization might require. It was in fact light religious content delivered straight into audiences' homes, which did little to assuage fears it could dilute or even replace more traditional activities, such as attending Sunday services.[102]

On the topic of debasement, Sheen, by virtue of his aristocratic position within the institutions of the church, had to contend with these accusations more carefully than his Protestant peers. After all, rather than maintaining and honouring the ecclesiastical hierarchy which he represented, as the criticism goes, Sheen essentially flattened it. By writing and speaking in the vernacular and participating in the low mediums of paperback novels and television, Sheen was guilty of taking religion out of the churches and cathedrals – away from the baroque and the grandiose elements that had defined Catholicism since the Reformations – and reducing the prestige of Christianity into morsels for the masses. In other words, Sheen was criticized for being guilty of promoting a spirituality that lacked the grandeur, trials and sacrifice that true religion demanded.[103] Additionally, among his fellow Catholics, numerous columnists noted their "mixed feelings" about having a man of Sheen's stature not only host a program sponsored by the Admiral corporation, but also occasionally pitch their products while dressed as a veritable spokesperson for the church.[104]

While today, it is understood to a certain extent that commercials and sponsorship are needed to ensure a program stays on the air at a desirable time slot, the mingling of consumer goods with discourses aimed at soothing a person's soul was then a novel sort of oddity, one that was seen as both odd and intrusive.[105] In many ways, this critique would mirror the criticism levelled at the later televangelists, where the intersections between television, religious, and advertising were said to have contributed to the "commodification of American religion."[106] Sheen was likely aware of this tension and the possible issues it could lead to, doing his best to soften things. In one episode he promoted Admiral by giving it a tongue-in-cheek appraisal: "At the end of this television program, there is going to be a great burst of applause … You will have heard something the likes of which is not given on any other television program. You will have heard something that delights every father in the United States, that thrills every mother, that pleases every child. Namely, a commercial about an Admiral refrigerator."[107] Still, to defer any criticism that he was profiting from his celebrity during what was in essence a public service broadcasting program, Sheen frequently reminded his viewers that all proceeds generated by the sponsorship and his own salary would – in an act of personal austerity – be sent to charity rather than his personal coffers.[108] And so, while the presence of a bishop appearing to shill for a corporation certainly raised some eyebrows, Sheen thus nevertheless found ways in which his celebrity could contribute to his own personal sanctification behind the scenes.

## Celebrity, Sanctity, and Persona Negotiated

Like other celebrities, the celebrity preachers of the 1950s were not isolated in their formulation but were part of a wider discussion and negotiation of celebrity that defined the television personalities of the era. Though their programs were decidedly religious by nature, the American public did not necessarily see men like Sheen, Peale, and Graham as representing radically different enterprises than celebrities such as Berle or Sinatra, as both categories of entertainers essentially competed for *the same* viewing audiences.

Note, for instance, how the downward trajectory of Berle's program and popularity began in 1952, the same year that *Life Is Worth Living* went on the air. This suggests that Sheen was not simply able to draw fresh audiences to television whom might otherwise have had little interest in the medium, but that he was also able to draw audiences *away* from Berle.[109] Thus, the same people who might tune into the *Texaco Star Theater* in search of a comedy routine would also tune into the DuMont Network for a lighthearted and often enlightening lecture from Bishop Sheen. From our current vantage point – one which can see the past seventy years of television history neatly mapped out – it might be tempting to look back and categorize both programs as discrete genres, one being a comedy show and the other being a public service lecture. However, to suggest that audiences at the time had the same level of awareness about genre and format as we do is, perhaps, anachronistic. Television was a new medium at the time, not fully formed. Audiences then were likely less discerning about such differences, viewing the personality-centric programs as two sides of the same coin at the 8:00 p.m. timeslot. In such a case, Sheen's star power and celebrity draw could be compared with not only his fellow celebrity preachers but also wider configurations and expectations of this newfound form of American celebrity as it unfolded. As such, that Sheen's program – which was essentially a mandated public broadcast – not only survived but *thrived* is itself telling not only of the kind of programming Americans craved, but also of the kinds of celebrities they desired.

As a Catholic bishop, however, Sheen's celebrity was nevertheless required to navigate and contend with additional facets of his celebrity and specifically *sanctity* that his peers – whether preachers or otherwise – did not. As a celebrated member of the Catholic clergy, Sheen was not simply a preacher but also a sanctified individual, a man who had taken the cloth along with its accompanying vows of obedience and celibacy. As we have seen, since his death, Sheen has also been put forward as a candidate for sainthood, with his cause slowly progressing toward its ultimate goal. Thus, when examining Sheen's appeal, it is not necessarily clear where – if at all – the dividing line between the celebration of celebrity ends and that of sanctity begins, posing a unique problem in understanding his fame. What does it mean then when a sanctified person is also a celebrity (and not because of their sanctity)? What happens when this person is self-aware of this dual positionality? How do they reconcile these two halves?

Sheen's relationship with his celebrity, as we have previously seen, is tenuous at best. As discussed in chapter 1, throughout his career and in his autobiography, Sheen exerted an active effort to keep the topic of his celebrity at arm's length whenever he was given the chance to discuss it, often relying on his well-known tactic of self-deprecating humour to deflect any acknowledgement of his star power.[110] If we recall, I cited a quote from Sheen's autobiography where he cheekily remarked that three of his classmates had gone on to become famous personalities – and if the reader is feeling charitable, perhaps they will consider him the fourth.[111] Thus while other television celebrities of his era were focused on negotiating a form of fame that could make them culturally relevant without going the route of the "real" stars who hailed from Hollywood, Sheen's fame required additional negotiation, even if there was little in his confident television persona during *Life Is Worth Living* that suggested it. It could be tempting to say that such concerns only troubled him later in life, such as during the composition of his autobiography in the twilight of his years with his full legacy to look back upon. However, we can see in other early instances that he was aware of the dilemmas associated with his fame.

During his appearance in *What's My Line?*, the panellists were tasked with identifying the mystery guest. In their attempt to garner more information about his identity, the panellists asked Sheen whether he was "a familiar figure in public life." He replied "Un peu, oui" (A little, yes), causing host John Daly to jovially chime in with a correction, "I would say our guest is well known." In the following question, Sheen was asked whether he was well known in television. Sheen looked lost in thought a moment, like it had never occurred to him, before hunching his shoulders and responding "Je ne sais pas" (I don't know) and again having Daly add a resounding "'Yes' on our guest's behalf."[112] If we go further back, even as early as 1946 – several years before the inaugural run of *Life Is Worth Living*, when he was still riding off the popularity of *The Catholic Hour* – Sheen reportedly rebuffed a reporter seeking to interview him. When asked why he was uninterested in the coverage, Sheen stated that publicity was "as artificial as rouge on the cheek."[113]

Sheen's comment about fame being of little more value than "rouge on one's cheek" is perhaps ironic – as will be explained below – and doesn't really tell the full story of his relationship toward his own celebrity and persona. Sheen was known at times to have an obsessive tendency toward managing and perfecting his own image – especially as it appeared before the cameras. According to his one-time assistant and two-time biographer, Daniel P. Noonan, Sheen was drawn to the camera from the first moment he walked on set, becoming immediately and intimately aware of the power the lens had for capturing his already well-honed persona as a powerful orator and preacher.[114] On set for *Life Is Worth Living*, he was reported as being controlling and perhaps even domineering toward crew members, instructing camera operators how to position the shots to capture his best angles, and making heavy use of underlighting to give his face an air of added gravitas whenever he broke into the more serious elements of his monologues.[115] He never appeared before the cameras unless his hair was immaculately coiffed, his cheeks and chin clean shaven, and his attire perfectly washed and ironed. His choice of wardrobe was equally telling – by choosing to dress up in the full ceremonial regalia of a bishop, replete with a grand sash and cape, Sheen signalled his status while instilling a sense of presence and grandiosity before the cameras that no one could ignore.

Actions such as these suggest that Sheen was hardly impervious to the draw of celebrity and were by no means the only defining marks his fame had on his life. In *The Bishop Sheen Story*, James C.G. Conniff comments on the fact that the bishop owned a "long black Cadillac" with a chauffeur, who not only ferried him to his engagements at the Adelphi Theatre for his weekly program but also out to brunch with his film star friends – who included fellow Catholics and Hollywood starlets Loretta Young and Irene Dunne.[116] When he played his occasional round of golf, he would show up at the club "dressed for the sport like a men's fashion magazine ad model."[117] Sheen also owned a home in the Upper East Side made from white brick and limestone, and another in Washington, DC, with a stairwell modelled on one he'd seen in the Vatican and which had left an impression on him. Commenting on the stairwell at the Washington house, a gushing Conniff remarks that a "wired gold and aluminum ceiling fixture centered above it reflected in a circular mirror set in the basement floor. It gave the illusion that you were gazing down into fantastic depths at least two stories beneath the very foundations of the house."[118] However, lest the reader be taken away by the ostentatiousness of the buildings themselves, the author quickly highlighted how Sheen furnished his living spaces with "austere furniture ... especially the bedroom," with the mention of the bedroom simultaneously drawing attention to a very personal space while neutering it more appropriately for his person.[119]

Examples such as these highlight that Sheen was in some ways drawn toward the ostentatious, often manifesting itself through the material. While owning a stairwell that reminded him of a similar one in the Vatican could be made out to be a material reminder of a spiritual experience, such an artifact is hardly a pilgrim's memento or other keepsake. An imposing automobile, a home that instills awe in its visitors, and lunch companions that turn the heads and inflame the passions in bystanders are visibly powerful. These are symbols of privilege and influence in society – a passive means of signalling Sheen's celebrity to others in perhaps less than subtle ways – and likely contributed to the frequent accusations of pride levelled at him, as well as the concern his cause had taken to ensure that his more ordinary and "down to earth" aspects were emphasized.[120]

It is thus here where Sheen's success in cultivating a comfortable and entirely familiar "everyman persona" in the way that television facilitated falters upon closer examination. Regarding so many of the aspects that were meant to come across as accessible, a closer examination also suggests that they were perhaps not so. Take for example the dressings he chose for his set, choosing to make it appear like a rector or professor's office. While useful for conveying authority, these were not spaces with which the average American would have been familiar or perhaps even comfortable. Where television of the 1970s and onward increasingly focused on family spaces, even having entire shows taking place predominantly in the living rooms of its characters, the 1950s still encouraged a certain remoteness or idealization of its spaces.[121] Furthermore, Lynch remarks that while the content of Sheen's program was designed to be inclusive, inviting and form bonds of attachment with his audience, his choice of ceremonial clothing – rather than more comfortable, informal wear – had the effect of putting up certain barriers and creating detachment between himself and the viewer.[122] His choice of clothing also pointed toward his status as a veritable aristocrat within the American church, causing one to wonder how his body can be understood – does it represent the fulfillment of the American dream, or does it represent its unattainability?[123] As much as he sought to become the familiar face and voice to millions of Americans, by mingling with his fellow celebrities, counting himself among them, meeting the opportunities they presented him, living in his palatial home, and even appearing behind the screens of the television rather than in person, Sheen was perhaps on some level maintaining the difference, distance, and grandeur expected from a man of his stature within the church. Though he sought to be ordinary and approachable, he was in reality living far from such ideals.

Regardless, in calling attention to all these quirks of Sheen's celebrity, it is not my intention to debase the figure, nor to argue that he was hypocritical. Rather, I would like to highlight the complexity and contradictory demands of balancing two halves of a single life – one steeped in austerity and the other in a world deeply embedded in conceptualizations of secular celebrity. While we might be tempted to see both halves in opposition and conflict, the reality is not so stark. Scholars Marguerite den Berg and Claartje L. ter Hoeven remind us in a recent article that where celebrity is concerned, faith and secularity should not be understood as two opposites separated by rigid boundaries; they often mix, overlap, and blend in unexpected ways in the popular arena.[124] I suspect Sheen – and even Peale and Graham in their own Protestant ways – likely equated the two, and that he saw no conflict between fame and sanctity, between *celebratio* and celebrity, perhaps even believing them to be intertwined. Sheen, through his celebrity, was in many ways the most visible representative of the church in America. Seeing him on screen was seeing the church, in all its glory, personified and dignified, there to guide and console Americans through a challenging time. By embodying the persona to the fullest of what his faith would allow, Sheen was perhaps also pushing the church for all his celebrity could allow. All his grandiose gestures drew attention to himself and by extension to his Church, and because of that, he had to find ways to present himself as an impeccable, successful, and larger than life, representative of that institution.[125]

## Conclusion

Cultural theorist Stuart Hall once remarked that "popular culture … is an arena that is profoundly mythic. It is a theatre of popular desires, a theatre of popular fantasies. It is where we discover and play with the identification of ourselves, where we are imagined."[126] The traits and individuals that a given society finds themselves drawn toward are fluid and unfixed, operating in both real and imagined spaces and constantly finding themselves in ongoing negotiation with wider audiences and their expectations.[127] Celebrity then – as a social construct – acts as a guidepost for drawing attention to the particular assortment of traits and individuals held in high regard by a given society at a specific time or place. Of this era, as Timothy H. Sherwood writes, "Americans wanted to be reassured," and individuals who could provide that reassurance were afforded a previously undiscovered route toward celebrity of which television was the pivotal medium of allowing for its conceptualization.[128]

The celebrity preachers who personified this newfound form of celebrity were able to thrive in the early postwar years because they offered Americans an accessible access point into the problem-solving capabilities of religion, through shared, ecumenical access points. As we saw, despite hailing from across denominational lines, Sheen, Peale, and Graham were not so much competing voices but complimentary ones in America. What bound them together was the suggestion that religion was intimately grounded in the material and emotional concerns of the viewers and their own interests in the here and now. As Erin A. Smith suggests, "The same readers who read Peale's *The Power of Positive Thinking* were also quite likely to watch Catholic Fulton Sheen's prime-time television program, *Life is Worth Living*, write fan letters to the Jewish Liebman, listen to liberal Protestant Fosdick's sermons on the radio, and/or follow Graham's enormous evangelical Christian revivals through the media."[129] Where denominational lines had previously been defining factors in the identification of Americans – an identification often related to ethnic boundaries – the atmosphere, as we have previously discussed, had markedly changed by the 1950s. The suburbanization of America in the aftermath of World War II had helped break down many of the previous barriers that physically and spatially divided Americans. It also helped that none of these celebrity figures were unduly concerned with highlighting the particularities of their respective traditions or suggesting their superiority, but instead sought to highlight the common ground represented by the "triple melting pot" of their shared Judeo-Christian heritage and the ecclesial foundations of the nation.[130]

For the most part, the celebrity preacher excelled at disseminating what Smith refers to as a "middle brow" theology that came across to its audiences as educated and informed, all the while being immanently accessible and uncritical.[131] Tuning into one of their programs or picking up a paperback of theirs, one would immediately see that their messages were was targeted to everyday lay people, the labourers and workers among America's public, rather than its theologians or learned elite. In effect, as a remedy for the spiritual and political malaise of their day, these celebrity preachers sought to position religion as an easy-to-understand but ultimately transformative force, one that could aid individuals in letting go of their fears and insecurities. In other words, spirituality was rendered as the non-denominational route to health, happiness, prosperity, and the American dream. However, in many ways, the religion being disseminated by celebrity preachers sometimes appeared to be a distant cousin of the version of Christianity being preached from the pulpits of churches across the nation – a version of Christianity that was often looked down upon by scholars, intellectuals, fellow clerics, and at times even the community of devout itself. While this distillation of religious fundamentals into its more approachable format caused many to argue that something was being lost, it was nevertheless necessary to reaffirm these very same values on a massive scale. Such is the paradox of massive appeal and accessibility.

Though Sheen and the other celebrity preachers of the era were prolific across numerous media – including radio and paperback publishing – it was their television presence that had the greatest effect on shaping this form of celebrity personality. As Christine Becker remarks, "In the private spaces of American homes, early television progressively deconstructed the mythologies of stardom that the film industry had systematically cultivated for decades."[132] In other words, by ushering in modifications of the celebrity tropes and expectations that were once solidified, dominated, and closely guarded by the then-dominant visual media – Hollywood – television, with its focus on the authenticity and "real" personas of its stars, allowed the medium to propel figures like Sheen to the spotlight, figures whose presence could be read as a challenge to the prevailing norms of celebrity.[133] In this, I am not necessarily arguing that Sheen's show, or Peale's, or any of the other celebrity preachers of this era were themselves responsible for changing the norms and expectations of celebrity as some proponents have argued.[134] Rather, these were men who were able to recognize the shifts in the atmosphere and seize the possibilities afforded to them. As such, the success of the early religious television programs and the rise of the celebrity preachers in the 1950s points to both the fluidity and variety of celebrity found in mid-twentieth-century American popular culture as well as the adaptability of personal sanctity that allowed these men to enter into stardom as religious leaders.

While this form of celebrity continued to live within the ongoing careers of these men – Sheen enjoyed his aura of celebrity well into the 1970s, even after his fiasco in Rochester, Peale remained a popular orator and bestselling author, and Graham was no less visible and beloved until his death in 2018 – the circumstances that allowed for their rise and creation was not as long-lived. On the one hand, television transformed rapidly. While Sheen could achieve success with little more than his good looks and a piece of chalk, later viewers were more demanding in terms of what they expected from a thirty-minute program – as was evidenced by his diminishing returns in later years. Even the much beloved variety program of the early 1950s rapidly lost ground as more ambitious, scripted drama programs like *Gunsmoke* or *Wagon Train* became the norm. Religious programs would evolve, too, not by following the lead of entertainment television but by borrowing from the playbooks of commercial marketers and focusing on promoting a single product: salvation.[135] As the personalities hosting these programs transformed their celebrity personas into the televangelists we continue to recognize today, these preachers bore little of the markers that defined the early celebrity preachers. Gone was any semblance of ecumenism, with many Evangelical televangelists routinely arguing that others or outsiders were destined for hellfire while only the righteous "we" would benefit from God's transformative grace.[136] Rather than focus on inclusivity, these celebrities tended more toward the exclusive than the belief of an America defined by shared values. They would also increasingly compete for slots on Sunday mornings, competing with traditional religious services to draw audiences to their programs.

Still, when we consider the men who rose to fit the mould of the celebrity preacher in the postwar era, Sheen stands out from his peers through his choice to remain denominationally *visible* during his televised talks. While other celebrity preachers of the era, such as Peale and Graham could wear tan suits and focus their talks on a soft sort of ecumenism and doctrinally loose positivity, Sheen's program was necessarily Catholic in appearance, if not doctrine. By dressing in his full ceremonial regalia and not the more casual clothing one would assume he was likely to wear at home or in private company, Sheen was simultaneously subordinating himself to the cultural expectations placed upon a Catholic bishop as well as slowly subverting such expectations of otherness through his performance.[137] By making himself a visibly (and undeniably) identifiable symbol of the Catholic faith, he was reminding his viewers of his status within the church, while also normalizing the visibility of its most defining elements. In the role of television host, and wearing the guise of the bishop, Sheen was demonstrating that the Catholic bishop was to an extent just another performer, just another television persona, just another fellow American.

Speaking to this, Mark Massa argues that Sheen's popularity and career helped facilitate the final stages of American Catholicism's long-term transition from cultural minority to part of the cultural mainstream.[138] Reeves similarly states that "Bishop Sheen's phenomenal success on television was a sign that millions of Americans had gone beyond the crude caricatures so familiar in the nation's history and were willing to accept Catholics as Christians and friends."[139] Indeed, by relying on overtly Catholic symbols, and playing upon the possibilities of familiarity engendered by the medium, Sheen's presence can be read as sign of the increasingly commonplace familiarity with Catholic symbols in American popular culture. Even if the average American might not encounter Catholic bishops going about in their day to day lives, they could apparently now encounter them in their living rooms if they so chose to do so.

The optimism and ecumenism brought about by the celebrity preachers wasn't without its cracks, however. Though Sheen was widely admired across denominational lines, his prominence caused lingering nativism to flare up. One noticeable example was when *Time* magazine featured him on the cover of one of their 1952 issues, proclaiming him as the "first televangelist." At the sight of his face alone, with cassock, collar and zucchetto, the magazine received a flurry of protest letters from Protestant ministers, one of whom railed that Sheen's cover was a symbol of "Roman Catholic totalitarianism."[140] Additionally, the perceived success of Sheen in reaching wide swatches of audiences across denominational lines was perhaps more anecdotal and optimistic than grounded in the data.[141] Though, I would argue that what matters more than whether these claims about the ecumenical nature of their approach and diversity of audiences were factually grounded or not, is that commentators and proponents of Sheen *imagined* and *desired* them to be true.[142] After all, the belief that an American cleric from a minority faith could so effectively unite Americans of all backgrounds under a single, simple message, was effectively also a belief in America itself and its possibility of more fully becoming a nation built on democratic pluralism.

Finding strength in Sheen's apparent ability to unite Americans is itself a far cry from the discourses touted a generation prior, which communicated messages of suspicion and distrust about minorities wielding too much national influence – something epitomized in the backlash to the Al Smith presidential campaign.[143] While in the 1920s and 1930s it was untenable to imagine that a Catholic spokesperson could unite various communities around a similar, shared identity as Americans, by the 1950s, not only had it become a viable prospect, but one in which commentators sought to assert and solidify.[144] In this sense, there is some truth to the coming-of age adages about the Catholic reception by and acculturation into the American mainstream. However, as is discussed in the following chapter, this process was far from a linear trajectory that merely came to fruit in the postwar climate of ecumenism. Indeed, where American visual media and culture was concerned, the process of "rehabilitating" Catholics into the American mainstream began much earlier than Sheen's prominent appearance during the television. A full generation earlier, back in the 1930s, Catholic stories, culture, and identities were already becoming part of the mainstream American visual language and memory, notably by turning the most totemic emblem of Catholicism – their celibate, sanctified priests – into leading figures with which Americans could identify. And so, while the medium of television was not necessarily responsible for this gradual change in perception of Catholics in America, as we see in the following chapter, it did in many ways inherit the momentum previously built up by an unlikely ally – Hollywood.

# 4

# From Suspicion to Stardom

## *Realism and the Hollywood Priests*

### A Good Year to Be Entertained

In 1954, *Life Is Worth Living*, was in its third and final season on the ailing DuMont Network, with Sheen's nationwide visibility and popularity showing little sign of slowing down. However, parallel to his program, another American work of visual media replete with Catholic themes and characters began receiving widespread critical acclaim. Coming off the tail of his controversial appearance before the House Un-American Activities Committee, director Elia Kazan released the film *On the Waterfront*, a tale of corruption, violence, and one man's crisis of conscience while working as a longshoreman on New Jersey's docks.[1] Marlon Brando portrayed Irish American protagonist Terry Malloy, a rough and tumble working-class American figure, able to exude – as film critic Allen Almachar remarked – "both a dangerous thug and a vulnerable man at the exact same time."[2] Though Brando's performance of a man struggling with his conscience and the demands of his blue-collar masculinity garners most of the film's laurels, Karl Malden's supporting turn as Father Pete Barry – a hard-smoking, rough-talking, and afraid-of-nothing Catholic priest – was no less remarkable as it pointed to a significantly harder shift in the portrayal of Catholic priests from prior generations, and from a then-concurrent television program.

Hollywood has had a long-lasting fascination with Catholic clergy, so much that by the 1950s, there was no shortage of Irish American priests in its catalogue. Popular films from the 1930s and 1940s helped build up a repertoire of expectations and visual imagery for on-screen depictions of these priests that were largely framed against a backdrop of suspicion. Nativist sentiments were in an upswing in America, and these sentiments painted Irish Catholics as a subversive "fifth column" incapable of becoming truly American – a portrayal that frequently made them targets of persecution. Rather than give in to the ripe atmosphere of suspicion that surrounded American Catholics at the time, these films depicted their protagonists as safe and paternal figures who selflessly worked for the greater good of their communities – thus avoiding any nuance or moral ambiguity that could paint them in a negative light. While this type of characterization risked making Catholic priests appear weak or "soft" to audiences, the movies in question evaded this reading by painting them as authority figures who embodied a responsible and controlled (and often superior) masculinity and who were typically portrayed by highly charismatic leading men. The way priests of this earlier generation were portrayed was thus a far cry from *On the Waterfront's* Father Barry, who embodied a form of masculinity more typically found in the "hard-boiled" genre, where gangsters and detectives (often Irish Americans Catholics themselves) glorified toughness and the reaffirmation of masculinity over that of femininity in a world of violence and competition.[3] This characterization of Father Barry suggests that, by the 1950s, the American audience's perception of priests had grown beyond these earlier archetypes, and that grittier, less conventional, and more nuanced characterizations were now possible and even expected.

However, far from the gritty docks where Father Barry ministered, Sheen's Emmy Award-winning performance made for decidedly safe and family-friendly viewing.[4] While American audiences had – thanks to Hollywood – grown accustomed to seeing priests in either relaxed black cassocks or black suits with clerical collars, Sheen performed each episode in the unambiguous garb of a monsignor.[5] In contrast to the more challenging and realistic figures Hollywood was moving toward in the 1950s, Sheen's series and televised performances seemed to be a throwback – perhaps even an anachronism – that pointed to an earlier era of visual culture surrounding priests and one where the foundations, and even expectations, of his performance of celebrity priesthood along with its appeal can be rooted.

This chapter examines how Sheen's televised performances in the 1950s, rather than being read as a novel development in the then-current visual repertoire of American priests, were instead indebted to an earlier tradition of Irish American priests in American visual media – namely, a tradition established by Hollywood in the 1930s and 1940s. By discussing certain tropes, perceptions, and evolutions of Irish Catholics in America, along with the portrayals and embodiments of their masculinity, we will be able to understand the disproportionately dominant role Hollywood has had in shaping the American public's perception and expectations of Irish American Catholic priests against racially and religiously charged nativist stereotypes. As we shall see, Sheen was in many ways the inheritor and continuation of the celebrity priest archetype shaped by these earlier on-screen portrayals, as his own "brand" of performative clerical masculinity reflected many of the same tropes found in these films – and, moreover, he continued to embody these characteristics even after their prominence had begun to fade as more challenging and ambiguous depictions had become the norm.[6]

Therefore, while the story of Sheen's success owes much to his medium, time, and place, the earlier story of Hollywood's depiction of priests also factor into this and to better understand his celebrity appeal, we need to examine the cultural and visual histories that helped enable it. To do so, we will use several Hollywood movies as our primary source material – specifically, *Going My Way*, *Angels with Dirty Faces*, and *Boys Town*.[7] While Sheen's performance might have come across as old-fashioned, it nevertheless resonated with audiences, and while it is my contention that this has largely to do with the differing set of expectations audiences brought to the medium of television, Sheen was nevertheless highly adept through his own televised performances at giving second life to an earlier portrayal of priesthood that had largely disappeared. Though, lest we view this visual lineage as being entirely linear in its trajectory, we will also examine how the depiction of Father Barry challenges these earlier tropes as well as the reasons why they were necessary in the first place.

## Irish Catholics, America, and Hollywood

### *Irish Catholics in America*

By the mid-twentieth century, Sheen and many of his Catholic contemporaries, such as fellow priest and CUA scholar John Tracy Ellis, were both unequivocal and nonchalant about the Americanness of the nation's Catholics of Irish descent. To Ellis, in particular, Catholics were not outsiders but the greatest representation and fulfillment of the nation's promise and values.[8] However, even in the decades prior, the integration and acceptance of Irish Catholics into the nation's membership was hardly a given.

While Irish Catholics have been on America's shores since the time of the Thirteen Colonies, they were a marked minority. Their numbers, however, increased exponentially following the Great Famine of 1845–49, when nearly two million Irish men and women arrived as refugees, with another 650,000 arriving in the 1880s owing to increasing political violence and land wars back in Ireland.[9] The number of dioceses in America at the beginning of the nineteenth century had quadrupled by the twentieth century, making the largely immigrant Catholic communities the single largest denomination by membership in the nation.[10] The growing presence of Irish Catholics, however, did not signal a seamless amalgamation into the American pastiche. It was widely believed they were resistant to acculturation, and, as a result, did not achieve any sort of immediate nor widespread cultural acceptance from America's patchwork Protestant majority.[11]

Prejudice directed against Irish Catholics in America during this earlier era can be understood as an amalgamation of two historical currents. The first was a long-standing history of anti-Catholicism among English Protestants. As historian Kyle E. Haden puts it, "Footed in the Reformation, anti-Catholicism bore fruit among the various Protestant settlers in colonial America and passed in the genetic structure of American national consciousness. Like a roller coaster, its manifestation in social and political behavior has risen and fallen over the course of U.S. history, but has never been eradicated."[12] The Catholic adherence to the foreign institution of the papacy was deemed at best to be medieval and backward, and, at worst, evidence that Catholics held a tenuous dual allegiance to the Pope in Rome.[13] Additionally, certain liberal proponents of American democracy argued that the tenets of their young nation rested on non-dogmatic premises, and therefore Catholics, by their dogmatic nature, could never become true democrats and thus never become true Americans.[14] Catholics would continue to face this type of perpetual questioning about whether they were *really* American until the midway mark of the twentieth century.

The second current was rooted in English colonialism – both of Ireland and of North America itself. Just as the Catholicism of the Irish was made into a trope to assert the power of English Protestantism, their expanding presence in America could also point to anxieties about the ruling class's inability to fully dominate and control their colonial subjects back in Europe.[15] This class-based opposition against the possible acceptance of Irish Catholics had an additional confounding element in the United States, where it was estimated that of those who migrated to the nation, a mere 3 per cent arrived with any professional or artisanal skills, making the vast majority of the arrivals unskilled labourers in desperate need of work.[16] As such, the majority of the newcomers settled in America's industrial centres – New York City, Chicago, and Detroit – or in what remained of the old frontier, where manual labourers were in high demand for railroads and other infrastructure projects – work which did little to elevate them from their generally impoverished background as recently landed immigrants looking to settle in a foreign and often hostile culture.[17] As labourers, "their days were spent draining land, grubbing, mucking, or digging ditches … [they] endured brutal working conditions, punishing state and company politics, and hostile community reactions."[18] Worse, the Irish newcomers, many of whom did not speak English, appeared to outsiders, as Irish studies scholar Christopher Dowd puts it, as "poor, uneducated and insular. They did not seem compatible with American society."[19] All the while, this ostracism coincided with a surge of self-awareness about their own ethnic difference, which, in turn only exacerbated the feeling of division between them and their American peers.[20]

Becoming recognized as Irish American Catholics as opposed to "Irish Catholics in America" was thus a slow and unsteady process and not without its setbacks. For instance, the 1928 presidential campaign of Democratic candidate Al Smith showcased the extent to which the Protestant majority was unwilling to accept that a Catholic could be fit to lead the nation. Smith, a four-times-elected (and popular) governor of the state of New York (from 1919 to 1920 and again from 1923 to 1928), was in many ways the poster child for a rags-to-riches story showcasing the promise of the American dream. A second-generation American, Smith grew up in Manhattan's notoriously rough Lower East Side. Linked to Tammany Hall, the Irish American–run political machine that controlled most of New York's politics and the Democratic Party in that state, he eventually became a political reformer who campaigned against Prohibition. Smith sought the Democratic nomination for the presidency first in 1924, and then successfully in 1928. Despite going forward as a popular candidate in the Northern states, his Irish Catholic identity did him no favours as he lost in a landslide.[21]

Interestingly, by all measures Smith appeared largely detached from his faith in public life, and repeatedly denied that dogmatic matters could ever overrule the loyalty of Catholic Americans to their nation.[22] Yet, despite presenting himself as something of a liberal, urban gentleman, the image of the hard-drinking, hard-fighting Irishman tainted by Catholic suspicion was hard to fend off. Classist opponents saw Smith as having been cut from the same rough cloth as Irish labourers.[23] Others took issue with everything about Smith, from the people with whom he socialized (dockworkers, Catholic priests) to the urban colloquialisms he deployed in his speech, to the cut of his suits, finding fault and proletariat sensibilities in all of them. It just went to show that even after putting on a suit and becoming governor of the nation's most populous state, the cigar-smoking presidential candidate was, at the end of the day, unable to shake the pejorative stereotypes that branded every Catholic Irish American.

As this prominent example of anti-Catholic sentiment demonstrates, any historical analysis that supports the notion of there being radical change in America's attitude toward her Catholic minorities during this period would seem misguided. Thus, rather than acting as a herald for equality and the positive acceptance of diversity, Smith's presidential campaign instead ended up giving new life to America's long-standing tendency toward "ethno-religious bigotry."[24] While nativist sentiments in late nineteenth and early twentieth-century America were by no means homogenous, Catholics inspired sentiments of "fear and loathing" in the Protestant majority – a sentiment perhaps owing to their perceived racial proximity and similarity to the majority, along with the enduring prejudices inherited from Protestant Europe.[25] Smith's campaign thus became the linchpin for a revival in intolerance not seen in the states since the Know-Nothings of the 1850s.[26]

While the backlash against Smith proved that America's Protestant majority was clearly not ready for the presence of prominent Irish American Catholics in politics (and least of all in presidential races), the late 1920s and 1930s nevertheless marked a turning point of different kind and in a different arena. In the years following Smith's failed presidential bid, Irish American Catholics went on to achieve acceptance and even acclamation in the most privileged and rapidly dominant medium of entertainment culture: Hollywood.

## *From Suspicion to Stardom*

While the Midwest of Sheen's upbringing and the urban metropolis where he forged his career were far removed from the balmy reaches of Southern California, it was there, during a generation prior, where seeds that would help move the nation toward Catholic acceptance – and by extension, elements of his own celebrity success – were being sown.

At the turn of the twentieth century, Hollywood was little more than a small, unassuming municipality that straddled the edge of Los Angeles and the Santa Monica mountains. In 1910 the small city in the foothills voted to merge with their much larger neighbour, and just two years later some of the first motion picture companies settled around Los Angeles. Owing to its balmy weather and spacious potential for studio lots – as well as the distance it put between filmmakers and Thomas Edison's New Jersey–based Motion Picture Patents Company, which had a penchant for suing filmmakers – the area quickly became the centre of America's fledgling movie industry.[27] By 1917, major motion pictures were being made, and the lead actors in these films – figures like Charlie Chaplin, Douglas Fairbanks, and Mary Pickford – would quickly go on to become Hollywood's first stars. By the following decade – which saw the erection of the famous "Hollywood" sign on the hills – the suburb was producing several hundred feature films each year. While radio was still the dominant medium of entertainment in households and public spaces, movies were rapidly growing in popularity, and, as a result, Hollywood quickly became the dominant producer of not only films but also American visual culture more generally.[28]

Despite coming from often disenfranchised socioeconomic and cultural backgrounds, the 1930s produced no shortage of Irish American and Irish-born American actors landing leading roles in Hollywood pictures, meaning that, in a peculiar twist of fate, Irish American Catholics were being widely disenfranchised in labour and politics at the exact same time they found themselves – and their stories – ascending in entertainment media.[29] While some film representations of Irish issues and identities were played for little more than cheap laughs – as in in the infamous and widely boycotted 1927 film *The Callahans and the Murphys* – others offered more positive and far less prejudicial roles for Irish American actors to play.[30] Contrary to expectation, given the climate of distrust and prejudice, American films with staunchly Irish Catholic stories helmed by Irish leads were hardly niche either. Remarking on this, Gary D. Rhodes states that "rather than being produced specifically for working-class Irish immigrants in urban areas like New York … it is clear that moving picture companies targeted Irish-themed films at the general American audience who attended screenings in small towns and big cities across the country."[31] Not only were many popular movies of the era carried by Irish American actors, the stories themselves were fundamentally stories about the Irish underclass in America – and, by extension, Catholics in America.

Importantly, these films did not shy away from depictions of Irish American hardships – their struggles and reconciliations with Catholic morality and their challenging interpersonal stories. Well-written screenplays and strong direction helped expose these themes in a way that became meaningful and even acceptable for wider American audiences and values. While the first Irish American celebrity actors of the 1930s and 1940s indeed became celebrities through their portrayal of "Irish ethnic types," these portrayals did not characterize the Irish ethnicity nor the Catholic religion as wholly other – rather, here in these early films, Irish American Catholics were portrayed as being both fully ethnic and fully American.[32] This more nuanced portrayal of Irish Americans – one that simultaneously reminded viewers of their differences while at the same time closing the divide that separated them from the Anglo-Saxon, Protestant majority – reinforced the vision of America as a diverse, melting pot of a nation. As a result, from the 1930s onward, American moviegoers became familiar with what would become quintessential Irish American figures, such as the hard-boiled gangster with a kind heart underneath and – more significantly for our work – Catholic priests.

That priests – the most visible markers of Catholic otherness – would come to be major and often critically acclaimed characters in early Hollywood productions of this era was by no means a certainty; and yet, it can hardly be considered a cultural fluke that slid under the radar of production studios. If a single figure can be said to have helped usher in not just the presence of priests in cinema but their casting by top actors in both leading and supporting roles, it would be Joseph Breen. Breen was the son of Irish immigrants raised in a devout Catholic household, who became a prominent journalist in the early 1930s before being before appointed by the Motion Picture Producers and Distributors of America as the head of the newly created Production Code Administration (PCA).[33] While production studios had previously self-censored their work voluntarily, minimizing graphic violence and sexual content, the PCA made censorship requirements legally binding.[34] Breen, inspired by his staunch Catholic upbringing and enduring faith, approached his duties militantly.[35] Thus, as head of the censorship board, he acted as both the gatekeeper of Hollywood's content and the enforcer of its morality. For Breen, few characters held as much appeal – or significance as symbols of morality – as Catholic priests, and he ensured they would be portrayed as exemplary Americans in Hollywood's films. While priests thus could be (and were) routinely mocked and feared in other areas of American culture, Breen ensured that their representation on screens across America would be consistently upstanding.

While Breen ensured that there would be no shortage of material for our discussion, three films in particular from this pre-war era of Hollywood stand out for our investigation as prime examples of the ways in which Irish American actors portrayed Irish American Catholic priests during this period – either in a leading role or as a major supporting actor: *Boys Town*, *Angels with Dirty Faces*, and *Going My Way*. Each of these films stands out for our discussion of this period, not only for their narrative content but for how they reflect broader cultural attitudes through their depictions of clergy. While each performance has its own nuances, three common elements of their depictions of priests stand out in particular: priests as characters with clear goals and relatable story arcs; priests as moral authorities and exemplars; and, perhaps most importantly, priests as familial figures with an overarching concern for the well-being of their communities. Taken together, these characteristics exemplify the positive portrayal of priests sought by Breen and others associated with the PCA, a portrayal which characterizes priests as "safe" figures who appear far removed from any of the negative stereotypes typically cast on them – and which in many ways give a backdrop to, as well as mirroring, the later on-screen performance of Sheen himself.

## Hollywood Archetypes

### *Safe Adults, Reckless Youths*

*Boys Town*, released in 1938, and just two months before *Angels with Dirty Faces* hit the theatres, was among the earliest mainstream Hollywood pictures to focus on a Catholic priest in the leading role. In the film, Spencer Tracy portrays a fictionalized version of the real-life Father Edward J. Flannagan, who established the titular orphanage and associated organization in Douglas County, Nebraska in 1917. The movie opens with Flanagan hearing the final confession of a murderer on death row, who describes the troubles he had as a homeless youth and his inevitable spiral toward crime. Refusing to let other men follow the same path and believing – as he declares – that "there is no such thing as a bad boy," Flanagan makes it his life's goal to set up a sanctuary for delinquent young men.[36] Over the course of the film he encounters and overcomes a variety of opposition, from legal and jurisdictional matters to trouble among the young men he shelters at Boys Town. One in particular, Whitey Marsh – played by Mickey Rooney – idolizes his older brother Joe, who is in prison awaiting trial for murder. After failing to be elected "mayor" of Boys Town by his peers, Whitey flees, intending to catch up with his brother who has recently escaped from prison. However, one of the other boys follows Whitey and is tragically killed after being abandoned by him. Still insistent on finding his brother, Whitey finally meets up with Joe during a robbery where he is accidentally wounded by a gunshot. Eventually, the delinquents give in, allowing Father Flannagan to come to their rescue while Joe and his criminal associates are captured. As a reward, Boys Town is flooded with donations and Flannagan begins planning an ambitious expansion for the sanctuary.

The image of the priest responsibly looking after delinquent youths and attempting to steer them away from a life of gangsterism is as important culturally as it is central to the film. The eleventh-hour reversal at the beginning of the picture – where the sinner on death row speaking to Flannagan sees the error of his ways and turns toward the church – succinctly conveys the Catholic theory of redemption and salvation. Though, as the film demonstrates, Flanagan's interest in the salvific process is not only spiritual and moral but also physical and communal. While Flanagan is indeed working to save the souls of the youths at the titular Boys Town, his most pressing concern is to give them a better life in America. Not unlike our celebrity preachers who would later blend temporal concerns with spiritual messaging, the film seems to suggest that all Catholic priests follow a similar social and religious imperative. As well, both the plot of *Boys Town* and the characterization of Flannagan specifically situate the priest as a caretaker and surrogate father for young boys. As such, the characterization of Flanagan as a safe, paternal figure whom the boys can look up to inherently challenges the then-pervasive suspicions cast on priests as agents of a foreign power or as possible corrupters of the youth.[37] Thus by portraying Father Flanagan as a caring, intelligent figure who desires to "save" the youth of the neighbourhood – not through proselytizing or doctrine, but rather through clothing, shelter, and safety – the film maps Catholicism onto local and material concerns, grounding its supposedly superstitious and airy doctrines. Importantly, the movie reminds audiences that this was not some work of fiction: not only was Flannagan a real-life figure, but his Boys Town experiment still exists, its mission intact and ongoing.

## *Fighting Stereotypes … and More*

Narratives that showcased the concern of priests for their parishes and the youth of America directly countered stereotypical fears about the role of priests as indoctrinating foreign agents with malevolent agendas. Priests such as Father Flanagan were men you could trust around your children and were men who were concerned with securing a better future for America itself. As Irish studies historian Christopher Shannon remarks, "The success of *Boys Town* marked a sea of change in American attitudes toward catholic priests … it was one thing to show a priest taming adult Irish gangsters in an urban ghetto; it was something entirely different to trust one with the children of America."[38]

Hollywood's depiction of Flannagan as a heroic Irish Catholic priest with very American sensibilities appeared in stark contrast with many of the stereotypes and representations of Irish Catholics in America at the time. Since the first waves of Irish immigration, Irish masculinity had inspired both fear and fascination in the American imagination. As discussed previously, the majority of the newcomers found themselves employed in industrial centres, performing hard labour in frequently unsafe conditions. Historically, the workplace acted not only as a space of male competition and rivalry for blue-collar workers and labourers, but also as a space of comradery and companionship that could extend beyond the working hours and into their shared spaces and activities.[39] Heavy drinking was common among blue-collar workers and labourers, so much so that then-contemporary commentators saw boozing and brawling – two activities that seemed to occupy their work and leisure times – as "inherited traits" of the Irish in America, something "embedded" in Irish culture.[40] The stereotype of the drinking Irishman was, however unfortunate, not entirely mythical. As was the case with many labourers in America, the harshness of their working conditions often promoted – even necessitated – the consumption of alcohol on the job and after.[41] For many Irish left with no choice but to work in abhorrent conditions out of fear of remaining destitute, alcohol was valued as a "critical component of their transplanted culture and masculinity," becoming a crucial component of the construction of their masculinity and self-identification as "rough, daring and formidable" workingmen.[42]

Unsurprisingly, the preferred pastimes and hobbies of Irish Americans reflected their often hard, dangerous, and violent lives. Boxing became a favoured and often uncouth pastime of Irish Americans, even if certain Catholic leaders sought to align athleticism with their ministerial work.[43] As a physical sport that relied on martial prowess, boxing matches were important tests and displays of manhood – here, Irish men could "affirm their masculinity" against others, including their oppressors, with boxers standing in metaphorically for the parishes or communities they represented, effectively putting the collective manhood of their supporters on the line.[44] Victories would be vicariously felt and enjoyed by their supporters while defeat brought with it a feeling of utter castration and impotence.[45] Sports and their associated activities allowed men to "escape from the domestic sphere and fraternize with other men, experiencing camaraderie and affirming their sense of male identity."[46] Bars – where watching sports and gambling often took place with plenty of alcohol – where quintessentially male spaces.[47] Owing to this, the Irish, as a people, were perceived to be more indulgent than others, "given to drink, sex, and generally revelry, which stood in stark contrast to stifling influences of Protestantism, lingering Puritan habits, and conservatives mores."[48] Such a rough and challenging masculinity was therefore framed as the embodiment of the existential threat to America's morality and moral sovereignty so feared by early nativists.[49]

However, the paradox of much of Irish masculinity in America at this time was that Irish masculinity was often times also fundamentally Catholic masculinity, effectively imbuing many Irish men with a sort of ambiguity: they simultaneously embodied characteristics of rough, hardened, and amoral labourers, as well as the more "feminine" qualities typically assigned to the religious. As Catholics, devotional life and religious culture inevitably seeped into their habits and informed their character, much of it carried over from their past in Ireland.[50] Discussing this ambiguity in his 2008 article "The Sword and the Prayerbook," Joseph Nugent notes how Irish clerics in the nineteenth century were often themselves the purveyors of this dual-natured masculinity. Initially, the Irish clergy emphasized a sort of heroic manliness that was rooted in martial prowess yet still connected to the spiritual. They emphasized that the ideal Irishman was like Christ both "in body and spirit," able to navigate both the secular and the sacred.[51] While models of tough, heroic and ultimately virtuous masculinity were initially emphasized through figures already present within the tradition – such as the world-travelling Ignatius Loyola and Francis Xavier, both of whom stood out as exemplars of manliness and transplanted identities – the ideals gradually shifted toward the ordinariness of priests as everyday people, as positive models for the community.[52] While Irish Catholic men may have revelled in and celebrated their working-class credentials and its "harder" male activities and pastimes, they were nevertheless bound through their association to the church.

This markedly religious aspect of Irish masculinity came to clash with hegemonic ideals of American masculinity that had largely relied on a separation of the public and the private – of home life and work life, of the secular and the religious – relegating duties such as child-rearing solely to the domain of women and deeming its associated activities as "unmanly."[53] As John Beynon remarks, there was a clear dichotomy espoused around the ideal of manhood, in that being hard, physically powerful, and mentally strong, as well as competitive, aggressive, dominant, rational, unemotional, and objective, are often advanced as typical indexical markers of the masculine. These traits, traditionally attributed to masculinity, present it as a superior state to femininity, whose attributes of softness, emotionality and nurturing are seen as wanting in comparison and, as a result, often employed in censure.[54]

In the case of Father Flanagan's real-life masculinity and his on-screen portrayal, both his religious calling and desire to act as a paternal figure to help raise young men are presented as important, heroic, and manly. Without a strong, caring, and spiritual father figure – in this case, a celibate man – the young men in *Boys Town* would stumble into the more dangerous and destructive aspects of the harder masculinity that they idolized. While on the one hand, this characterization supported the age-old belief that young men require the active presence of masculine role models to support their proper development, the fear here is not that they would become too soft or feminine, but rather that they would fall into more untamed and unconscionable patterns of masculinity – and by extension further away from the safety and sanctity of the values of the church as well as America itself.

## *American and Catholic*

As much as this movie sought to combat and counteract nativist stereotypes about the "Catholic other," there is a second reading to Flanagan's depiction that is just as important as the first: by seeking to transform the lives of these unruly and ethnically marginal young men, Flanagan can also be understood as bringing them more fully into the folds of a shared American identity.

One most pivotal aspect of Flanagan's characterization for our study was the filmmaker's decision to root his heroism and morality not only in his Catholicism but also in his acquired or perhaps earned Americanness. Though Irish-born, Flannagan was consistently portrayed through the film as a role-model worthy protagonist *because* he was a great American; his background and even his vocation as a priest were merely incidental.[55] In other words, the way in which Flanagan is portrayed by Tracy – as a morally upright protagonist looking after youth and opposing crime – is not inherently Catholic, and the traits he embodies focusing on the good of the community, growth, and giving the boys the potential to achieve the promise of the American dream, could be those of any paternal moral exemplar. Moreover, in the same manner that this film reminds us that even an immigrant priest could become a great American, Flanagan's role as caretaker gave him the opportunity to teach the boys to "become good American citizens, instilling strength of character and civic virtues."[56] As such, we can see that the character of Flanagan was portrayed as upstanding not necessarily because he was a Catholic priest, but because he was an upstanding American making more upstanding Americans. As such, though Flanagan displayed heroic virtues in his service to others, he was neither a caricature nor necessarily depicted as being superhuman. Rather, his exploits were depicted as taking place in the realm of the ordinary, the normal, and in doing so the film helped underline the relative "ordinary" goodness in priests – a trait as well that viewers of *Life Is Worth Living* would also come to witness later in the televised performances of Sheen.[57] Nevertheless, and also much like Sheen, while the film strives to portray the bravery and humility of Flanagan as being admirable qualities in an ordinary man, his real-life counterpart was hardly an obscure figure given new life by the film. Rather, Flanagan was very much feted like a celebrity until his death in 1948 and his fame wasn't merely limited to the area in which he operated, but rather, his home for boys became, according to a *Time* magazine article from 1931, "a source of pride to Omaha [and] a model institution for the nation."[58] Above being simply a refuge for young men, some of the nation's most widely known celebrities of the era also visited the institution to help promote it further, among them baseball star Babe Ruth, boxing champion Jack Dempsey, and the Oklahoma-born entertainer Will Rogers. So great was his reputation that President Truman sent him on as something of an ambassador to tour postwar Europe and review the state of the children care facilities there and see if his now American model could be brought there. Upon his landing in Ireland, he was initially greeted like a returning hero as his work in the United States were already well known and widely adored.[59] While his time in Ireland ended in failure, with the church in Ireland wanting little to do with listening to a celebrity cleric who had spent so much of his life abroad, and he returned with a sense of dismay shortly before his death, it's important to note that rarely was a member of the Catholic clergy celebrated in America to this extent during the 1930s and 1940s as one of their own – and likely would not have been had his life and film not been so successful in bridging his Catholic identity with American values.

### *Soft Priest, Hard Gangster*

Tracy's portrayal of Flanagan as the heroic priest was well received by the viewing public and film critics alike, earning Tracy an Academy Award for Best Actor at the eleventh Academy Awards in 1939. His portrayal would also help pave the way for a string of similarly well-received representations of priests in cinema. Just two months after the successful release of *Boys Town,* the 1938 picture *Angels with Dirty Faces* reminded American audiences that priests could be equally benevolent and caring as well as masculine figures. Though not the leading man of the film (that spot would be taken by James Cagney), the character of Father Jerry Connelly (played by Pat O'Brien in the first of several movies where he portrayed a Catholic priest) stands as another example of the way early Hollywood filmmakers portrayed clerical figures as relatively safe and paternal figures who nevertheless understood the harder masculine attributes of living in rough neighbourhoods – and whose reformed character trajectory can, by extension, be read as mirroring the change in perceptions surrounding Irish American Catholic – and notably, priests – by wider audiences.

The film opens with a delinquent youth named Rocky Sullivan, (played by Frankie Burke during his adolescence and then James Cagney during adulthood) who gets sent to reformatory school (a.k.a. hard labour) after a failed trainyard robbery ends in his arrest. From there, a montage introduces us to a series of newspaper clippings and quick takes showcasing how Rocky spent the next fifteen or so years of his life in and out of the correctional system and taking part in an increasingly violent series of crimes. Upon returning to his old neighbourhood after taking a final "rap" on the advice of his lawyer and criminal associate Jim Frazier (played by Humphrey Bogart), he encounters an old friend from his youth, Jerry Connolly. Jerry – a reluctant accomplice in the robbery at the start of the film – has now become not only reformed but also a parish priest concerned with preventing the kids from becoming – as Rocky proposes – "hoodlums like me."[60] Over the course of the film, Jerry attempts to help Rocky reform, but Rocky's old life and associates continue to pull him back toward crime. Rocky soon becomes a male role model to the unruly youths of the parish who come to admire his criminal ways and whom Jerry fears will follow him into a life of crime. At the end of the film, after killing two of his former criminal associates (including Frazier), Rocky takes Jerry hostage and is once again arrested by the police and sentenced to death. Jerry – who knows that how Rocky dies will affect whether the young men in the gang idolize or dismiss their mentor – pleads with Rocky to act like a coward on the way to the electric chair. Rocky initially refuses to let go of his pride but eventually acts terrified in the moments before his execution, screaming for mercy. The young men later learn in the papers that Rocky apparently died a coward's death and lose respect for their one-time idol – and by extension, with the masculinity he embodied – with the controlled, priestly masculinity of Father Jerry coming out as the victor and more desirable role model for the boys.

*Angels with Dirty Faces* did several remarkable things for the portrayal of Catholicism and priests in American visual culture. First, the movie mapped Catholicism to America's inner-city ethnic parishes, nestled among overcrowded and often gritty streets – a pairing which would continue to resonate, even with academics, to some extent into the twenty-first century. In numerous shots, the movie pans over the busy streets outside the parish showing viewers the relative grime, chaos, and poverty of the community in which Jerry's church is situated.[61] The exterior shots situate the church within the immigrant community, an element of their toil and hardship on the still-unfamiliar shores of America, but also as a beacon of hope and promise. Jerry's church is thus subtly positioned as being a place apart, a place that is connected to the Old World immigrant community but also the means of moving away from it toward fulfillment in America. By virtue of being a priest, Jerry could be said to be acting as representative of both the church and America in his community.

Second, like in *Boys Town*, Jerry's main charges in the film happen to be the unruly young boys who make up his choir. Part of Jerry's challenge in the film is about instilling order and domesticity in the neighbourhood, as the boys in the movie are initially shown to prefer hanging out far from society in an abandoned basement over going to events being organized by the parish. Rather than depict Jerry as a matronly character who could be perceived to be soft or weak, the movie positions the cleric ministering and watching over the boys as being manly. In this case, Jerry's athleticism is first and foremost on display as he coaches them at basketball and other sports, suggesting that priests are not so far removed from quintessentially male activities. While the movie pits different archetypes of masculinity in competition – the tougher, "hard-boiled" masculinity that the boys idolize, and the safer, paternal masculinity of Father Jerry – it also pits two different visions for Catholics in America against each other. Rockey, by virtue of being a gangster, shows little interest in acclimatizing himself to American society, preferring to go his own way, while Jerry, by virtue of his pastoral work, seeks to instill the positive values of American society into the boys. Importantly, this competition isn't a subplot but rather the primary focus of the film. In typical hard-boiled fashion, Rocky "is a man of action who defines himself and his masculine identity in opposition to forms of non-masculinity";[62] however, his eventual submission to Father Jerry's plea is not depicted as unmanly, but rather as heroic and Christlike and a rejection of all that he previously stood for, suggesting to audiences that his hard-boiled toughness and failure to acculturate is a sham and that real toughness lies in sacrifice and submission. In effect, by becoming more Christlike and less like his past self, Rocky becomes more American.

Much like in *Boys Town*, then, it is the socially responsible, approachable, and paternal masculinity embodied by the reformed Father Jerry that "wins" against the harder gangsterism embodied by Rocky and initially idolized by the youths. While the film suggests that there is a place for a reconfigured tough-guy Irish Catholic masculinity – Jerry himself used that life as a stepping-stone toward his fulfillment as a priest – ultimately it is Rocky's debasement and sacrifice at the end, which, though not seen as manly by the youths, nevertheless steers him more closely to the ideals espoused by Jerry's reformed masculinity. Such behaviour also reminds us of the duality of Irish Catholic masculinity, whereby the spiritual is entwined with its configurations and performances, and ideal men are those who follow their moral compasses, whether priests or martyrs.[63] However, this film, along with *Boys Town*, seems to be suggesting that the pairing of the spiritual with temporal concerns isn't simply some form of behaviour reserved for priests and other elites, but rather for Catholics integrating themselves with America, and in doing so they could become great Americans. In other words, to be American is to be concerned with both the spiritual and the temporal, and priests, as well as reformed gangsters, could become exemplars for both in times of need.[64]

### *Irish in America Versus Irish Americans*

The third and arguably most important priest for our examination is Father Charles "Chuck" O'Malley from 1944's wartime film *Going My Way*. Played by Bing Crosby – who won an Academy Award for the role – Father O'Malley stands out as a quintessential Hollywood priest and a culmination in many ways of those who graced the screen before. Crosby's depiction of O'Malley combines the safe, paternal masculine qualities of Father's Flanagan and Jerry, while superseding them in terms of charisma, charm, and star presence.

In the film, O'Malley is initially represented as an outsider from Illinois who arrives in New York City to take charge of an ailing parish named St Dominic's. The parish, we're told, "is in a bad way" owing to the current pastor, a man named Fitzgibbon, who is old and apparently unwilling or unable to turn things around.[65] Though the newcomer and the older priest initially clash in their pastoral styles, the two men eventually bond – over *Irish* whisky, no less. With the help of O'Malley's talents as a songwriter, mirroring Crosby's own musical fame, and ability to orchestrate the boys of the parish into an effective choir, the priests are able to raise the necessary funding to save the parish from inevitable closure and decay. Though O'Malley is successful, the church is ultimately destroyed in a fire at the end of film. However, despite the tragedy and the failure to effectively "repair" the church, the lingering good of O'Malley's presence nevertheless had an immense positive impact on the lives of everyone associated with the parish – with their hearts and minds ultimately being what was repaired. At the picture's end, O'Malley disappears, much like the hero of an American Western – his job done, he allows the other characters to carry on with their lives – which further roots him into the visual repertoire of heroic American images.[66]

While certain plot elements of the film (such as the musical elements) might seem hokey by modern standards, the Best Picture–winning movie put both the Irish American experience and Catholicism front and centre. The main plot of the film revolved around the administration and repair of a Catholic parish, and although only a minority of the film's audience would be able to identify with this plot on a personal level, it was nevertheless translated in way that allowed the wider American audience to connect with the characters as they navigated a rapidly changing world. Viewers could root for the priests in their underdog struggle to rescue their parish through their own ingenuity, talent, and the American way. Of course, it did not hurt the film that the main character was played by Crosby, who was arguably the premier A-list celebrity of his era (and himself Irish American). Though he first rose to acclaim as a jazz singer, by the 1940s, as film historian Stephen C. Shafer writes, "Crosby was known to Americans on the radio, in records, in film, and in stage.""[67] As a man of remarkable charm and personal magnetism, as well as a highly visible public profile, it was no surprise then that Crosby's celebrity often superseded or at the very least overlapped with that of the character he was portraying in any given film – and *Going My Way* is no exception.

Before the film's release, there were fears that the character of O'Malley might become too conflated with the actor's own status as a heartthrob and celebrity – which is unsurprising as most of his film roles up to that point had him playing romantic leads or thinly veiled versions of himself. To ensure Crosby's celebrity and reputation didn't taint the celibate priest, the Production Code Administration under Joseph Breen gave special scrutiny to every scene Crosby shared with his co-star Risë Stevens to ensure the film did not convey an unacceptable amount of romantic tension between the two characters.[68] Furthermore, after the film was released to critical and box office success, its run grossing the equivalent of over $250,000,000 adjusted for inflation, making it a major blockbuster for the era.[69] So successful was Crosby in elevating and endearing the character of this Catholic priest to wider audiences that even Cardinal Spellman feared that any controversies in Crosby's personal life could tarnish O'Malley and by extension the church in America.[70]

Though celibate and something of a musical dandy, O'Malley is not depicted as being "soft." The film presents him instead as a man of action, a decision-maker who displays a consistent strength of character. He is not afraid to hold his ground and lightly butt heads when it comes to it. For example, at one point in the film, O'Malley accidentally breaks a window with a ball and apologizes to the man from inside for his mistake and tries to make amends. The man, however, repeatedly chastises him about the incident before boldly declaring that he doesn't understand or like priests because he doesn't believe in anything. He eventually, and reluctantly, throws the ball back to O'Malley who then jokes "You even throw like an atheist," drawing a contrast not between traditional masculinity and femininity, as one might have expected the line to go, but between Catholic and irreligious masculinity, with Catholic (and even priestly) masculinity as the superior and more manly of the two.[71] Thus, though he is a priest being derided by the man in the scene, O'Malley nevertheless comes across as being both the humbler character and more athletic man.

Like we saw in *Boys Town* or *Angels with Dirty Faces*, *Going My Way* also depicts masculinities in conflict, albeit in a more subtle manner. In the film, there is an open competition between clerical and non-clerical masculinities as well as American and immigrant ones. O'Malley's restrained, productive, and ultimately socially beneficial masculinity is contrasted with that of Tony Scaponi (played by Stanley Clements), the young leader of a gang of delinquents. Scaponi, an Italian American and fellow Catholic, is depicted as wayward and as embodying a competing ethnic model of masculine authority. O'Malley acts as the voice and embodiment of order, holding a particular disdain for rougher, uncouth patterns of masculinity. In one scene, a visiting friend, who is also a priest, offers to take O'Malley to play a couple of rounds of golf, to which he declares "a golf course is nothing but a poolroom moved outdoors."[72] It is through the force of his will that O'Malley steers the youth of the parish toward a model of socially acceptable masculine behaviour. Scaponi begins the movie as a model offering the opposite pull, toward a harder masculinity that proves itself through being a nuisance to authorities and his unwillingness to become acculturated in wider society. In this sense, Scaponi's masculinity is decidedly working-class and outsider, a model which Catholic Americans themselves were widely purported to follow. However, it is O'Malley who ultimately befriends Scaponi and reforms the younger man, reconfiguring the standards by which Scaponi rates himself as a man. By the end of the film, Scaponi becomes a choir leader, someone so transformed that he is no longer recognizable as the young man at the beginning of the movie.

Assigning wild, unruly, and ultimately immature masculine qualities here to the character of non-Irish immigrant descent transfers these unpopular and demeaning elements of masculinity away from O'Malley – a priest who exhibits control and caring – and Irish Americans more generally. By portraying O'Malley as the embodiment of a calm, cool-headed, caring, and ultimately noble man – someone the audience could identify and sympathize with – the film helps dispel and break stereotypical representation of Irish Americans as rough working-class gangsters. Equally so, by associating a disdain for authority and a more lowly, earthy iteration of masculinity with Scaponi's waywardness, the movie suggests that such masculine behaviour is somehow un-Catholic. The film therefore presents Irish Americans as model citizens seeking to reform society in a socially beneficial manner, while at the same time depicting the masculinity of the priest as one who restores and upholds order and its institutions without requiring violence or an ill temper to do so. Ultimately, O'Malley is revealed to embody a more powerful masculinity than Scaponi, thus informing the viewers that the calm, nurturing and ultimately celibate masculinity of the priest is greater than that of the brash, troublesome youth that Scaponi – and by extension, any ethnic stereotype – embodied in the film's opening.

It is worth noting that such representations of priests were not so far removed from the representations being produced by Catholics themselves in other media at the time. Catholic publishers were keen on showing the younger generation that priests, while heroic, were not altogether different than they were.[73] They still enjoyed sports, male camaraderie, and all the things young men should enjoy, except they happened to have found vocations within the church as opposed to outside. Catholic comic books and visual novels aimed at younger audiences also routinely depicted priests as being young, dark-haired, and often handsome men who were physically fit and in the prime of their lives.[74] While this difference could be attributed to the changing demographics of the priesthood – the first half of the twentieth century saw far higher numbers of young recruits – it also acted as a reminder to audiences that priesthood was a viable, fulfilling profession, one in which a man, though celibate, was no less of a man.[75]

While the representation of O'Malley certainly bears a number of similarities with that of Flanagan and Jerry, his characterization differs in the way the film emphasizes his *Americanness* first and foremost over any aspects of his Irish heritage. For example, from their first scene together, O'Malley is meant to stand in contrast with Fitzgibbon, not only in their administration styles or age differences, but also in their identities. Fitzgibbon – as we learn from a scene where he expresses longing for his distant homeland – is an example of the *Irish in America*, whereas O'Malley has no such longing and is more firmly

*Irish American.* As such, O'Malley is everything Fitzgibbon is not at the start of the film – youthful, courageous, innovative, and hopeful. One might argue that as Fitzgibbon acclimatizes himself to the new younger priest, he is simultaneously acclimatizing himself with the America O'Malley vicariously represents. In this sense, O'Malley, in particular, came across as not simply an idealized priest – but an ideal American. Ultimately, in portraying O'Malley, Crosby presents audiences with a good-looking, talented, and all-American man, who effects changes in his environment through his own hard work and labour – the epitome of what every citizen could aspire to become. All the while, he just so happened to be a priest.

## The Fulfillment of Those Who Came Before

A decade after *Going My Way* made waves in cinemas across the nation, Sheen was the most popular and well-known priest in America. In 1954, his program, *Life Is Worth Living*, was in its third season and showed no sign of stopping even with the closure of his original network.[76] The bishop had just won an Emmy Award and now found himself nominated once again. And yet as novel as his program was for the early days of television, many components of his performance and messaging mirrored these priests from the past generation of Hollywood movies, both in terms of the kind of values he sought to share with his viewers and his self-representation as a Catholic spokesperson – and by extension, his celebrity persona.

While *Boys Town* and *Angels with Dirty Faces* were both released in a decade that saw ongoing tension between the Protestant majority and the nation's Catholic minority that affected the ways in which priests were represented, Sheen emerged as an active participant in the relative ecumenism of the early postwar years. Nevertheless, he was no doubt well aware of the history of prejudice against Catholics in America, as well as its enduring elements of which even his fame faced backlash.[77] Had Sheen been interested in sidestepping any lingering nativism toward Catholicism, he could have chosen to perform in less ornamental garb, taking on the more comfortable black suit and upturned collar that marked virtually every priest in these Hollywood movies and which he himself wore during his more relaxed guest appearances at dinner and television specials.[78] Instead, he approached his role as television host and spokesperson for the church head on, with full ceremonial regalia and stage dressing. It could be argued, then, that he chose to confront this nativist legacy on *Life Is Worth Living* not by combative words or actions, but by choice of attire and set dressing. Like the earlier priests from Hollywood, Sheen approached his duties unafraid of challenge and with confidence, turning what could be perceived by some as a weakness – his overt identification with a minority religious tradition – into a strength. More importantly, by becoming as visibly Catholic as he could, Sheen was also reminding his audiences that Catholic priests were just as American as Milton Berle, Frank Sinatra, or any other personality they encountered in prime-time programming.

Curiously, much like the figures of Fathers Flanagan and Jerry from these films, Sheen also seemed to have been aware of the importance of representing priests as caretakers for the youth, or at the very least, as *safe* figures. While there is little evidence of Sheen having spent much time during his lengthy career in the company of children or even young adults, he appears to have embraced this representation in his anecdotes, frequently opening his episodes with stories involving children. In one episode, he talked about a little girl who was being taught catechisms by her mother and is quizzed about the difference between mortal and venial sins. The little girl said, "The mortal sin makes God angry, the venial sin makes Him nervous."[79] He also told stories in which children shared positive or humorous impressions of him. In one episode, he tells the audience about a girl studying at Rosemont College. She tells the sister running the class that "I just finished reading Bishop Sheen's work on *Three to Get Married*. God and I are willing, but we can't find the man."[80] In another, Sheen informs the audience that he received a letter from a mother who watched his program. She wrote to tell him that Cathy, "our little two-year-old adores watching you … you get many kisses" when it's time to say goodnight, and that she sits "in her rocker almost spellbound during your entire talk."[81] The veracity of these stories, along with how he came into possession of them, is unclear – perhaps they were among the mountains of mail he received, or perhaps they were mere inventions of his own imagination. Whatever their origin, it is telling that he shares them at all in the first place as stories such as these – which detail a certain level of intimacy between Sheen and children – speaks to his ability as well as desire to convey himself to audiences as a safe, paternal, and familial figure who could be entrusted around the nation's youth.[82] While part of this certainly had to do with the medium and the way television celebrities were more approachable than Hollywood ones, it also seems to suggest a lingering need on Sheen's part as a stand-in for *all* priests to represent them as friendly fellow Americans akin to the ways that *Boys Town* and *Angels with Dirty Faces* did. In this manner, Sheen can be read both as positioning himself in this lineage of priestly depictions, even if it perhaps wasn't as pressing to do so by the 1950s.

Though, out of the priests we discussed, Sheen unsurprisingly has the greatest mirroring with Crosby's depiction of Father O'Malley, both of whom communicated a similarly powerful celebrity magnetism of their own. Despite being in his fifties when *Life Is Worth Living* aired, his clean-shaven face, perfectly slicked-back hair, and meticulous grooming made him appear as a man far younger than his years. Indeed, his good looks hardly went unnoticed, by viewers and historians alike. Scholar Thomas Doherty comments on the "penetrating" quality of Sheen's eyes and his "silver fox hair," even going so far as to describe him as a "dashing Don Diego Zorro … a suave Count Dracula."[83] He further recounts television critic Marya Mannes as stating "the man has magic … he could probably qualify as a leading man at any studio" in Hollywood.[84] Like the character of O'Malley, Sheen was a man of many talents, industrious levels of energy, and unafraid to take action, and both men had began arcs that saw them begin as newcomers and relative outsiders – each hailing from Illinois, no less – assigned to revitalizing institutions in New York. While O'Malley was sent to rescue a sagging parish, Sheen was first sent to tend to the SPOF, where he filled its coffers with donations from his fundraising, before going on to Rochester to usher in the optimism of Vatican II, albeit without the spirit of success granted to O'Malley at the movie's end.

As popular as O'Malley became, he would always be a work of fiction, a character portrayed by real-life celebrity Bing Crosby. Sheen, on the other hand, was a living example of the ideal kind of celebrity priest Hollywood created a decade past, which makes it so peculiar that at the same time he was endearing himself to viewers of his television program, an altogether different representation of a priest was making waves in Hollywood.

## A Break in the Lineage

In the Hollywood movies of 1930s and 1940s, the rash, abrasive, hard-hitting and hard-drinking masculinity typically imparted to the Irish was avoided, sublimated, or replaced with more socially conscious patterns of masculinity. Instead of being in any way similar to the stereotypes floating around at the time, the Irish American priests of *Boys Town*, *Angels with Dirty Faces*, and *Going My Way*, were decidedly safe and paternal figures who embodied the spirituality expected of their position while simultaneously coming across as distinctly *American* figures in the process. However, by the 1950s, Hollywood and American itself were transforming, and rather than need to depict priests in a safe manner, it became possible, perhaps even enviable, to show priests in more challenging and possibly realistic performances and characterizations than what came before.

Movies such as Alfred Hitchcock's thriller *I Confess* (1953), involving a priest who becomes a suspected murderer after he fails to break the seal of confession, and Mark Robson's *Edge of Doom* (1950), which saw a priest being beaten to death by a crucifix, pushed the envelope of what sort of stories were now acceptable to involve priests, even if the characterization of them as upstanding community leaders was only marginally altered. However, Karl Malden's performance as Father Barry in *On the Waterfront* is largely emblematic of a wider shift ways a priest's character could be depicted.

*On the Waterfront,* as mentioned earlier, came to cinemas at the same time Sheen was at his peak of hosting *Life Is Worth Living*. The main plot of the film revolves around a young man named Terry Malloy (played by Marlon Brando). Terry is a dockworker, and, like many of the men working in that part of the city, is inherently tied up with the mob. Though initially bound to a pact of silence that binds many of the men together (and lets the mob thrive), he eventually faces a crisis of conscious and a change of heart. At the urging of Father Pete Barry (Karl Malden), a combative reformer priest, Terry admits to his sweetheart Evie that he had an unwilling role to play in her brother's murder at the opening of the film and later goes on to testify publicly against mobster-union boss Johnny Friendly. Terry's testimony causes a rift between him and the other men, who effectively ostracize him for his commitment to the good of the community over the unspoken code of silence. In the end, Terry confronts Johnny Friendly and is badly beaten by his goons. However, rising up from his sacrificial state and marching to the dock to work wins him the respect of the men who shied away from him, and in turn he triumphs on the side of communal good over that of the mob.

Though Malden's Father Barry is only a supporting character in the story, he holds a powerful presence in the film that challenges many of the previously established tropes associated with Hollywood priests, as his real-life counterpart, Father Corridan, was the figure who inspired the story in the first place.[85] While Father Barry is still a man looking out for the good of his community like the priests we previously examined, rather than need to stand in as a paternal figure and guide for children, his wayward charges are working-class adults: Irish American longshoremen and the mob influencers who hold sway over them. As such, to connect with those to whom he ministers, the masculinity displayed by Barry's character is stripped of any of the safer, gentler attributes associated with men like Fathers Flanagan, Jerry, and O'Malley. Barry's masculinity is undeniably hard-boiled and immigrant-inflected, not unlike that of Rocky and that which *Angels with Dirty Faces* worked so hard to distance from Irish American ideals. As a "manly" man thrust into the middle of unruly dockworkers, Barry fully inhabits a world of violence, ambushes, competition, and death and must be strong enough to stand up to it.[86] Where the earlier priests of Hollywood were often treated with reference and deference, even in conflict, Barry finds no such camaraderie as the dockworkers freely heap insults on him and even consider having him murdered.

In terms of personality and physique, there is nothing "soft" about Father Barry. He smokes cigarettes and drinks beer. He walks into bars and dockyards without a moment's hesitation, and he comes into every scene with a sort of fiery, righteously angry energy that threatens to erupt at any moment. When the men pelt him with fruit and beer bottles in one scene, he remains still and unflinching, keeping himself calm and controlled while they succumb to emotional outbursts and petty antics. He also explicitly proves his toughness and grit when he enters a bar and slugs Terry in the face. By entering a traditionally masculine space and exerting his authority through physical prowess, against a man who was himself a boxer no less, Barry demonstrates – not just to the men who work in the docks, but also to the viewer – that there was nothing to be questioned about this priest's hardened masculinity. Yet there is a curiosity here: though reflective of their present circumstances, Barry's masculinity, like that of the longshoremen he strives to rescue, is rooted in the grittier demands of the immigrant past, oblivious to the gains made over the past generation in terms of perception, attitudes, and acculturation toward Irish Catholics in America.

In this regard, Malden's performance as Father Barry (filmed in the same year that Breen retired, no less) comes across as an intentional rejection of many of the values Hollywood previously ascribed to priests and which were currently winning Sheen praise. Unlike Father Flanagan, who was American first and priest second, or Jerry, whose reformed ways stood in for the transformative promise of America, Barry is unapologetically Irish and Catholic and perhaps only incidentally American. For example, in one scene, Father Barry embraces his Irish roots by referring to himself sarcastically as "just a potato-eater" – which is somewhat ironic, as Malden out of all the actors discussed in this chapter, was the only among them without Irish ancestry.[87] In another scene, where he delivers a monologue to the men at the docks imploring them to turn away from the mob, he powerfully invokes Jesus in a novel manner. "[Christ] sees you selling your souls to the mob for a day's pay!"[88] he declares with righteous anger, adding that Jesus isn't someone you only encounter back in the church, but "kneeling right here beside you."[89] Barry thus brings religion out of the church, away from civilized society and potentially "feminine" spaces, and into the harder, ethnic, and "masculine" spaces of the docks. In doing so, the story echoes a hard-boiled trope of placing masculine and feminine spaces in contrast and opposition, two halves separated by a ranked dichotomy whereby manly spaces and the values believed to be inculcated there (courage and heroism) are what all men should strive toward.[90] In this regard, Barry's Jesus is as tough and challenging as the Irish American dockworkers. Hardly a sissy who died on a cross and never got his hands dirty, Barry tells them that "Jesus stands alongside" the dockworkers every morning as they line up for work, and is crucified anew whenever a good man is prevented from doing his duty or getting an honest day's pay from the mob.[91] A similar sentiment about the toughness of religious figures is echoed by Evie, Terry's love interest, when she asks, "Did you ever hear about a saint hiding in a church?"[92] In this, she suggests that true saints – whether priests or laypeople – are the ones out there in the muck and mire of the world, working where they're needed most, much like Barry is doing in the neighbourhood. It also questions to what extent the church itself still stands in for the promise of America.

As startling as it might seem, Father Barry, was nevertheless presented as an ideal priest for his circumstances and setting. Even as the Catholicism depicted on screen and vicariously embodied by Malden's portrayal would seem a sharp contrast from the hopeful optimism of the earlier films, Father Barry was very much a community worker, albeit a gritty one, focused on saving the men in his environment. Where the earlier movies depicted priests in almost neutered terms – presenting them as ideal members of society that Americans need not fear – Father Barry spoke directly to the rougher side of the Irish American and immigrant experience that those same films fought so hard to distance. This would seem to be largely intentional on the part of the filmmakers. Both Kazan and screenwriter Budd Schulberg had previously met Corridan, with Schulberg being moved by the man's "earthy" street smarts and Kazan apparently asking after his meeting whether Corridan was in fact a real priest or just a dockworker in disguise.[93]

While it is possible that American viewers of the 1950s were simply growing more accustomed to increasingly challenging films and characters, as cinema often subverts its earlier tropes, Father Barry's on-screen portrayal and turning away from earlier priestly archetypes speaks volumes about the changing perception of Catholicism in America by the mid 1950s – or at the very least, the potential for a change in perceptions. Though there was lingering nativism, as evidenced by the backlash against Sheen's appearance on the front cover of *Time* in 1952, there would also appear to be a parallel current of progress that suggested that postwar Americans of immigrant backgrounds need not shed their ethnic past but should actively embrace it – that the ethnic American was no longer an outsider but an expected component of the wider American experiment.[94] Hollywood's move to explore more challenging characterizations of priests can thus be read as mirroring a change in the overall social climate: studios no longer had to defend the priests in the face of nativist prejudices and could instead depict them as complicated characters, they way they would other Americans. Taken as a whole, this makes it strange that Sheen – perhaps the safest priest of all – would rise to celebrity stardom at precisely the same moment in time.

## Comfortably Anachronistic

Films like *On the Waterfront* made for decidedly more challenging viewings than any of the earlier films discussed in this paper – with the possible exception to *Angels with Dirty Faces*, which also employed many of the tropes and characterizations of hard-boiled masculinity while simultaneously questioning their merits. However, despite this purposeful break in the trajectory of priestly depictions, the filmmakers were certainly aware of them and sought to engage them, even if it's not entirely clear to what extent they sought to establish Father Barry simply as an about-face or the logical, more mature extension of these earlier depictions.

In the early 1950s, while the project was still in development, screenwriter Schulberg apparently spoke about wanting his depiction of Barry to be the "antidote to the stereotyped … Bing Crosby" image of the priesthood that so affected audiences and Hollywood alike. Corridan, too, apparently agreed that such a depiction wouldn't be fitting for the movie and encouraged Schulberg and Kazan to approach the religious themes differently, by making their own *Going My Way* but "with substance."[95] Curiously, not only was this approach explicit in the film, but it was also deployed in its marketing. Take for instance, one of the trailers reissued for the film after its sweep of the Academy Awards in March 1955, where it tied the record for most wins set previously by *Gone with the Wind*. The short trailer opens with a message from the producers imploring viewers to go see the sensational film for themselves. After calling attention to its "superb acting" and "inspired direction," a text crawl proclaims that at the heart of the film is a story "as warm and moving as *Going My Way*."[96] However, lest the audience think that this is a fluffy feel-good film like the predecessor it just referenced, it quickly adds a qualifier to the above statement that wears its character on its sleeves "with brass knuckles!" On the one hand this suggests that even a decade after its release, the reputation and success of *Going My Way* was still widely remembered as a sort of benchmark for religiously themed movies to meet. It also suggests that even a movie as successful as *On the Waterfront* could still ride its coattails to a certain extent, simply by drawing attention to the specifically Catholic elements of the film's plot, setting, and characters. However, the comment about brass knuckles, connecting violence with these themes, also suggests an uneasiness with the ways in which the religious themes were portrayed previously in cinema, or possibly that an optimistic, family-friendly religiously inflected movie wouldn't be of interest to audiences in the 1950s unless it contained brass knuckles and harder depictions of masculinity.

This reading would appear to at least partially be the case as the trailer the moves through highlights from the film, beginning with Brando's performance as Terry before moving to Malden as Father Barry. Out of all the scenes they could have picked, the trailer rather sensationally chooses the one where Barry comes to confront Terry in the bar. However, the trailer cuts away to a different scene moments before he throws his famous punch at Terry's jaw. While having a priest strike a man was now acceptable content for a film, but decidedly not for a widely released trailer, the trailer nevertheless plays ominous, almost menacing music at the appearance of Father Barry who then stands over Terry, looking down on him the way a person might an ant. Even this brief scene would tell audiences that this film's priest was a far cry from O'Malley, who was often filmed from a higher vantage, allowing him to look upward and optimistically toward the camera and the audience alike.

Though Malden would fail to secure an Academy Award for his supporting role in the film, losing to Jack Lemon in wartime comedy-drama *Mister Roberts*, critics nevertheless praised the "realism" he brought to the role, suggesting that Kazan, Schulberg, and Corridan's efforts to reimagine a Hollywood priest were largely successful. Roger Ebert suggested that if Brando hadn't been in the film, it would have been Malden's performance that would have received widespread attention.[97] However, as much as I find Malden's portrayal moving, I don't feel that it was the kind of role, nor Malden the kind of personality, which had the capacity of creating widespread popular acclaim the way Crosby was able to achieve with O'Malley. Though the attention to realism can give substance to the study of a character, it does little to create awe for the viewers. We only need to look at the case of Father Corridan, Barry's inspiration, who remains something of a minor historical figure, remembered mostly by Jesuits and film afficionados. Even after the release of the film, Schulberg was disappointed by how little it did to catapult the magnanimity of Corridan's work and subsequently wrote the novel *Waterfront* (1955) about him. While also highly acclaimed, the work did little to elevate the central figure. Ultimately, Corridan's work with the longshoremen failed to draw them away from organized crime, and he moved on to become a teacher at LeMoyne, before settling later in life as a hospital chaplain.[98]

It is here that we can draw a few important points from our discussion about the nature of celebrity in religious figures along with its reception during this period. The first is that critical acclaim does not necessarily lead to widespread popular acclaim. Malden's performance nearly earned him an Oscar, and Corridan's advice on set helped make the movie a major success, and yet neither seemed to make the same cultural impact as Crosby's portrayal of O'Malley the previous decade. Second, while realism can propel actors in secular roles to the heights of stardom, as the film did for Brando, the same isn't necessarily true for actors portraying religious characters. Malden's performance, and by extension Corridan's real-life work, didn't show the potential for the American promise, dealing instead with contemporary problems that rooted the viewer to an immigrant past that the work of generations had strived to overcome. It comes across as a reminder of the ugly, earthly imperfections that people carry and stands in stark contrast to the ways in which the widely acclaimed priests from the earlier generation of films were received – particularly the case of Father O'Malley. In this sense, O'Malley, more than all the other priests we discussed in this chapter, comes across as being almost too perfect – a larger-than-life character or even a "fantasy priest," as Crosby biographer Gary Giddins put it.[99] "Liberated from romance, venality and vainglory," continues Giddins, "Father O'Malley emerged as a superhuman font of liberal wisdom, empathy and action."[100] It was these very superhuman qualities which made O'Malley such an important idea in wider culture, and who needed to be upheld as an exemplar as much as he needed to be protected. For instance, while Cardinal Spellman feared the ways in which Crosby's celebrity life could affect the image of O'Malley and the church, he never felt such concern over the reception of any of the priests since then, least of all Father Barry. As such, we can see that celebrity during this era is in some ways tied to a sense of optimism, of looking to the future – that audiences would rather rally around figures who show us where we're going, rather than reminding us of where we came from.

Unsurprisingly, we can apply many of these elements of O'Malley's popularity to our reading of Sheen. As a celebrity preacher guiding Americans with spiritually accessible wisdom and empathy, Sheen also might have come across as a perhaps too perfect priest, a fantasy. This, of course, potentially problematizes our earlier discussion about television as being an approachable medium that emphasizes the ordinariness of its subjects and series' hosts. After all, what does it mean when a television host and celebrity at once strives to inculcate a sense of ordinariness in their approach and presence while at the same coming across as a fantasy? This is not to say that Sheen necessarily played a version of himself that was far detached from reality, as was perhaps the case with other early television presenters such as Milton Berle whose well-document egocentric, crass, and domineering self was at odds with his television persona. Rather, it serves as a reminder that the celebrity persona who appears on television screens is a highly orchestrated and heavily mediated presence. In the same vein that Crosby's turn as Father O'Malley required help from the costume and makeup department to make him look the part, and he could draw on his own lengthy career in show business to help with the characterization, Sheen's immaculate presentation, too, was the product of lengthy and meticulous grooming, vocal training, and years of experience as an orator. As such, despite Sheen's appeal to ordinariness and approachability on *Life Is Worth Living*, his brand of celebrity priesthood, like those of the movies that came before, was hardly emblematic of the average Irish American priest, but rather an idealized realization of it.

There also remains something to be said about the medium of television that continued to make this form of celebrity possible. In the 1950s, cinema continued to enjoy its elite status among America's visual media, itself seen as a medium worthy of serious critical study, while television had yet to find its footing as a medium producing anything other than friendly, familiar, and safe for the family. People could go to the cinema to be challenged, whereas viewers of Sheen's program did not tune in to be challenged, any more than audiences expected to be challenged by Berle's antics on the *Texaco Star Theater*. In this vein, scholar Thomas Doherty remarks that Sheen was largely a "pure product of early television, a time when a singular face in close up on the small screen could still lull viewers in a trance of attention."[101] He was popular because his series fit so comfortably with what was expected of early television by its audiences and their cultural memory – whereas a priest like Barry, who embodied many of the harder stereotypes often ascribed to Irish American masculinity, would not be welcome on the smaller screen for decades to come. Therefore, if Sheen's visual performance and priestly persona was a living, breathing anachronism that called back to an earlier era of optimism and which was no longer needed by the time his television program first came on the air, that was perhaps the point.

## Conclusion

Film historian Christopher Shannon suggests that the rising prominence and visibility of Catholic priests in early to mid-twentieth-century American popular culture can be read as the "test case" for America's emerging conception of itself, not as a nation built around a single ethnic group as was frequently the case in Europe in the preceding century, but as an evolving pluralistic democracy.[102] In a similar vein, Christopher Dowd observes, "The origins of American popular culture are rooted in immigrant life, cultural concerns about assimilation, and attempts to define common American experiences across class and social boundaries."[103] Accordingly, "popular culture provides a dynamic, discursive space in which communal identity constructions (including ethnic identity constructions) can take place. It allows for identities to be proposed, tested, rehearsed, revised and (sometimes) rejected."[104]

Where the late 1920s saw revivals of anti-Catholicism, from the 1930s onward Hollywood sought to demystify and lionize the image of Catholic Americans and priests as their most visible symbols. Priests were presented to the American viewing public, not as agents from an insidious foreign power but as heroic and socially minded community organizers and educators of youth who sought to bring their communities more fully under the folds of their newfound American identities. They stood out as masculine role models, too, offering powerful alternatives to the rough, elemental forms of masculinity often stereotypically ascribed to their immigrant ancestors. This was of particular importance as at the time of these films' release Catholicism was still very much an underdog religion in the American landscape, with its adherents predominantly still living in parish neighbourhoods of a single ethnicity up until the end of World War II.[105] This only began to shift in the 1940s and then dramatically in the early 1950s when Catholics were presented with new horizons and the means of leaving behind their close-knit parish communities that had bound them together for so long. It was thus there, in the newly built suburbs, that Catholics more fully reached the end of a long trajectory that took them and their stories from despised, dangerous outsiders to ideal examples of Americans. As such, these early conception of priests in American popular culture foreshadowed the gentrification process that Irish American Catholics themselves underwent from the era of nativism to the postwar suburbs. It was thus from this canon of popular culture that we can understand a little more about the appeal of a figure like Sheen and what made his presentation to millions of viewers on a weekly basis so easy to accept, as well as how those same audiences may have already been prepared for and expectant of a priestly performance like his.

Bearing this in mind, Sheen's television show was hardly responsible for this change in perception. Rather, it occurred at a time of confluence when America was beginning to come to terms with its diversity as well as accept its identity as a multi-ethnic, multi-religious society. Sheen was not one to hide away in a church anymore than the saints Evie or Father Bary spoke about on the docks – rather, as a celebrity preacher, he was a public figure, one who could at once cling to and shed the rigidity of his Catholic identity and speak to the whole of America, even as a minority. Sheen, as heir to a lengthy tradition of depicting priests in morally upright and positive roles, encapsulated the possibility of the societally benevolent religious minority member who stood out as a quintessentially American figure who could lead others toward their shared values and that which these films were so keen to promote. In the same way Hollywood presented Irish Catholics as part of America's broader urban village, Sheen's television could now do the same for institutional Catholicism, taking the tradition and its doctrines out of its austere and ornate churches and cathedrals and presenting them to Americans in a way that was broadly appealing, recognizable, and familiar. Though there would continue to be lingering doubts about the character and allegiance of Irish Catholics in the early 1950s, Sheen nevertheless was living, breathing, performing proof that Catholics of Irish descent had become part of the larger patchwork of what an American man could be – both on screen and off.

Yet, there is nevertheless some irony here. While film historian Christopher Shannon argues that these films offered varied representations of Irish Americans that were meant to represent and encapsulate the diversity and difference of America's minority populations in a generally non-judgmental manner, taking strides to paint Irish American Catholics as fellow Americans, they also sought to distance these upstanding characters from any overt connections to their immigrant past.[106] Such traits that signalled their ethnic heritage and diversity were in fact used as markers that pointed the characters, and the audience, toward a previous time and place rather than the present in America, and were thus largely folded under, used as backdrops, or depicted as something to be opposed. We can see instead that the characters of Fathers O'Malley, Flanagan, Jerry – and even Sheen himself – became more acceptable to mainstream Protestant viewers not by embodying Irish "ethnic" types but rather through their portrayal of a familiar and almost Protestant-inflected masculinity, as society might see it, even when visibly identifiable as priests. In other words, the differences their immigrant ancestors or present communities might have embraced were now homogenized, resulting only in vestigial differences, such as an antiquated pining for Ireland in *Going My Way* or the lightly spoken brogue in the case of Sheen. Not so for depictions like Father Barry, of course, whose characterization sought to reclaim these ethnic differences and markers of Irishness that had been considered unfashionable to depict on screen in the previous decades, and whose realism still marked him as something of an outsider who wouldn't fit in postwar American society.

That said, it is important to remember that neither Sheen's performance nor the characterization of Father Barry in *On the Waterfront* can be read as having occurred in a vacuum. While both appeared on screen at the tail end of a long tradition of priests in Hollywood films, what is perhaps equally relevant is that both of their on-screen debuts coincided with a particular moment in American history – the onset of the Cold War. On screen, Barry could be read as embodying a certain Cold War no-nonsense toughness that the nation craved in its leader, not unlike the largely fabricated persona Joseph McCarthy cultivated, and whom we discuss further in the following chapter. Sheen, on the other hand, was largely a comforting and safe persona that brought Americans back to simpler, stabler times. Yet, in reminding audiences that to be American required a moral and religious underpinning of the self, he also spoke to an urgent need against the backdrop of geopolitical turmoil. As such, one element of Sheen's celebrity that has hitherto remained unexplored is his own capacity, performance, and portrayal among his proponents as an anti-communist Cold Warrior. While he never slugged a man in a bar, he was not without a hardness of his own, albeit one that was spiritually transfigured from what was expected of America's leaders participating in discourses about the conflict – and to which we turn to in the following chapter.

# 5

# Hard Bodies, Hard Nation

## *Catholic Bodily Responses to the Cold War*

In 1959, New York's *Herald Tribune* ran an extensive and largely flattering ten-part biography of Fulton Sheen titled "The Bishop Sheen Story."[1] Written by journalist Francis Sugrue, the series was intended to build excitement around Sheen's imminent (albeit short-lived) return to television after the cancellation of *Life Is Worth Living* two years prior. Ostensibly seeking to provide a tell-all, behind-the-scenes review of the man whose face was by then well known across America, the reader was instead served carefully selected and highly flattering tidbits from Sheen's personal life that seemed intended to convey not only that a comeback was imminent but that Sheen was still at the top of his game.

In part five of the series, the article opened with a detailed section discussing Sheen's daily routine, hobbies, and, rather curiously, his eating habits. Giving a nod to his workaholic tendencies, it mentioned that Sheen – rather heroically – refused to "bow" to a forty-hour work week and spent the vast majority of his time undertaking work for the SPOF, writing books and articles, preparing speeches, and instructing converts, among various endeavours. While the article was keen to display Sheen's formidable output where publishing and other duties were concerned, Sugrue conceded that the aging Sheen did take some time off, enjoying several markedly gendered pastimes. The bishop, like his fellow Americans, was known to take the "occasional television glance at a baseball or football game," though he much preferred participating in said activities himself. At fifty-eight, Sheen was presented as a man of "ruddy good health, enhanced by tours on many a Washington golf course."[2] Sugrue also notes that Sheen was no slouch on the tennis court, a statement he supports with an apparently candid quote from a certain Freddy Botur, the local "tennis pro at the River Club on the Upper East

Side" which Sheen frequented. In Botur's professional opinion, Sheen was an "excellent player" – especially for a man of his age.[3] While the privileged status signalled by tennis and golf as sports hobbies – not to mention the status signalled by playing tennis with pros at a private club in New York's Upper East Side – might have been simply matter of fact in Sugrue's biographical work, the subtle nod given to an aging celebrity bishop's apparent late-life athleticism, vitality, and hardened work ethic was anything but happenstance.

It is widely reported that, in the 1950s, America experienced a moment of acute anxiety surrounding men's bodies – and, in particular, white, English-speaking men's bodies – often referred to as a "crisis of masculinity."[4] While America's men had spent the better part of the previous decade proving themselves on battlefields across Europe and the Pacific, the postwar years saw their society undergo a rapid and often bewildering transformation. Returning servicemen put away their fatigues and put on their ties, earning college degrees, securing white-collar jobs, and settling into the expanding suburbs outside America's growing cities. The decade also witnessed an unprecedented expansion of single-family households and the height of the "Baby Boom," which saw a skyrocketing birth rate rapidly turning a whole generation of men into fathers.[5] All this prosperity, however, led to a widespread belief that men were becoming alienated from the harder, more primeval elements of their manhood. Accordingly, advertisements frequently emphasized "male" activities such as backyard BBQs, camping, hunting, and fishing.[6] At the same time, a slew of then-contemporary literary works – such as Arthur M. Schlesinger Jr's *The Vital Center* (1949), David Reisman's *Lonely Crowd* (1950), Sloan Wilson's *The Man in the Gray Flannel Suit* (1955), and William H. Whyte's *The Organization Man* (1956) – asserted that these transformations were inherently detrimental for America's men, leading to feelings of isolation and detachment from traditional masculine values that would have normally kept them grounded.[7] Scholars have equally observed how American men were widely perceived to be falling away from "hardness" and sliding toward "softness" – a state of physical, mental, and even moral weakness that alarmed even the nation's leaders.[8]

More pressing was, from the 1950s onward, both popular culture and government policy connected men's bodies with the nation's domestic and international struggle against communism, vicariously linking the vitality of men's bodies – particularly those of its political leaders and celebrities – with the health of the nation, its institutions, and its ideologies. As scholar Susan Jeffords argues in her 1994 monograph *Hard Bodies*, the Cold War helped construct and establish an embodied dualism in America whereby "bodies were deployed in two fundamental categories: the errant body containing sexually transmitted disease, immorality, illegal chemicals, 'laziness,' and endangered fetuses, which we can call the 'soft body'; and the normative body that enveloped strength, labour, determination, loyalty, and courage – the 'hard body.'"[9] It bears noting that in hierarchical systems of social organization marked by race and gender, soft bodies inevitably belonged to women, people of colour, foreigners, and men of non-normative sexuality, while the hard body was inherently male, white, and heterosexual.[10] Men with hard bodies were presented as standing in for good health, physical strength, and virility, not only in themselves but as vicarious representations of the nation and its values at large. In contrast, soft bodies were everything that hard bodies were not – sites of weakness, illness, deviance, and treachery – which in turn pointed to a weakness of the nation and its institutions. In the political arena of the Cold War, the repercussions of this bodily dichotomy could also be mapped to the then-current geopolitical positioning of the nation in a clearly defined manner: men with hard bodies were fit to lead the nation, showing how the values they embodied could stand up to the cultural, political, and military challenge posed by the Soviet Union, while men with soft bodies were at danger of losing the battle and going over to the other side.[11]

Important to our discussion is that minorities, such as America's Catholics, were neither detached nor sidelined by this dichotomy, but active participants in its propagation. Catholic anti-communism, like most anti-communism of the era, was therefore a gendered and bodily response to America's geopolitical situation, while simultaneously striving to install a sense of security to a decade of general malaise and unease. By finding figureheads to champion the hardness lionized by this dichotomy, these men could stand in for the vitality of the nation and the superiority of America's values and institutions against the ever-present spectre of communism. The most emblematic, as well as infamous, of America's Catholic men to become a figurehead for hardness was none other than Joseph McCarthy. Transforming himself from a relatively unknown junior senator from Wisconsin into a hardened Cold Warrior, McCarthy aggressively associated softness and weakness with otherness and treason while personifying a masculinity that was as brash as it was reckless. While his time in the spotlight was short-lived and ultimately self-destructive, he wasn't the only Catholic leading the charge against softness and communism. Fulton Sheen, too, through speeches on *Life Is Worth Living* and in his various writings, positioned himself as a leading voice against the Red Menace. However, rather than advocating for traditional hardness as was the case with McCarthy and others, Sheen lionized the moral integrity of America as a rallying point against his own reconfigured ideas of softness, which the communists embodied. Despite arguing for a hardening of spirit and intellect, proponents nevertheless rallied around Sheen's celebrity and found ways of idealizing his body and habits. On the one hand, this could be read as an effort to eliminate any suspicion of softness around an aged member of a minority clergy, while on the other it also demonstrates the lengths to which a nation will go to create idealized heroes in their popular cultures – even when those figures were likely far from the ideal being espoused. Ultimately, in examining how Sheen reconfigured, deployed, and was understood by others to embody hardness, we can identify an additional, urgent configuration of celebrity in the early postwar period – that of the hard-bodied Cold Warrior.

## Hard Bodies, Hard Nation

Men's bodies exist and are understood differently according to their historical and cultural contexts. As such, unpacking the societal need and striving for hard masculinity that shook America in the postwar years cannot be understood without also examining the so-called crisis of masculinity that was widely reported to have occurred during the era.[12] While numerous troubles, real and perceived, contributed to the sense of the malaise, it was the looming threat of the Soviet Union that cast an ever-present spectre over men's bodies that could not be ignored.[13]

While formerly allies, the cracks in the Soviet-American World War II alliance began to show in the span of a few short years following the conclusion of the war, and the two superpowers quickly found themselves in a state of mutual fear and mistrust. In 1947, America made anti-communism – once a fringe political position – mainstream foreign policy by adopting the Truman Doctrine, a geopolitical and economic precursor to NATO (the North Atlantic Treaty Organization), which sought to curb, combat and ultimately contain not only Soviet expansion but the spread of communism globally, effectively setting the tenor for American global relations moving forward.[14] The following year, the Marshall Plan was approved as a comprehensive and American-led plan for the economic recovery of war-torn Europe, with the provision that a modernized, revitalized Western Europe could stand on its own two feet against Soviet expansion.[15] However, despite these measures, by 1950 the Soviets had developed their own atomic bomb, communists under Mao had finalized their seizure of mainland China, and the communist northern half of Korea was erupting into a full scale war with the South. As communism spread rapidly across the globe, taking seed in countries from Southeast Asia to South America, the American principle of democracy appeared to be losing not only its previous geopolitical footing but also the vigour and vitality it needed to endure.

Although the 1962 Cuban Missile Crisis – perhaps the height of tension between these two superpowers – was still some years away, the 1950s were nevertheless a time of uncertainty and escalation in America's geopolitical relationships as well as with the bodies within its own borders. In December 1953, anxieties connecting men's bodies with anxieties about the nation came into full effect when the *Journal of the American Association for Health, Physical Education, and Recreation* published a rather unsettling article titled "Muscular Fitness and Health," which painted a dire portrait of the health and fitness of the average American. The article's study revolved around a systematic examination of the fitness levels of American boys between the ages of six and sixteen. Comparing American with European youths in the same age bracket, the study suggested that the average levels of physical fitness among Americans paled in comparison to their transatlantic counterparts.[16] Shortly after the publication of this article, a disturbing trend was noted in army recruitment offices: a drastic upsurge of young men were failing to meet the basic physical fitness requirements of America's armed forces.[17] America's men, it would seem, were in danger of becoming "sissies."[18]

In response to this apparent laxity in America's physical capabilities, President Eisenhower launched the President's Council on Youth and Fitness, a nationwide program for raising awareness about the health and fitness of America's young men, and by 1957 the Council began implementing a nationwide program focused on setting targets and standards for schools to implement.[19] Although the Council's initial focus was on America's youth, the program's benefits were expected to continue with the participants into adulthood, resulting in a new – and harder – generation of American men.[20] Dr Shane MacCarthy, the executive director appointed to head the Council, was unequivocable in communicating this goal of internal transformation – as he explicitly remarked just before the 1956 Olympic Games in Italy, "Perhaps as we consider the next Olympics, the theme should be not so much 'Win in Rome' as 'Win at home.'"[21] As this remark suggests, it was MacCarthy's hope that, by demonstrating their vigour on the international stage, these athletes would inspire a larger reinvigoration of the nation. In other words, it was important for America's Olympic athletes to be successful, young, and powerful, not only to win metals but also to act as representatives of the dominant ideology their nation espoused and hoped to inculcate into its populace.

The Olympics were, in fact, a major driver behind America's desire to demonstrate the vigour of its men. In the geopolitical context of communist expansion, the visibility of Soviet bodies made possible by the recently revived Games represented a source of anxiety. Though the first postwar Games were held in 1948 in London, the 1952 Games in Helsinki would be the first time Americans and Soviets squared off against each other in competition.[22] Just as the Soviets were mistrustful of America's growing world influence and ideological hegemony, they had similar worries about the potential danger of American bodies and their domination in international sports.[23] Sports scholar Ekaterina Emiliantseva argues that, for Soviets, "results oriented competition was [seen] as a way to expand the realm of ideological agitation abroad and strengthen legitimacy at home" – put differently, sporting competitions came to be understood as ideologically potent "Cold War weapon[s]."[24] That the 1952 Games would be a highly televised event was hardly overlooked by the Soviet leaders. Television would become the ideal means to increase the visibility of hard Soviet bodies and the ideology they represented while exposing the potential softness of America's own. As Susan Jeffords remarks, "A nation exists … as something to be seen," and there was no better way of being seen than through manly athletic competition.[25]

Similar fears and anxieties surrounding men's bodies would later be echoed by President-elect and American Catholic John F. Kennedy, who penned an article for *Sports Illustrated* magazine in December of 1960, shortly after winning that year's presidential election.[26] Titled "The Soft American," Kennedy used the editorial to lament what he saw as the ongoing loss of American vitality and manhood since the closure of World War II. In voicing his apprehension over this increasing frailty, Kennedy drew a direct contrast between American weakness and Soviet vitality: "We face in the Soviet Union, a powerful and implacable adversary determined to show the world that only the Communist system possesses the vigour and determination necessary to satisfy awakening aspirations for progress and the elimination of poverty and want. To meet the challenge of this enemy will require determination and will and effort on the part of all Americans. Only if our citizens are physically fit will they be fully capable of such an effort."[27] Here, Kennedy effectively draws a connection between the vigour of a nation's people and the vitality of its ideology and global ambitions, by pointing out the apparent dangers of a physically unfit or "soft" civic body in the face of an implacable ideological foe. His statement suggests that the hardness of Soviet bodies represented a challenge, not only to the physical fitness of America's own men but also to the vitality of its institutions. American weakness was thus not only a threat to its efforts overseas – it also had the potential to jeopardize the freedoms and aspirations of its citizens within its own borders. As such, Kennedy's article and the Eisenhower administration's edicts can be read as part of a wider trend in America that "connected male physical fitness … to patriotism."[28] In other words, by embracing and embodying the harder attributes and expectations of masculinity, men could also embrace and embody a firmer definition of American patriotism and vicariously protect its institutions against the communist danger.

## Hardness and Hegemonic Masculinity

Rooted in the physiological ideals of the male body, hardness has long been conceptualized by the muscular and the erectile.[29] Social scientist Robert Brannon also notes that hard masculinity equally tends to encompass a concern for a hardness of character.[30] While Brannon analyzes this hardness of character to mean that men need to have tightly controlled emotions, American handbooks for young men from the postwar era also associated hardness of character with the ability to strictly adhere to moral codes. Take, for example, Catholic ex-marine John Cross's *Let's Take the Hard Road*, which portrays the ideal man, not only as one who strives for hardness of body through exercise and healthy eating, but also as one who also exerts discipline over his emotions, desires, and any temptations that may arise – such as having sexual relations outside wedlock or even smoking cigarettes.[31] In effect, the idealized hard male is a man made of contradictions and opposing pulls – one who is simultaneously hard of body and mind, stoic yet virile, disciplined yet utterly detached from his emotions.

In trying to understand the operative patterns of hard masculinity and the anxieties surrounding the male bodies which fail to conform to those standards, R.W. Connell's theory of "hegemonic masculinity" is helpful.[32] Noting the hierarchical organization of masculinities and femininities at the societal level, she argues that hegemonic masculinity is driven by the need to dominate and the fear of being dominated by others, a drive that pools social power in the hands of "hard" men at the expense of women and subordinated masculinities. Accordingly, hegemonic masculinity is not a "fixed character type … but a pervasive force."[33] Such a system thus reinforces and is reinforced by a perceived gender dichotomy: "real" men are rational, stoic, tough, and independent, while women – and subaltern men – are emotional, superstitious, weak, and dependent. Scholars such as Rotundo and Meyer comment on the contradictions inherent in setting such impossible standards for men to live by – while hegemonic ideals propose the means of asserting oneself and overcoming anxiety, they are at the same time the causes for those very same anxieties.[34]

Throughout the twentieth century, the integration of hard masculinity with religious bodies has largely occurred under the hegemony of white, heteronormative – and in particular – Protestant Christianity. The roots of this trend can be traced to the "muscular Christianity" movement that emerged out of mid-nineteenth-century England.[35] In stark contrast to earlier iterations of Protestantism that abhorred all forms of sport, as well as prejudicial views that associated such activities with the lower classes, clergyman Charles Kingsley and the jurist Thomas Hughes posited that the Church of England was becoming "overly tolerant of physical weakness and efficiency" and wholly unsuitable for the manliness demanded of the British imperial enterprise.[36] In a pair of novels exploring these themes, Kingsley's *Two Years Ago* and Hughes's *Tom Brown's School Days*, these men argued that bodily strength and manly virtues were prerequisites for the dissemination of strong Christian values, often stressing "action rather than reflection and aggression rather than gentility."[37]

Initially based out of England, the movement could in many ways be read as a reaction to a changing world – such as ongoing demographic changes brought about by the ongoing Industrial Revolution, and more pressing by the growing participation of women in church functions, as well as the increasing visibility of the "other" bodies of Britain's colonial subjects.[38] When transplanted to the United States in the 1880s, it retained much of its anxiety about change and the need to look back to an imagined past, while also taking on new dimensions more suited to its new environment. While hardly universally accepted, leading Americans including future president Theodore Roosevelt were deeply moved by the tenets of the movement, connecting masculinity to nature and conquest, effectively refashioning themselves into manly exemplars who could stand apart from the perceived effeminacy and emasculation brought about by the excesses of the Gilded Age.[39] Into the twentieth century, elements of the movement and its ideologies would continue to persist and permeate deep into America's culture and religious identities. White Protestant Americans founds means of using biblical frameworks (notable those espousing male "headship") to reinforce a broader cultural trend toward masculine hardness and ideal social configurations. Importantly, as historian Kristin Kobes Du Mez outlines, during the 1940s and 1950s a revitalized Evangelical identity seemed indebted to these earlier ideals as it lent itself to an overlapping focus on militarism, traditional gender roles, and patriarchal authority that inspired religious and popular culture.[40] For many Evangelicals, the figures who embodied virtuous American masculinity – John Wayne, for example – "would come to define not only Christian manhood but Christianity itself," regardless of their actual religious affiliations.[41] In other words, America's moral core and ecclesial foundations were becoming increasingly rooted in conceptions of hardness and the bodies upholding those same conceptions. Even Billy Graham, who might seem an unlikely candidate for such a position, given our recent discussion of the man as an accessible, family-friendly celebrity preacher, was nevertheless still a celebrity and a man within whom the vitality of a nation and its values could be rooted. Graham seems to have been aware of this, as he made conscious efforts to project an image of being a "seasoned yet virile male."[42] He was frequently photographed with his well-attired wife, stable of children, massive dogs, and illustrious home property, showcasing the health of emblematic American values of home, family, and stability. Elements of his bodily fortitude also overlapped with his message of moral fortitude, as he was a strong advocate for moral hardness, arguing that practices such as sobriety, fidelity, and honesty took precedence over more macho characteristics, suggesting "real men" were man enough not to fall into vices and misbehaviour in the first place.[43]

## A "Hard-Scrabbled" Catholic Response

Catholic masculinities figured into this negotiation, too, but in a more complex manner. Largely owing to their historical associations with immigrants and working-class men, Catholics have often been positioned as subaltern in relation to the dominant (i.e., Protestant) modes and aesthetics of manhood.[44] As we briefly alluded to in the previous chapter, due to their adherence to a ritualistic devotional culture, Catholics in America are intrinsically inflected with a religious angle to their manhood that differs sharply from their Protestant peers.[45]

Catholic priests, in particular, embody a pattern of masculinity that is markedly different from the norms of hegemonic expectations. By virtue of their celibacy and positionality as religious leaders, priests have been contending with these issues since the Middle Ages as they seem to shirk the traditional signifiers of masculinity – biological fatherhood, sexual conquest, and so on.[46] Nevertheless, we have already seen ways in which Catholics have sought to combat accusations of softness by invigorating the roles and bodies of priests. In the case of Father Jerry from the previous chapter, for example, we can see how traditional framings of hegemonic ideals were rebutted and reconfigured whereby the spiritual and the moral authority of his position as moral authority and community leader is what makes him a man and is thus hierarchically above the muscular, the erectile, or any other components of masculinity that could be deemed as hard or hegemonic. Equally so for lay people, as Maldonado-Estrada has demonstrated, Catholic men have found ways to associate activities performed for their parish (such as physical labour and craftsmanship) as being simultaneously manly and religious.[47]

This is not to say that depictions of Catholic manhood have shied away from markers of hard masculinity (such as aggression, willingness to fight, emotional stoicism, etc.). The successes of Notre Dame University's football team, and the invigorating effect they had on the wider community, led theologian Alister McGrath to remark that "Catholicism can equally well be said to promote muscular Christianity."[48] Bishop Sheil's Chicago ministry, particularly his work with the Christian Youth Organization, was also a clear Catholic iteration of the muscular phenomenon. Sheil had apparently been something of an athlete in his youth, passing up on a career in sports to become a preacher.[49] Similar to Protestant worries about the city and its vices, Sheil saw sports and physical activities as an alternative to draw young men away from more problematic pastimes and possible criminal activities.[50] Boxing was his preferred sport, which he promoted vociferously over national radio and in magazine interviews, and was even feted by President Roosevelt for his work with the youth.[51] Though Sheil was keen on promoting the moral aspects of his ministry, in averting vice among the nation's youth, much of his persona and personal charismatic appeal was nevertheless derived from, as scholar Timothy B. Neary would remark, "his vigorous athleticism."[52]

The Korean War (1950–53), however, was among the first major armed conflicts between communist and Western-aligned states, and it provided an early and fertile battleground for formulating American Catholic hardness and opposition to the ideology. Catholic opposition to communism had been long-standing by that point, with the official Vatican stance on the ideology being hardly nuanced, though few anti-communists within the ranks had a chance to meet their opponent head-on until the conflict.[53] One prominent figure during the war was Father Emil Kapaun, a heroic American army chaplain captured by North Korea. Kapaun, by virtue of his posting to the front lines, was inscribed by his proponents as being representative of a hard-bodied paternalism, encapsulated by the inscription on a statue honouring him: "All Man, All Priest."[54] On the battlefield, he gained a reputation for being fearless as he ministered to the troops and bravely tended to the rescue of dozens of men before being captured. In captivity, he would die from malnutrition but later be awarded the Medal of Honor for his actions. Like other chaplains ministering along the front lines, he found novel ways of expressing hardness by appropriating jeeps, ammunition, and other elements of war as makeshift altars for their sermons, effectively reinforcing their masculine credentials and those of the religious tradition they vicariously represented, demonstrating that times of geopolitical turmoil both bodies and beliefs were ripe for manly reification.[55]

Stateside priests, too, injected themselves into these dichotomies, like the Jesuit Edmund A. Walsh, who framed the Catholic response to communism as hinging upon hardness of body and character. Walsh had been an ardent anti-communist since the 1920s and arguably was the most visible among America's Catholic leadership until Sheen took the spotlight.[56] In the 1930s, he was tasked with directing relief work for the National Catholic Welfare Council in the then-famine-stricken Soviet Union. Having witnessed atrocities against local clergy, along with the shuttering of the Catholic presence in Russia and show trials condemning priests, he very much seems to have emerged a changed man with a singular mission to combat the existential and cosmological threat he saw in communism.[57] According to Walsh, the reason communism threatened the United States and was growing worldwide was owing to the fact the Soviets perceived Americans and democracy to have gone soft, and he can be read as being among those who felt that the presence of a yet fully understood global geopolitical conflict necessitated that the church powerfully reaffirm its moral and spiritual systems.[58] As such, the remedy for America's lack of physical hardness was to embrace its inner moral hardness. What this meant in practical terms was that, by the 1940s, he was all but advocating for a pre-emptive atomic strike against the Soviet Union. Arguing the moral legitimacy of atomic war, he believed that only by utterly annihilating their atheistic opponent could they ensure the preservation not only of democracy but of their Judeo-Christian values. For Walsh, only hardness could resist the communists, as softness and "the belief that you can win over a totalitarian government with sweetness and light is a delusion that time is gradually uprooting."[59]

Though Walsh's fiery posturing could be read as something of an outlier, no man better encapsulated the image of hard masculinity than that of the hard-bodied Cold Warrior Joseph McCarthy.[60] Emerging to the national spotlight after delivering a surprisingly fiery speech in 1950 at the Republican Women's Club of Wheeling, West Virginia – during which he held up a list identifying some two hundred or so Communist Party members supposedly operating within America's government – the junior senator quickly and infamously became the nation's most visible anti-communism and a household name.[61] Biographer Allen J. Matusow comments that this quick rise into the spotlight had the capacity to elevate McCarthy to the status of a celebrity, and that "there was a time in the early 1950s when Joseph R. McCarthy, junior senator from Wisconsin, commanded more national attention than the president of the United States."[62] Appointed as the chairman of the Senate Committee on Government Operations, which put the vaguely defined Senate Permanent Subcommittee on Investigations under the purview of his office, and backed with the counsel of prosecutors Roy Cohn and Gerald Schine, McCarthy had a near limitless ability to pursue his agenda of rooting out suspected subversives within America's institutions.[63]

Likely little needs to be said about the efficacy of McCarthy's investigations and the hollowness of his show trials.[64] However, and key to our discussion, we can see that in his quest to purge communists and communist sympathizers from America's bureaucracy, the core of McCarthy's activities hinged on the association of errant bodies with national weakness. Implying through innuendo that soft-bodied men were inclined to side with traitorous communism, he suggested that America's political class had not only grown weak, but by their own softness allowed communism to take root in America.[65] He used words such as "vile" or "indecent" to describe adherents to the opposing ideology, and because American had gone soft on rooting out communists before his arrival, going so far as "coddling them," he argued that subversives operating freely inside the nation have done more harm to democracy than the whole might of the Soviet army.[66] He directed the same invectives toward his critics and anyone siding with those he persecuted, referring to them as being "perverted."[67] He referred to politicians opposing his work as being part of "the lace handkerchief crowd," not so subtly implying that their lack of support for his tactics demonstrated a lack of masculinity but also that it brought their sexuality into question.[68] At one point, McCarthy was asked to compare his list of subversives from the Tydings Committee with the

State Department's own loyalty files and dossiers. Finding little in there to support his own claims, McCarthy declared publicly that then President Truman had the dossier "raped" to cover any data that might have exposed potential subversives, hinting that not even the nation's commander in chief was immune to softness and deviancy.

In contrast, the senator did whatever he could to portray himself as a "self-made man of the people" who had come from a rough background before emerging as a champion of America's values.[69] Though McCarthy, a law school graduate, was hardly the humble figure he portrayed, he leveraged the immigrant background of his parents, carrying his "hard scrabbled Irish Catholic roots as a point of pride," effectively embracing an almost stereotypical image of the Irish.[70] His close associate Roy Cohn remarked with some praise that the senator, though busy at work in the soft city of Washington, DC, was essentially "rough-hewn … never managing to throw off his country-boy origins" and emphasized his athleticism by remarking that McCarthy "liked to swim and water-ski and would occasionally play golf."[71] Like a true adherent of *The Drinking Man's Diet,* he did nothing to hide his copious consumption of alcohol – whiskey was his beverage at choice – and was rarely seen eating anything but steak and other large cuts of meat.[72] Speaking to his persona, scholar Andrea Friedman remarks that "he cultivated a reputation as a fighter, a gambler, and a womanizer. McCarthy made much of his college career as a boxer, glorying in his depiction as a 'slugger' rather than a man of skill."[73] McCarthy rooted much of his hardness in his own physicality, demonstrating that he was a man of action, unwilling to be slowed down by decorum or by taking the time to gather evidence to support his accusations. After all, as the nation's foremost anti-communist, any setbacks to his person were setbacks for the nation – in other words, his personhood and strength was the strength and defence of the nation.[74] When McCarthy weakened, so, too, would the nation.

In his associating of softness with deviance, we can also see that McCarthy drew inspiration from already established Catholic positions against communism, effectively rooting *moral* normativity with hardness – a fact that was likely deeply rooted in his own Catholic faith.[75] According to biographer David Oshinsky, McCarthy was a devout Catholic who "went regularly to confessions, observed meatless Fridays, gave generously to Catholic Charities, and rarely missed Sunday Mass."[76] In a 1952 issue of *Catholic World*, a woman who claimed to know some of the senator's friends assured the magazine that he was "a deeply religious man ... Joe always takes time out to pray, even in the heat of a tight political campaign."[77] McCarthy himself even spoke openly about his faith to a certain extent. He told *Time* magazine that he was a "good Catholic," but – lest someone think his faith made him soft or subservient, a person of questionable loyalties as many Catholics had historically been stereotyped – he reminded them that he was not a "kiss-the-book, light-the-candle" kind of Catholic.[78] Still, to McCarthy, like many Catholics – especially those who supported him – the fundamental difference between America and the Soviet Union wasn't so much the difference between two competing political and economic systems, but between good and evil, between moral hardness and immoral softness embodied by each nation, respectively.[79] "The greatest difference between our western Christian world and the *atheistic* Communist world is not political," he declared, "ladies and gentlemen, it is *moral*."[80] Such proclamations were perhaps empty posturing, like much of what can be said about the senator.[81] However, the frequency in which he deployed a similar line of reasoning would suggest that it was at least in some part rooted in his faith – the underpinnings of which necessitated a hardness of body, character and spirit – and a position that would mirror much of Sheen's own anti-communist posture.[82]

## Hard Body, Harder Spirit – Bishop Sheen and a Reconfiguration

By the mid-1950s, Sheen's opposition to the Soviet Union was long-standing and well recognized. Daniel P. Noonan, who spent several years in Sheen's employ, paints the man as something of a prophetic figure who foresaw the eventual cooling of the relations between the United States and the USSR long before it happened.[83] Scholar and Sheen biographer Kathleen Riley also positions Sheen as something of a forerunner, suggesting he was a part of the anti-communist "vanguard" in America. She writes, "By crusading for social justice and against the threat of communism, Sheen was among those socially conscious priests who helped move the Catholic Church out of the confines of the ghetto mentality and into its rightful place in the mainstream of American life and thought."[84] Though any claims to Sheen having been a lone voice against communism during the pre-war years are fanciful at best, he was certainly one of the most prolific celebrity figures to take up the cause.[85]

As Timothy H. Sherwood reminds us, before hosting *Life Is Worth Living*, Sheen made his position about communism known on his *Catholic Hour* radio appearances in the 1930s.[86] He argued that the church alone, out of all the forces in America, had consistently stood strong against the threat of the modern error of communism, tying it alongside Nazism and fascism as a trifecta of anti-American ideologies – albeit arguing that communism was the most dangerous as it came under the guise of friendship, as it would during World War II when uniting with the Allied powers to defeat the Axis. However, the church had seen it for what it was all along, and "the only solution to the threat of communism" was through the Christian principles, such as those espoused by the Catholic Church.[87] Like other Catholic anti-communists, Sheen can be read as having understood the opposition of the Soviet system "not as a matter of geo-politics or justice, but as a challenge to the moral and spiritual authority" of the teachings underpinning the church and America.[88] Sheen would go on to claim to have been personally urged on by then Pope Pius XI – himself an outspoken critic of communism – to take a stand against the ideology even while America was in the process of cementing their wartime alliance with the Soviet Union, effectively bestowing him with something of a divine mandate to combat the opposing ideology.[89] From there, Sheen devoted considerable time and energy to combatting the ideology, consistently pouring "forth a gushing stream of books, articles, pamphlets, sermons and speeches detailing the theory and dynamics of Communism."[90]

Though both Sheen and McCarthy hailed from the rural Midwest, the bishop embraced little of the earthy populism that defined the senator's hardness in his approach to combatting communism. While Sheen did selectively emphasize his rural upbringing in his autobiography (as discussed in chapter 1) and was re-envisioned as a country boy by his later devotees (as discussed in chapter 2), Sheen opted instead to take a more spiritual and learned – though no less impassioned – stance against communism that might seem at odds with hard masculinity. In 1948, Sheen released *Communism and the Conscience of the West*, a book that greatly expanded many of his *Catholic Hour* discussions about communism. He argued that America and other Western nations rested their success, freedoms, and national character on the strength of their moral foundations – foundations that were predominately shaped by Christianity. As Timothy Sherwood elaborates, "Sheen tapped into the general mind-set in America that equated religion with anti-communism," whereby American democracy could not survive if it was ever separated from its Christian foundations.[91] "Religion, especially Christianity," writes Sherwood, "therefore became as much of an identifying mark for being American as mom, baseball, and apple pie."[92] Thus, as long as the American people upheld its moral underpinnings, the nation would not only be able to fend off ideological threats but retain its most recognizable institutions along with the very core of its identity. Similar to how Kennedy and others equated a loss of physical vigour with susceptibility to foreign invasion, Sheen argued that when a nation loses its moral tenor, it becomes susceptible to rot, which in turn creates a space where other ideas – such as communism – can enter and fill the void.[93] Where much of the nation in the 1950s would connect bodily hardness with ideological strength, Sheen was advocating for a somewhat novel sort of spiritual, moral, and intellectual hardness that prefigured all other discussions of the body. In elevating spiritual hardness, Sheen was perhaps able to circumnavigate some of the expectations of bodily hardness that McCarthy and others so readily emphasized and sought to have applied to their person.

As American popular culture and politicians were readily channelling the dichotomy of hard and soft to link men's bodies with national vitality, Sheen used similar language to shift the dialogue toward what he perceived to be the more pressing softening taking place within America – a softening of spirituality, morality, and intellect. In 1947, a quote of his found its way into the pages of *The Observer* (an edition of *Our Sunday Visitor*), where Sheen opined on America's spiritual laxity, stating that "Communists have zeal and no truth, we Americans have truth but no zeal."[94] In the same article, while discussing an apparent postwar lack of ingenuity and intellect in America compared with America's earlier achievements, Sheen would comment on bodily hardness, albeit not as one might expect: "There has been a softening of our brains. We [now] appeal for a *hardening* of brains."[95] Sheen's interest in the male body here was specifically rooted in the brain, where man is responsible for his spiritual and intellectual reasoning. He further developed this interest in an episode of *Life Is Worth Living* where he declared that "the fatigue which concerns us presently is not physical fatigue, but rather mental fatigue. Why is there so much apathy and dullness and indifference in the world, and such a want of fire and enthusiasm … the chief cause of fatigue is not exhaustion, but stagnation."[96] Unlike the examples discussed in the previous sections, which primarily rooted softness in the base physicality and athleticism of men, to Sheen, the fatigue and weakness afflicting Americans was only rooted in the physical insofar as it could be connected to morality and intellect. In effect, the weakness affecting America's men was a pressing concern, not due to their diminishing build or musculature, but because a stagnation of morals and intellect at the personal and national level together threatened the nation's global standing and ideologies. Thus, where Kennedy and others would equate physical fitness with patriotism, Sheen went further, equating patriotism with spirituality and explicitly Christian morality. In other words, physical and mental fitness were important primarily because they gave rise to a strong spiritual and moral character. In Sheen's worldview, Americans had the choice of either bowing to the flag of a beloved nation based on Christian principles or of bowing to a totalitarian regime based on emptiness. Commitment to one meant restoring the health of the nation, while the other meant corrupting it.[97]

Like McCarthy, who tied moral and bodily softness with vulnerability and potential sites of supervision, Sheen, too, saw the nation being vulnerable to communist incursions, albeit from the entry point of spiritual and moral softness instead. In one episode of *Life Is Worth Living*, he made an explicit connection between communism's rise and a nation's weakened moral fibre. In comparing the nation to a body, he stated that "whenever a civilization begins to die morally or spiritually, there begin to appear vultures. That is the mission of Communism in the world. Communism is the scavenger of a decaying civilization."[98] Just as bodies open themselves up to incursion when experiencing moral weakness, when a national body loses its sense of morality and strays from its Christian foundations, it, too, opens itself up to the danger of weakness. For Sheen, spiritual and moral weakness were thus more pressing concerns than mere physical weakness in warding off communism. He elaborated on this in another episode, by stating "we need the kind of revolution in the United States … that pours out of a man's heart pride, and covetousness, and lust, and anger, and envy, and gluttony, and sloth. In other words, then, the battle against communism begins with the hearts of every single American."[99] Here, like

McCarthy, he explicitly situates the cosmological underpinnings of the battle of democracy versus communism in the body, linking the decline of Christian morality and bodily integrity to a potential communist incursion.[100] Sheen would continue to emphasize this link when he declared that "Communism is strong only when it borrows some of the moral indignation that has been inherited from the Hebraic-Christian traditions; Communism is weak when it departs from that tradition."[101]

Though Sheen seldom referred to men's bodies in as explicit a manner as other anti-communist figureheads, he does expressly connect the American nation and its ideologies with the body of Christ. When speaking of Christ's sacrifice on the cross in an episode of *Life Is Worth Living* titled "Pain and Suffering," Sheen states that "his blood was his royal purple. It was the foundation of democracy, the worth of a single soul."[102] Here, Sheen is effectively suggesting that, as Christ's bodily sacrifice was the bedrock upon which American democracy rested, the battle for its future continued inside the hearts and souls of its present-day inhabitants. However, what is perhaps more remarkable is that the hardness Sheen advocates is explicitly rooted in Christ's suffering and ravaged body, making this a stringently Catholic reading of Christ's body and its connection to America's ideologies. Unlike American Protestant depictions and conceptualizations of Christ's hardness – see, for example, Warner Sallman's immensely popular painting *Head of Christ*, which emphasizes a glowing, virile and "manly" Christ – Sheen's Catholicism inverts these more traditional depictions by asserting that true physical hardness has ties to suffering, and that Christ's noble sacrifice was the wellspring not just of the nation's religious foundations but of democracy, the most cherished of America' ideologies.[103]

It was this very spiritual hardness that Sheen so effectively embodied when positioning himself against the hardest embodiment of communism – Stalin himself. Where Truman once referred to Stalin in hardened terms as the "world's bully," Sheen casually remarked in a *Time* magazine piece from 1954 that "he prays every morning for Joseph Stalin" the same he would for any wayward soul – effectively debasing the Soviet leader to the status of a common sinner, of a man experiencing moral softening.[104] However, his most poignant rebuke of the Soviet leader occurred in an episode titled "On the Death of Stalin." Using a clever play on words, frequent allusions, and his own creativity, Sheen delivered an episode-length monologue heavily indebted to Shakespeare's *Julius Caesar.* Envisioning a fictitious scenario in which the Soviet leadership was forced to react to and contend with the sudden death of supreme leader Joseph Stalin, Sheen interspersed scenes from the tragedy with his own biting criticism of communist principles and leaders by name. In one scene, Sheen played with the famous speech given by Marc Antony to the Roman people after the death of Caesar, replacing him with the Soviet leader Malenkov giving a similar speech to fellow members of the upper echelon. "Friends, Soviets, countrymen," he began, "lend me your ears; I come to bury Stalin, not to praise him."[105] Where Marc Antony's speech became a clever double entendre that turned the people against the conspirators, Sheen's Malenkov was not intended to offer praise to the recently departed leader – as he states in his final, dramatic pronouncement of the episode: "Stalin must one day meet his judgment!"[106] At the time of its original telecast, the episode was very much a work of fiction. Stalin, the Soviet leader, was very much alive and there were no plans pertaining to the succession of his leadership. However, nine days later, Stalin suffered a sudden cerebral hemorrhage. After three days unconscious in a coma, he was pronounced dead.

Stalin's death further cemented Sheen as one of the nation's foremost anti-communist crusaders – a celebrity who both promoted America's values through his televised appearances and defended them against the unseen enemy. Moreover, by predicting Stalin's death, he became something of a prophet against communism, too, suggesting that he perhaps understood the weakness tied to the ideology better than anyone else. Notably, by condemning Stalin's soft moral integrity, only to have him die a few days later, Sheen showcased the link between spiritual hardness and bodily integrity.[107] Because Stalin's outward hardness lacked the internal hardness afforded by a strong religious and moral foundation, he ultimately lacked the bodily integrity to persevere. And so if the vitality of male bodies was understood to stand in for the vitality of the nations and its ideologies, Stalin's death demonstrated an inherent weakness in both the Soviet nation and its ideologies, suggesting that they were not as secure – or hard – as may have been previously thought.

## *A Most Healthy Body*

Sheen's personal focus was on the importance of philosophical, moral, and intellectual hardness in the ideological war with communism. He spoke about these issues as a celebrity, and in turn saw the further expansion of his celebrity character owing to the visibility of his stance promoted through his television show and other media output. However, it was by this very virtue of his being a celebrity figurehead that he could never be completely detached from wider discussions and imaginings of the physical elements of the hard/soft dichotomy and how they related to his own body.

In her 1994 monograph, Susan Jeffords argued that leading figures in America could capture the imagination of popular culture and act as emblems of the American identity, vicariously standing in for the strength of the nation and its values.[108] Though her monograph and case study largely focused on the aging body of American President Ronald Reagan as a leading anti-communist in the 1980s, along with the nation's then-current stable of celebrity action film stars, we can nevertheless witness the same process in effect in the 1950s whereby hard bodies become the collective symbols that anchored the nation. As Jeffords writes, "These hard bodies came to stand not only for a type of national character … but for the nation itself."[109] Of equal importance, it could be said, were that those national figureheads and celebrities themselves be perceived to embody hardness without any potential stain of softness or suspicion. This is potentially one reason which made the 1950s rooting out of communist sympathizers – partially orchestrated by Ronald Reagan, then head of the Screen Acting Guild – among Hollywood's elite so pressing: If not even the nation's celebrities could stand up to Soviet incursions, then what chance did the rest of the nation have? And so, though Sheen was aging, and hardly an athlete by any normal metric, mattered little; what was more important was the perception and the symbiosis between his body and wider culture.[110] After all, as Jeffords remarked, the fixation on the bodily health of elderly leaders often coincided with a surge in popularity in sports, along with an increased scrutiny of diet and physical wellness. By propping up and idealizing the health of Sheen's body, the body of the man who so vigorously defended and promoted America's values, proponents could do the same for the values he represented. Through this, though clearly aging, Sheen's body and bodily habits became points of fascination, intimately linked with the vitality of the national ideologies and its efforts to combat communism.

To take one instance, during the 1950s, Sheen's eating habits had a habit of making their way into newspaper exposes of his life, interviews, and other biographical instances – as Sugrue's biography of Sheen at the start of the chapter demonstrated. However, *The Bishop Sheen Story* was hardly an outlier in these matters. In a 1952 article titled "The Seven Deadly Sins of Our Time," which included an interview with Sheen, the author remarks that when Sheen "adjourns for dinner" it occupies no more than "one half hour" taking place like clockwork from six to six thirty.[111] It goes on to state that "he contents himself only with a few vegetables, a glass of milk or black coffee, a tiny unseasoned salad, or a lamb chop no bigger than a delivery stamp … he contents himself to eat frugally." Not only does Sheen eat little, with no garnish, but he takes little pleasure in eating – seeing it more as a daily chore than anything else. In another article introducing Sheen to his parish shortly after his installation at Rochester, one journalist remarked that Sheen's "breakfast is frugal – orange juice, hot water and toast."[112] In case readers didn't happen to associate Sheen's healthy yet skimpy breakfast with the traditional Catholic virtue of asceticism, Atwell makes the reference explicit, by stating that Sheen's morning meals are "a combination of mortification and practical necessity … he's suffered from ulcers but they don't bother him much now." Remarkably, the article suggests that Sheen's austere diet combined with his personal asceticism improved his health – making his meals both healthy and holy. Sheen's eating habits were thus a source of much fascination and were frequently linked with the discourse surrounding physical fitness being espoused nationally. In other words, Sheen's aging body was represented as a site of both physical and moral strength in the face of America's perceived growing luxury, decadence, and laxness.

Interest in Sheen's physicality extended far beyond his food preferences. In *The Bishop Sheen Story*, Sugrue casually refers to Sheen as the "ex-farm boy from Peoria."[113] Much like how the current Diocese of Peoria has been seeking to refigure Sheen as a rural Catholic, Sugrue declared that though Sheen resides in bustling New York City, he "can't get enough of fresh air."[114] As remarked in chapter 2, at his museum in

Peoria, in the small children's corner behind the main display housing some of his vestments sits a stack of colouring books. The first quarter of the book depicts idyllic and imagined images of Sheen's past, as a young man growing up on the farm. We see him riding a horse and smiling. In another image, he uses his muscular arms to work the dirt in the field with a shovel. By all accounts, the Sheen depicted in these images for children to view and colour is a strapping young man in the prime of his life, more of an athlete than a bookworm – far flung from the perfumed man who was immaculately coiffed in well pressed suits or full clerical garb he came to be.[115] Ironically, these accounts contrast very much with scenes from his autobiography and even his own aversion to manual labour and farm work.[116] As was the case with McCarthy, Sheen's rural origins – no matter how far removed he might have become in becoming a veritable New York dandy – became a point of fascination, an earthy marker of his identity that grounded him among average Americans rather than singled him out as a member of the nation's intellectual – and often perceived to be effeminate – elite.[117]

The extent to which Sheen's supporters lionized his aging body reached near comical proportions. A year before his death, Sheen endured serious heart trouble that required prolonged hospital stays and repeated surgery. Shortly after leaving the hospital, he was apparently back to his old self, giving speeches and presentations and refusing to rest. A story in the *Twin Circle* at the time by Angela Canade and Paul Fisher remarked that "at 83 years of age, Archbishop Sheen has bounced back with vigor … his voice booms."[118] They also commented on his appearance twice in the article, observing that "the famous silver hair is carefully parted above a baby-smooth skin that glows with a healthy blush" and "there is a glowing quality about his eyes … you bask in their warmth." It would seem that even on the cusp of death, Sheen's body was not only glowing but had somehow gotten younger, almost childlike in terms of vitality. In a later obituary after his passing, the same newspaper remarked that even into his eighties, Sheen "spoke with the same vigor that characterized his earlier TV shows" some twenty-five years prior.[119] Similar stories would also run at various stages of his later life, notably during his troubled tenure in Rochester and his retirement shortly thereafter. In the *New York Times*, Paul Hoffman wrote a not-so subtle piece titled "Bishop Sheen's Vitality Startles and Delights Rochester."[120] The author would declare that Sheen had "the agility of a man much younger than his 72 years." Two years later, in the *Democrat and Courier*, George Murphy remarked that even in the "Autumn" of Sheen's life, he "remains young in spirit" after serving as a priest for 50 years.[121]

What we can see through these various sources is that, though advanced in years and well past his prime even by the mid-1950s, Sheen was refigured and reimagined as embodying the hard masculinity the nation so dearly craved and saw as essential for preserving and defending its values. While his body never achieved the same, almost fetishistic, heights to which McCarthy's and later Reagan's body would, Sheen's body, like his anti-communism and devotion to America's institutions, was nevertheless rendered hale and hearty through symbiosis, able to stand up to the ideological and geopolitical threat created by the nation's Soviet rivals. For as long as the aging bishop, a stalwart and outspoken defender of the nation's ideologies, was firm in his resolve against communism, so, too, would his body be the mirror reflecting these values – so, too, would the superiority of America be evident for all. Coupled with his discourses on the need for spiritual, moral, and intellectual hardness, even the potentially more problematic elements of his masculinity – such as his taste for luxury, ostentatious automobiles, and, notably, his celibacy – could be variously overlooked or reconfigured as was necessitated. The image we are left with, then, is both a man who was celebrated because of his hardened anti-communist stances, but also by virtue of his public celebrity required that he be imagined embodying all elements of hardness for the good of the nation.

## Conclusion

The Cold War was not only a conflict of political ideologies, but also a conflict over the interpretations of men's bodies. As historian Marko Dumančić observes, "Anxieties about mental and physical toughness consumed not only the leadership of Cold War governments; those in charge of cultural production also found themselves fixated on (re)presenting appropriate versions of masculinity."[122] Masculinity – or rather, the idealized perception of certain hardened hypermasculine traits – became a stabilizing agent in American society, with the bodies of predominantly white, heteronormative celebrity figureheads acting as the main vessels through which the nation could shape its hard character, avoid suspicions of softness, and render the identity of the nation more secure. What this investigation and that of similarly themed literature reveals is that bodies and ideologies overlap, become entangled and otherwise are used to read one another.

During the Cold War, men's bodies were imagined as mythical spaces where the conflicts of the competing ideologies of democracy and communism were played out. There was a rhetorical and imagined correlation between hardness and softness envisioned variously as good health and athletic fitness, but also in terms of morality and mental faculties. Sheen warned not of Soviet military aggression, but rather that the greatest threat was the corruption of the mind and soul – and, as he demonstrated in the case with Stalin, a weakened moral faculty inevitably led to a weakened bodily state. Fortunately, though America was suffering from a moral softening, every American had the possibility within them of standing up against the Soviets, of hardening themselves, and, as scholar James Patterson remarked, it all "came down to the Cross."[123] In particular, Christ's bodily sacrifice played a significant if not pivotal role in the potential for hardening America's men.

Despite a pronounced emphasis on spiritual hardness, understandings of Catholic bodies and Catholic understandings of the body were not wholly detached from wider discourses and perceptions in America but were brought into negotiation with ongoing currents of hardness in society. By virtue of his celebrity, Sheen's celibate, clerical, and Catholic body came into dialogue with the contradictory elements of hard masculinity intermixed with religious expressions in a novel manner. Though he was not the first or only Catholic leader to stand against communism and equate it with softness within the nation, "Sheen affirmed [the] general consensus by connecting it to the spiritual struggle between good and evil, virtue and sin, and life and death."[124] Thus while his position as a something of an intellectual dandy who paid close attention to his grooming may well have contributed to an image of softness, the hardness of his spiritually ideological stance against communism made his message compelling and solidified his position as a leading anti-communist. In this same manner, by his status as a celebrity Cold Warrior, it necessitated that he be rendered into a figurehead for America's own ideologies, where the health of his body stood in the health of the nation and its values. As such, he came to be perceived to embody hardness in all its elements, however improbable it may have been for a man of his age and position. Thus, while Sheen spoke of a hardness of spirit and mind, wider society's understanding of the binary demanded that he also have (or be perceived to have) a hardened body.

Nevertheless, in Sheen we can see how religious figures of this era – and indeed, of any era – have the potential to demonstrate hardness in the face of opposition without having to shy away from the intellectual, moral, and spiritual elements of their own existence. Sheen's Catholicism facilitated envisioning masculinity in this manner, and the same would be true for other anti-communist priests and church leaders of the period. As scholar Franklin Rausch argues in his study of Father Emil Kapaun – a Catholic priest who was captured and "martyred" during the Korean War – priests with hard bodies revealed that "religion did not make men, but instead gave them strength."[125] In the same manner that the ecclesial foundations of America were believed to provide fertile ground for the flourishing of the nation's values, identity, and character, religion did the same for the individual and their body. In this, Catholicism could argue that of all the forms of hardness moral and spiritual hardness reigned superior, and that Sheen, by virtue of his position as celebrity anti-communist, stood in as the ideal embodiment of these characteristics.

Nevertheless, as a final note of caution, Susan Jeffords remarks that hard bodies ultimately make for "dangerous role models" owing to the militarism and nationalism embedded within, but also because they hint at desperation, a last ditch for a nation to cling to what may be a dying, conservative framework whose influence has long been unable to keep up with cyclical and changing social conditions.[126] Societal change, as we have discussed, is a major precursor for male anxiety and the apparent need for hard, seemingly stable role models.[127] Yet, as noted in my introductory remarks, the conditions that led to anxieties around men's bodies in the 1950s were hardly unique, as they are equally present in the nineteenth century and at the turn of the century and could even be understood to have taken place again in the 1980s during Reagan.[128] This suggests that anxiety and the drive to hardness are inherent and pervasive in hegemonic masculinity, and that men in any era of change and uncertainty (as if there are any eras without either) will almost certainly experience a contradictory pull whereby hardened celebrity bodies can ease sentiments of anxiety while themselves being the sources of said anxiety. After all, envisioning the bodies of aged, leading men to be bastions of superhuman health and vitality is inherently contradictory, and hoping to see a reflection of oneself and one's values in such a proposition can only be unstable for the long term. And so, rather than truly lend themselves as the means of easing any anxieties over the perceived softness of men and their bodies, narratives and demonstrations of hardness in celebrity figures largely act to reinforce the binary and engender further anxieties. This is not to say that Sheen, as having been one celebrity figure who did little to detract from these readings of his body or other facets of his hardness, was willingly involved in furthering this cycle of anxiety. Rather, it serves to highlight yet another complex facet in the relationship between a celebrity and those who rally around them.

CONCLUSION

# The End and the Beginning

The second of December 2020 held the inauspicious distinction of being the one-year anniversary of the most recent major delay in Sheen's beatification ceremony.

In a markedly frustrated editorial composed for *Our Sunday Visitor*, Michael R. Heinlein – a frequent contributor and editor of *The Catholic Answer* magazine – railed against the ongoing delays in the process. As might be expected, he decried the surprising and vague nature of Rochester's request to throw another wrench into the cause and delay proceedings without a clear end date – even to the day of this composition in early 2025. However, more surprisingly, Heinlein extended some of the blame to Vatican officials themselves, calling attention to what he saw as an "all-too-familiar lack of clarity" in the canonization process on the part of the Holy See. Such disruptions and their lack of transparency should be a cause of concern not just for Sheen's devotees, he argued, but for the "whole Church."[1] In other words, until church leadership is able to offer more clarity, laypeople everywhere will be forced to continue toiling, not just for the cause of their celebrated patrons but also in the difficult task of finding answers that they should otherwise have been given.

On 4 February 2021, after several more months of no progress, the street outside St Mary's Cathedral in downtown Peoria was given the honorary designation of "Bishop Fulton Sheen Avenue." Msrgr. Stanley Deptula, the executive director of the Archbishop Fulton J. Sheen Foundation, commented on the location, noting how Sheen's family had moved from their farm to a home not far from the cathedral, apparently so that Sheen and his brothers could be close to the building along with the parochial school at the nearby Spalding Institute. As he states, "It is from these very streets that Fulton Sheen went on to change the world, not just the Catholic world, but the world, with a message that life is worth living."[2] While certainly hyperbolic, the monsignor's words, similar to Mr Heinlein's, indicate the extent to which Sheen continues to be viewed as something more than just the sum of his parts, and that his influence and significance extend far beyond his community. The honorary renaming of the street alongside the cathedral is of course symbolic of Sheen's spiritual connections to the church, an institution to which he dedicated his life. However, given that New York is still actively contesting Sheen's cause, the move to continue tangibly mapping Sheen to Peoria's geography may also be read as part of the larger struggle for rural Catholic visibility.

❍ ❍ ❍

Over the course of this work, I have sought to highlight not only the enduring importance of Sheen within the history and ongoing reality of American Catholicism, but also the ways in which celebrity and masculinity studies offer important theoretical supplements to the study of mid-twentieth-century American Catholicism.

In chapter 1, I demonstrated how Sheen's celebrity and sanctity both complemented and challenged each other. The church has never looked favourably upon celebrity, always seeming to fear its potential to grow beyond its boundaries and spill out of their control. Sheen, in the composition of his autobiography, demonstrated that he was in no way unaware of this tension, and sought to sublimate the elements of his life that led him to become a figure whose celebrity extended beyond the confines of the church. In doing so, he borrowed from the trappings and tropes of classical hagiography, and, in many ways, reimagined what it means to be an American celebrity – and, by extension, a sanctified figure. Ultimately, Sheen's desire for control over his narrative body led to the creation of a rather novel document that is neither fully biography nor hagiography but an unstable mixture of the two – much like his own personhood and body. This document highlights the possibility of undertaking similar readings of other biographical material produced by figures who straddled the twined poles of American celebrity and Catholic sanctity.

In chapter 2, I highlighted how Sheen's afterlife and body – that is, his material remains as they become holy relics – exposed rifts and power imbalances in the wider American church further compounded by his celebrity status. Since the late nineteenth century, rural Catholics have struggled for visibility and recognition amid the larger narratives of American Catholicism – narratives that have tended to be shaped, claimed, and otherwise dominated by the nation's urban metropolises, notably New York. Although the transfer of Sheen's remains to Peoria – the diocese responsible for his canonization proceedings – should have been simple, it became a veritable, and highly public, tug-of-war between New York and Peoria, between centre and the periphery, between the powerful and the underdog. This particular struggle, however, revealed itself to be not just a battle over Sheen's final resting place but also over his identity. Was Sheen a country boy at heart who never forgot his upbringing, or was he a member of the New York elite? Similarly, questions of Sheen's identity are also questions about situating American sanctity within one's body. Is sanctity derived by whatever kernels of one's upbringing remain deep within one's core, or is it demonstrated more so by the choices one made later in their life? In this case, we can see how the sanctity of the figures we adore is very much shaped by our own positionality. That Sheen could be both – country boy, rural Catholic and city-dwelling, elite celebrity – was perhaps never properly asked, but only tacitly admitted by Peoria as they commemorate him and keep his life on display at the Archbishop Fulton Sheen Museum. Nevertheless, one walks away from this ongoing ordeal asking to what extent his celebrity has also acted as a complicating factor in New York's decision to hold up his proceedings, and to what extent celebrity may also complicate the afterlives of fellow modern saints in the making.

In chapter 3, I contextualized Sheen's sacred celebrity alongside certain socio-religious trends that facilitated his rise along with his fellow celebrity preachers. While postwar America appears to have been in the process of experiencing a new religious revival, with Americans craving meaning and simple explanations to help them situate themselves in the aftermath of war, Sheen's rise (like that of Vincent Norman Peale) was made largely possible by new technologies of access. In ancient times, sacred figures were made known through local communities of adherents, through shared religious orders or institutional promotion. By the 1950s, radio, paperback publishing, and television effectively transformed the ways in which average people were able to connect with the figures they celebrate. Television, in particular, allowed for these connections to become more personal and familial, owing to the viewing experience itself and the types of content that Sheen and others in those pioneering years produced. Celebrity (as well as sanctity) became more accessible and approachable, something a person could invite into their living room, rather than experience at an absolute distance. Though not yet fully understood as an entirely different category, as Sheen competed with secular celebrities for the same ratings, and possibly short-lived as personalities performing religious television celebrity would rapidly transform, we can see the momentary flourishing of our new rubric in Sheen and others. Yet these friendly familiar personas embodied by Sheen and others still bore the marks of being manufactured and catered, with Sheen still putting himself at a distance with the viewer. In effect, Sheen's program embodied certain contradictions of accessibility and distance, which further emphasized his celebrity and sanctity.

In chapter 4, I positioned Sheen as the heir to a sizable repertoire of visual tropes and conventions established by Hollywood's depiction of priests in the previous generation. In contrast to the often-derogatory stereotypes of Irish in America (and in particular, their masculinity), priests – as the most visible symbol of Catholic difference – were played by charismatic leading men and demonstrated socially favourable traits with which Americans could identify. Sheen's later television presence is very much indebted to these earlier Hollywood iterations, even as Hollywood had by that time moved beyond these earlier archetypes and was depicting priests in more challenging manners. As I argued, the medium of television, with its emphasis on familiarity, allowed his then-anachronistic (albeit charismatic) character to thrive with his family-friendly content and affirming discourses. From these we may gather that American visual media – from cinema to television – had a hand in not only negotiating conceptions of American religion and celebrity to the masses but also in shaping and sculpting it in a way that resonates more closely with its audiences and their expectations.

Lastly, in chapter 5, we explored how the early postwar era, like much of the Cold War, was an era of anxieties where men's bodies were concerned. As the nation's men were perceived to be sliding toward dangerous softness, it necessitated the space for firm voices to vicariously embody and demonstrate that much needed hardness. While figures such as McCarthy dealt with bodily anxieties largely through a borderline stereotypical hardened approach, Sheen largely refigured hardness by tying it intricately to the spirit and one's moral compass. Firmness of character, morality, and mind – characteristics that Americans had within their reach owing to their shared Hebraic-Christian heritage – could allow the nation to overcome the threat posed by their own bodies. However, by virtue of his celebrity character, it necessitated that Sheen's proponents imbued him with the wider attributes of hardness – good health, fitness, diet, and the like – in order that their celebrity figurehead be a more complete reflection of the nation's vitality. In effect, Sheen's Catholic response to the geopolitical conflict signalled the ways in which body and religion can symbiotically inform each other during moments of increased national tension, crisis, and anxiety, and how celebrity adds an additional dimension of consideration to these dichotomies.

Ultimately, through these various discussions, I demonstrated how Sheen's body and body of work represent important sites of intersection between the institution of the American Catholic Church, the various identifications of its members, its understanding of sanctity, and its engagement with wider secular themes in American culture – my focus, of course, being on constructions of masculinity and celebrity. With respect to the former, I have demonstrated how Sheen's particular performance of masculinity represents a fascinating mediation of the concerns and expectations of both secular and Catholic expressions of masculinity; with the latter, I've sought to specifically call attention to how Sheen, as a sanctified celebrity, provides a powerful example of how the then-contemporary American context complicated traditional models of sanctity, forcing us to reconsider what types of secular attachments represent real or perceived impediments to the claim of sanctity. Through an exploration of his television fame – amplified by his careers as a bestselling author and radio personality – Sheen managed to tap into a particular moment of American history, reading the needs and expectations of his audiences to create a persona and performance that effectively blurred the lines of separation between religious and popular culture.

Sheen's blurring of such lines is not wholly unique: many mid-twentieth-century American Catholic figures have held secular attachments that might be read as complicating or being at odds with their claims to sanctity. Take, for example, Father Emil Kapaun, the US Army chaplain who died as a prisoner of war during the Korean War. While not necessarily a celebrity of the stature of Sheen, Kapaun embodied a sort of military heroism, making his body an excellent site to interrogate the ways in which Catholic and military identifications intersect.[3] Like Sheen, his physical remains have also posed problems for his cause, which up until recently had not been recovered nor identified.[4] With the "discovery" of his remains, the Diocese of Wichita, where his cause is based, is eagerly looking forward to continuing the process. It will be intriguing to witness whether his life among America's servicemen, while certainly one of the more hallowed of American callings, may disrupt or complicate understandings of his martyrdom and sanctity – and, if so, whether it will also need to be defused or refigured accordingly.

Equally intriguing investigations could be undertaken on Dorothy Day or Thomas Merton.[5] Despite Day's accomplishments, her early life – which flirted with communism and anarchism and saw her enjoy a "bohemian lifestyle" that led to an unwanted pregnancy and abortion – could prove to represent a complicating factor in her cause for canonization.[6] Though Merton (like Sheen), likely has fewer skeletons in his closet, during the peak of his celebrity, he nevertheless engaged in dialogue with other traditions and embraced a certain level of ecumenism and anti-war activism that might not have been expected for a typically reclusive Trappist monk.[7] Like Sheen, both Day and Merton wrote autobiographies that can be read as auto-hagiographical, in that each arguably sought to use these works to attenuate aspects of their character which might read as being at odds with their Catholic identity. In effect, the lives of all three (Sheen, Merton, and Day), were heavily intertwined with the workings of the modern secular world and its culture, making one wonder to what extent a potential modern American saint could exist without doing so. As such, the auto-hagiographical genre represents a fascinating window into the secular-sanctified tension inherent in these figures, demonstrating that they were, on some level, aware of this tension and anxious about attenuating it.[8] While the lives of all sanctified figures intersect with the secular to some extent, modern figures who find themselves celebrated beyond Catholic devotional circles inherently accumulate more secular attachments and significance than past figures – which, in addition to potentially complicating their claims to sanctity and the drive for their canonization, also drives home the necessity of studying these figures through an interdisciplinary rather than purely Catholic studies lens.

As a final concluding remark, I would like to momentarily turn our attention back to the theme of "ordinariness," and how both Sheen's and his devotees' attempts to frame his life in "normal" and "ordinary" terms speaks to a larger tension in the post–Vatican II canonization process. In Sheen's autobiography, the concern for ordinariness reads almost strangely: on the one hand, he uses the tropes of hagiography to signal his own sanctity, while on the other he emphasizes his "ordinariness" in his efforts to downplay his celebrity and frame his accomplishments modestly. His devotees have acted similarly, positioning him as a salt-of-the-earth Peorian rather than the New York aristocrat he read as during his life. In each case, we find ourselves continually being steered away from his career in New York City and the very aspects of his life that make him as recognizable as both a celebrity and sanctified figure. By moving to highlight such elements of Catholic ordinariness in his life, narrative, and image, Sheen begins to appear, both remarkable and unremarkable when viewed from different angles – something which seems to undermine the heroic nature and special character that would normally isolate a saint. Interestingly, this ambiguous framing speaks to a wider trend in modern saint-making post–Vatican II.

Since the late 1970s, papal figures, such as John Paul II and his successor Benedict XVI, have often stressed the "ordinariness" of figures on the road toward canonization, suggesting that the heroic virtues practised by these figures could be attainable for the average Catholic in search of a figure to emulate.[9] Coupled hand in hand with the reduction of the miraculous requirements for canonization, first by allowing for the founding of a religious order to replace one of the two required miracles, and then adapting the once-mandatory requirement for the second, we can see a top-down push toward emphasizing ordinariness in the lives of saints and those who would be counted among them. Such a push is, of course, paradoxical.[10] If all saints are simply normal people who embodied a slightly heightened sense of virtue, then what point is there to singling out the saints? It's a question that the post–Vatican II church has perhaps been unable or unwilling to answer.

Nevertheless, Sheen and his many intersections act as a reminder that our fields of study are seldom demarcated, that bodies move through many worlds, and that stories seldom play out the way they are written. In effect, given the prominence of similarly celebrated Catholic figures whose secular attachments can be read at odds with their sanctity, interdisciplinary readings that move beyond the confines of religious studies are crucial and, dare I say, essential. Celebrity studies can help us contextualize figures whose mass appeal extend beyond the domain of religious devotion and whose lives and careers touched those inhabiting non-denominational spaces. Under examination we can understand how secular tools of access and modes of being might inform the identities of these figures and their potentially contradictory embodiments of sanctity. Equally so, masculinity studies (or gender studies more broadly) for their part can help us navigate the often ambivalent and contradictory demands and expectations of both religious masculinities and secular ones. Figures such as Sheen effectively demonstrate the difficulty of being "read" according to a single rubric and the necessity for being viewed under a variety of lenses. Ultimately, the complexities I've outlined in the cause of Sheen and the causes of similar figures, along with their engagement outside purely religious milieus and their many intersections with wider culture, are what make them such engaging figures of study and which continue to draw devotees to their cause.

# Notes

## Introduction

1 In Fulton Sheen's recounting of events in *Treasure in Clay,* he describes it as a rather lighthearted accident. The store's errand boy – unnamed – was apparently smoking a cigarette and "fearful of his father, he threw it down the stairs." Unfortunately, it landed in a "fifty-gallon can of gasoline" and the whole business district was subsequently burned down. While the fire is documented, the details Sheen presents are less so – as will be the case with many of the anecdotes and recollections from his autobiography. See Sheen, *Treasure in Clay,* 8. Also Lynch, *Selling Catholicism,* 17.

2 While biographical sources make it clear that Fulton was his mother's maiden name, it is not fully clear why he came to be called this. One of his biographers, Daniel P. Noonan, states that Sheen was referred to as "P.J." as a boy and had a "slight preference for his mother's maiden name" over his own surname for undisclosed reasons. Sheen would himself echo something similar in 1953 to *Boston Post* journalist Ken Crotty, stating that he began calling himself Fulton during his school days to show filial affection for his maternal grandparents. However, biographer Thomas C. Reeves outlines a traumatic event in the Sheen family, when Sheen's younger half-sister (from a previous relationship of his father's) was forcibly removed by her Protestant grandparents owing to the household's "popery." Sheen began calling himself Fulton shortly after that event, implying it could have been in response to this incident. See Noonan, *Missionary with a Mike,* 2; Ken Crotty, "Bishop Sheen's Devotions Recalled," *Boston Post,* 9 May 1953, uncategorized box, Fulton Sheen Museum Archives, Peoria, Illinois; Reeves, *America's Bishop,* 11. For more on the topic of his name, see also Lynch, *Selling Catholicism,* 17; Riley, *Fulton J. Sheen,* 2.

3 Sheen, *Treasure in Clay,* 10.

4 Fulton Sheen has figured into several works addressing mid-century American popular culture, if not specifically focusing on his own celebrity. See, e.g., Massa, *Catholics and American Culture*. See also Sherwood, *Age of Extremes*.

5 Riley, *Fulton J. Sheen*, 3.

6 Though Fulton Sheen recounts it as a sort of epiphany, there was likely little doubt that he would become a priest. The only apparent issue was a matter of "when," as he also wished to become an academic. The question was thus which would come first, and as things unfolded his ordination took priority.

7 Sheen, *Treasure in Clay*, 23; Riley, *Fulton J. Sheen*, 3–6.

8 Sheen, *Treasure in Clay*, 27–8; Riley, *Fulton J. Sheen*, 7–8.

9 Fulton Sheen scholar Timothy H. Sherwood has remarked that Sheen spent so much time involved in speaking engagements, rather than teaching, that he was more of an "ambassador" than a lecturer for the CUA. Sherwood, *Rhetorical Leadership*, 17.

10 Despite being one of America's pioneering broadcasters, the DuMont Network would fold within the decade due to financial problems. Riley, *Fulton J. Sheen*, 65–6.

11 The exact numbers for his series are hard to pin down as the numbers cited in most sources appear to be largely anecdotal or "common knowledge" in that they do not reference any origin for these figures. Nevertheless, the range is typically given to have been between 20–30 million viewers at his nationwide peak.

12 During the first season, Fulton Sheen was cautiously paid $10,000 per episode, and shortly after upped to $16,000 by Admiral, which he also donated to the charitable branch of the SPOF. Massa, *Catholics and American Culture*, 83.

13 The audience rating would become more commonly known as the Nielsen rating. Though Fulton Sheen was highly rated, it is worth bearing in mind that the rating system only came into effect some three years earlier so that by the time of his broadcasts there were limited other programs available for comparison in the data. Massa, *Catholics and American Culture*, 83.

14 When Fulton Sheen went to accept his Emmy, Milton Berle, who had won that same award only a few years prior, is widely reported to have quipped that Sheen "got better writers – Matthew, Mark, Luke and John!" Sheen was also the three-time recipient for the Excellence in Television award by *Look* magazine. Lynch, *Selling Catholicism*, 7.

15 Elements of Fulton Sheen and Francis Spellman's frayed relationship during the 1950s, along with the abrupt termination of his television program, will be discussed in more detail in chapter 1 and referred to elsewhere.

16 *The Fulton Sheen Program*, which ran from 1961 to 1968, is the most well remembered of his latter television forays, along with various specials and guest appearance that went into the 1970s.

17 Fulton Sheen's canonization cause will be covered in more detail in chapter 2.

18 Fulton Sheen was both a vocal and vociferous anti-communist since the 1930s, regularly equating communism, fascism, and Nazism as what he saw were the three enemies of American democracy and Christianity itself. Other vocal anti-communist Catholic figures during the pre-war period include the now-infamous Father Charles Coughlin and the lesser known Edmund A. Walsh, S.J. For Sheen's most comprehensive treatise against communism, see Sheen, *Communism*. For more on Father Coughlin, see Marcus, *Father Coughlin*; and Warren, *Radio Priest*. On Edmund A. Walsh, see McNamara, "Russia, Rome, and Recognition"; and McNamara, "'Argument of Strength."

19 Some scholars have nevertheless gone to lengths to address the lives of 'other' Catholics. See Matovina, *Latino Catholicism*; Hendrickson, *Border Medicine*; Martinez, *Catholic Borderlands*; Cressler, "Black Catholic"; Matthew Cressler, "Black Power, Vatican II."

20 The oft-repeated adage that American Catholicism experienced a "coming of age" in mid-century America revolves around a narrative of linear progression – Catholics moved from being outcasts and immigrants to more fully welcomed and integrated, eventually becoming identifiably American sometime around the mid-century mark (variously pinned at the end of World War II or the election of John F. Kennedy). For the origins of this view, see Ellis, *American Catholicism*; Dolan, *American Catholic Experience*; and Dolan, *In Search of American Catholicism*. For examples of how this pervasive notion continues to inform readings of Catholic history – despite the fact that it often occludes important nuances and counter-narratives – see Lynch, *Selling Catholicism*; and McCarraher, "Saint in the Gray Flannel Suit."

21 Bearing the above in mind, I feel it appropriate to demarcate the scope and limitations of this project. Though I am examining wider societal trends in America, the focus of this work will predominantly be with concerns and issues associated with white, English-speaking Catholics of European descent. While features of power imbalances and inequality, along with social mobility and middle-class comforts, feature to some extent in my discussions in chapters 2, 3, and 4, considerations of race (apart from some discussions of Irishness), language, and economics are largely outside the purview of this work. That is not to say that these topics are unworthy of academic interest, but rather that they do not fall within the scope of my focus on Fulton J. Sheen, his particular performance of masculinity, his enduring celebrity status, and the theoretical implications that these intersections have for studies of mid-twentieth-century American Catholicism.

22 Charles Coughlin's first appearance on WJR radio took place in 1926, while Fulton Sheen would join *The Catholic Hour* in 1930.

23 Nathalie Heinich uses "Dieux" in the original French-language article. I have translated it for clarity. Heinich, "Des limites."

24 Heinich, "Des Limites," 163.
25 For a more thorough discussion of the role of charisma in celebrity/sanctity, see Kleinberg, *Flesh Made Word*, especially chapter 1.
26 Graus, "Visit to Remember."
27 Graus, "Visit to Remember," 57.
28 Boone and Vickers, "Celebrity Rites," 904.
29 Boone and Vickers, "Celebrity Rites," 909.
30 Boone and Vickers, "Celebrity Rites," 903.
31 Fulton Sheen is perhaps unique among many of his fellow celebrities in this sense as he had no official publicists, agents, marketers, or others acting for the promotion of his celebrity apart from himself. He largely dictated his own dress, makeup, appearance, and other aspects of his person, effectively taking the reins himself when it came to crafting his image. See Harris, "Celebrity Clothing," 233.
32 Marshall, "Promotion and Presentation," 39.
33 Marshall, "Promotion and Presentation," 39.
34 Marshall, "Promotion and Presentation," 43.
35 Conniff, *Bishop Sheen Story*, 26.
36 Christopher Lynch suggests that Martin Sheen contacted the bishop, asking to take on his surname for his own. If this is the case, it reveals a remarkable imbalance in fame and influence whereby the future Hollywood celebrity came calling to the bishop, who happened to be the greater celebrity at the time. Lynch, *Selling Catholicism*, 27.
37 Lynch, *Selling Catholicism*, 147.
38 See Bolton, "Beautiful Penitent Whore."
39 See Alpion, *Saint or Celebrity*; Alpion, "Why Are Modern Spiritual Icons?"; Alpion, *Saint and Her Nation*.
40 For scholarly works that explicitly address the celebrity of Aimee Semple McPherson and Billy Graham, see Sutton, *Aimee Semple McPherson*; Wacker, *America's Pastor*. While there is an abundance of recent academic and biographical works on Martin Luther King Jr., few acknowledge his celebrity, although a passing mention does occur in Duvall and Heckemeyer as an example of the intersection of black celebrity and activism. See Duvall and Heckemeyer, "#BlackLivesMatter." For a sampling of literature that addresses the celebrity of Catholic figures, see Henderson, "Media and the Rise of Celebrity Culture"; Fisher, *Dr. America*; Fisher, *Catholic Counterculture*; Massa, *Catholics and American Culture*; Clooney, "Thomas Merton's Deep Christian Learning"; Forsthoefel, "Merton and the Axes of Dialogue." While Amy Henderson's article does investigate Fr Coughlin's celebrity appeal, it does so only in passing in the context of a larger discussion of the role of radio in early American celebrity. Thomas Merton's celebrity is mentioned in both Clooney

and Forsthoefel, but neither author dwells upon or explores this connotation with much theoretical depth. Slightly more substantial treatments can be found in Massa and Fisher, for while Massa addresses Dorothy Day's fame via an exploration of her presence in and impact on American popular culture, James T. Fisher, likewise, does not shy away from addressing Tom Dooley's fame in his 1997 biography. Fisher also takes up Dooley's relationship to American culture more generally in a chapter in *Catholic Counterculture.*

41 Connell, *Masculinities*, 35.

42 Connell, *Masculinities*, 77. I am simplifying R.W. Connell's legacy and the trajectory of her own research. While *Masculinities* was the culminating work in her conceptualization of hegemonic masculinity and its operative patterns at the societal level, earlier investigations attempting to understand hegemonic patterns of masculinity in society can be reviewed in Carrigan et al., "Towards a New Sociology"; and Connell, "Hegemonic Masculinity." Connell also revisits her theoretical foundations at a later date in Connell and Messerschmidt, "Rethinking the Concept."

43 Eric Anderson's *Inclusive Masculinity* investigated the masculinity of college-age fraternity members and athletes, arguing that, with the decrease in cultural homophobia, men were slowly constructing softer "versions" of masculinity that allowed room for bonding and emotional connections. While his monograph can certainly be read as both provocative and iconoclastic in the field, the extent to which it offers a cohesive rebuttal or convincing refutation of Connell's theories is another matter altogether. In turn, Michael Moller – in "Exploiting Patterns" – criticized R.W. Connell for leaving little room in her theory for the lived experiences of men and the possibility for men to act in a selfless, beneficial manner. For a radically alternative theoretical stance that seeks to ground masculinity in actions rather than bodies – a stance I do not necessarily find convincing – see Schrock and Schwalbe, "Men, Masculinity, and Manhood Acts."

44 Michael Kimmel has argued that American masculinity is often shaped in emulation of perceived (and idealized) archetypes believed to have been formed in the early and pre-Revolutionary era, such as those of the noble artisan, the genteel patriarch, et al. Such archetypes acted as the repository of America's own mythologizing – notably, the potential for men to satisfy the conditions of father/providers and make a living out of their own labour or industriousness. The history of the nation and of men's bodies, of course, bears little semblance to this Golden Era mythologizing, yet the ideals would remain powerful archetypes overshadowing masculine self-understanding into the modern era. See Kimmel, *Manhood in America*.

45 See Kimmel, "Contemporary 'Crisis'"; and Starck and Luyt, "Political Masculinities."

46 See Gilbert, *Men in the Middle*.
47 See Horrocks, *Male Myths*; and Jeffords, *Hard Bodies*.
48 See Jeffords, *Hard Bodies*, especially chapters 1 and 2.
49 Du Mez, *Jesus and John Wayne*, 22–3.
50 Baker, *Gospel According to the Klan*, 20–2.
51 Maldonado-Estrada, *Lifeblood of the Parish*, 2.
52 See Rausch, "All Man, All Priest"; and Seitz, "Mass-Clock"; "Altars of Ammo."
53 See Holt, "Between Warrior and Priest"; and Karras, *From Boys to Men*.
54 Milton Berle's sexual appetite was infamous, as was apparently the size of his penis – which developed a mythology of its own as he was known to frequently flash it to his contemporaries with or without their consent. Needless to say, while Sheen's celebrity lifestyle brought him some of the glamour, the clerical vows took precedence over the other expectations of the celebrity male. See Calvert, "Similar Hats on Similar Heads"; Lewis and Berle, *My Father, Uncle Miltie*; Tierney Finster, "The Legend of Milton Berle's Supposedly Giant Dick," *Mel Magazine*, accessed 9 May 2021, https://melmagazine.com/en-us/story/milton-berle-penis-size.
55 See Du Mez, *Jesus and John Wayne*; and Baker, *Gospel According to the Klan*.
56 See, for instance, video of the episode "How to Psychoanalyze Yourself" posted on YouTube on 24 June 2014, which, by the end of 2024, has amassed over 700,000 views. See The Catholic World, "How to Psychoanayze [*sic*] Yourself | Bishop Fulton J. Sheen," 14 June, 2014, YouTube Video, 25:40, www.youtube.com/watch?v= k3rhPa7h4ro&ab_channel=TheCatholicWorld (defunct).
57 See Riley, *Fulton J. Sheen*; Reeves, *America's Bishop*; and Lynch, *Selling Catholicism*.
58 Daniel Noonan's two accounts of Fulton Sheen's life, while overlapping in many parts, nevertheless present two radically different opinions of the man – which in turn are reflective of Noonan's own disintegrating relationship with his former boss. Notably, where the first biography regularly heaped lavish praise on Sheen, the second included fairly scurrilous criticism, bordering on ad hominin attacks, on Sheen's character and personality, along with hearsay and gossip about the man. In conjunction with each other, they make for fascinating reads, albeit works with which one should proceed cautiously. See Noonan, *Missionary with a Mike*; and *The Passion of Fulton Sheen*.
59 See Crotty, "Bishop Sheen's Devotions Recalled"; Conniff, *Bishop Sheen Story*; and Sugrue, "Bishop Sheen Story."
60 Initially, I found Rochester's silence odd, especially considering the CUA and Peoria's rapid responses to my inquiries. However, revelations of the diocese's strained relationship with not only Sheen but also his unfolding canonization process – which is discussed in more detail in chapter 2 – were only then coming to wider attention.

61 See Marlett, "Harvesting an Overlooked Freedom" and Marlett, "Strangers in Our Midst"; and Bovée, "Church and the Land" and "Middle Way."

62 The notion that a religious revival, rather than a reconfiguration of existing sentiments, occurred in 1950s America has been proposed by several scholars, including Ellwood, *Fifties Spiritual*; Riley, *Fulton J. Sheen*; Weinstein, *Forgotten Network*. Other scholars have questioned this notion, suggesting instead that developments in media merely lead to the more widespread visibility of religion rather than a societal change in attitudes. See Hudnut-Beulmer, *Looking for God in the Suburbs*.

63 See Rosenthal, "This Nation Under God"; and Smith, *What Would Jesus Read?*

64 See Fisher, *On the Irish Waterfront*; and Shannon, *From Bowery to Broadway*.

65 See Jeffords, *Hard Bodies*.

## Chapter One

1 See Heinich, "Consommation de la Célébrité"; Andrea Graus, "Visit to Remember"; and Alpion, *Saint and Her Nation*. Derek Krueger has also commented on the paradoxical relationship between sanctity and celebrity, noting, "True saints seek anonymity, yet God wills their works to be 'shown forth' such that they can be known to the faithful." Krueger, "Hagiography," 227.

2 The specifics of his still-ongoing canonization process are discussed in more detail in chapter 2, but broadly speaking, his widely known public persona appears to have driven the need for closer scrutiny into the details of his life than the average candidate, and also caused fiercer rivalries over his remains and the control over his legacy,

3 While Fulton Sheen is the principal author of his autobiography, he was unable to finalize the manuscript during his lifetime. After his death, his close friend Edward O'Meara, who had recently become the archbishop of Indianapolis, hired the writer Patricia Kossman (also a friend of Sheen's) to prepare it for publication. It is therefore unclear to what extent Kossman might or might not have accented the hagiographical flourishes already embedded in the text as composed by Sheen.

4 Fulton Sheen devotes two entire chapters of this work to discussing his devotion to the Virgin Mother and elaborating on the "Holy Hour" of personal austerities he practised each morning. He also spends nearly an equivalent amount of time discussing his second of two trips to the Holy Land (in 1959). Both discussions eclipse the amount of time he spends addressing his twenty-five-year-plus radio and television career for which he is most widely known.

5 While the term has been used in popular culture to describe non-critical autobiographies that flatter the subject, it has found more critical use in academia. Medievalist Kate Greenspan makes extensive use of the term when

referring to autobiographical elements found in the larger writings of female medieval mystics such as Julian of Norwich and Catherine of Siena. In her use of the term, *auto-hagiography* is principally a characteristic of their writing, rather than a genre in and of itself. Others, however, have referred to it as a genre. Similarly, historian Clarissa Atkinson has referred to *The Book of Margery Kempe* – an early autobiographical work by the fifteenth-century English mystic of the same name – as a work of auto-hagiography owing to its reliance on the tropes of hagiographical literature. Elsewhere, literature scholar Milo Sweedler has likewise used the term to refer to Laure (née Collete Peignot)'s *Histoire d'une petite fille* and the other works that appear her *Écrits*, due to their mystical and confessional elements. In this regard, my use of the term hews more closely to that of Atkinson and Sweedler, but with some caveats as will be discussed later in this chapter. See Greenspan, "Autohagiographical Traditional"; Atkinson, *Mystic and Pilgrim*; Sweedler, "Autohagiography."

6 Fulton Sheen, too, touches upon the difficulties of composing an "authentic" biography of himself. As he states in his opening chapter, "there are [involved] three pairs of eyes," each of which see a man's life under different light – there is the man in question, the eyes of others, and the eyes of God. Taken at his word, any biographer will only be working with two out of three at best. See Sheen, *Treasure in Clay*, chapter 1.

7 As Robert Bartlett remarks, just as one generation of saints might take inspiration from the previous, so, too, does hagiography owe itself to past examples. See Bartlett, *Why Can the Dead?*, 511.

8 Eric Brook observes that one sometimes-overlooked element of hagiography is its function to preserve and perpetuate Christian *memory* from one generation to the next. See Brook, "Writing the Holy Image," 13.

9 Fulton Sheen biographers Thomas C. Reeves and Daniel P. Noonan have both remarked that Sheen was highly attentive where his image was concerned, particularly in the area of personal grooming and in what was being said about him by others. In one colourful story, when Sheen was asked by actress Loretta Young why he was always so well dressed and coiffed, he replied, "We dress for God, we are his representatives." Reeves, *America's Bishop*, 137.

10 Sheen, *Treasure in Clay*, 6.

11 There was no shortage of controversy during his lifetime, and this includes speculations about warring factions in the American Catholic Church. Most of these speculations involved either Cardinal Francis J. Spellman or Fulton Sheen's tenure as bishop of Rochester, which are discussed at various points in this book.

12 Michael DeAngelis and Mary Desjardin refer to celebrity biographies as a negotiation of authenticity and intimacy between the readers and the figure in question. See DeAngelis and Desjardins, "Introduction," 490. For

further discussion on authenticity in celebrity, see Thomas, "Celebrity in the 'Twitterverse.'" Scholars of religion have also previously examined the larger purpose of hagiography. In discussing Athanasius's *Life of Antony*, Aviad Kleinberg rather succinctly remarks that the ancient author had found a way of producing "a sermon masquerading as biography." Kleinberg, *Flesh Made Word*, 152.

13 It should also be noted that unlike most autobiographies, Fulton Sheen's *Treasure in Clay* contains an account of both his birth *and* his death, as the manuscript was completed for publication by a friend of Sheen's. See also Bartlett, *Why Can the Dead?*, 518.

14 On this note, *Treasure in Clay* is not organized purely chronologically. The first chapter opens with an essay espousing Sheen's own unworthiness as a biographer – much in the vein of classical authors – and midway through the book shifts to being organized by topic rather than the period of his life. See Bartlett, *Why Can the Dead?*, 518.

15 Bartlett, *Why Can the Dead?*, 513–4.

16 See Krueger, "Hagiography."

17 Curiously, there is an appendix in *Treasure in Clay* titled "Vita." This brief section reads more akin to curriculum vitae than biography, listing Fulton Sheen's many accomplishments and the honours he accrued over his lengthy career and busy life. This, however, was almost surely added by a later writer or editor before the text's publication.

18 See Thomas, "Celebrity in the 'Twitterverse'"; and McKenna, "Aging Film Actor."

19 Fisher, *Dr. America*, 9–10, 68.

20 Fisher, 12–13.

21 Fisher, 7.

22 McKenna, "Aging Film Actor."

23 Fulton Sheen speaks to this in the opening chapter of *Treasure in Clay*, commenting on the dangers of celebrity and its connection to vanity when he remarks how focusing on the limelight can make us forget a more important light. Sheen, *Treasure in Clay*, 6.

24 After losing track of their child, Mary and Joseph returned to the temple to find their boy sitting among the scholars as one might a peer. For a scholarly discussion of the remarkability of children in hagiography, see Weinstein and Bell, *Saints and Society*, 20.

25 Kleinberg, *Flesh Made Word*, 1.

26 See Pope, "Heroine Without Heroics."

27 See Payne, *Fathers of the Western Church*, 90–2; Augustine's most widely quoted citation on the matter comes from his *Confessions*, where he declares, "Grant me chastity … but not yet." Augustine, *Confessions*, 8:7.17.

28 The claims that he was a Satanic priest are likely an embellishment. Though they emerged from Bartolo Longo's own post-conversion recollections, it appears that they were later accentuated by biographers to highlight the immensity of his reconversion. See, e.g., Angelo Stagnaro, "Blessed Bartolo Longo, the Ex-Satanist Who was Freed Through the Rosary," *National Catholic Register*, 12 December 2016, www.ncregister.com/blog/blessed-bartolo-longo-the-ex-satanist-who-was-freed-through-the-rosary.

29 Hagiographies often play with and revel in dichotomies that reveal stark contrasts between right and wrong, good and evil. Weinstein and Bell, *Saints and Society*, 108.

30 In the case of Augustine, elaborating on one's troubled or wayward youth also acts as a means of debasing himself as author, and through this debasement a form of humility and humble authenticity are conveyed to the reader.

31 Referring to education as his "determining mold" is hardly an understatement when reviewing Fulton Sheen's hefty academic credentials and lengthy tenure as a professor at the Catholic University of America.

32 Sheen, *Treasure in Clay*, 17.

33 Lest readers think Fulton Sheen wishes to speak ill of his parents, he quickly concedes that his mother once explained that his father's lack of vocalized praise was due to his father not wishing to "spoil him" – he did, she asserts, speak of his son's accomplishments to their neighbours, albeit in secret. Sheen, *Treasure in Clay*, 10. Christopher Lynch, however, sees through Sheen's tacit explanation for his parent's behaviour and suggests they were in fact "firm disciplinarians." For instance, Sheen admits to having been hit by his father, but plays it down in a lighthearted manner by stating "there is nothing that develops character in a young boy like a pat on the back, provided it is given often enough, hard enough and low enough." See Lynch, *Selling Catholicism*, 17; Sheen, *Treasure in Clay*, 16.

34 Emphasis mine. Fulton Sheen further states that both he and his opponent had earned 100 per cent marks in the class up until this point. *Treasure in Clay*, 14.

35 Sheen, *Treasure in Clay*, 14.

36 Riley, *Fulton Sheen*, 2; Reeves, *America's Bishop*, 12.

37 Sheen, *Treasure in Clay*, 16; Lynch, *Selling Catholicism*, 17.

38 Reeves, *America's Bishop*, 26; Riley, *Fulton Sheen*, 3.

39 Lee, "Reading Celebrity Autobiographies."

40 DeAngelis and Desjardins, "Introduction," 490.

41 Fulton Sheen doesn't hesitate to add that he adored his classes on scripture and moral theology at seminary and would eventually pursue his education in that direction as far as it could take him. Sheen, *Treasure in Clay*, 20.

42 Sheen, *Treasure in Clay*, 25.

43 Sheen, *Treasure in Clay*, 26.

44 For the story of the Child Christ teaching in the temple, see Luke 2:41–52.
45 Sheen, *Treasure in Clay*, 16.
46 Sheen, *Treasure in Clay*, 14.
47 Sheen, *Treasure in Clay*, 12.
48 Indeed, while Fulton Sheen actively sought to distance himself from his television fame, it was through this celebrity that his fans came to know and adore him. It is no surprise that virtually all the obituaries published in both the religious and secular press after his death open with a mention of his television career and celebrity alongside his career in the church. A large collection of such clippings can be found in the archives of the Archbishop Fulton Sheen Museum in Peoria, Illinois.
49 Athanasius outlined his supposed inadequacies in the opening lines of *Life of Anthony* to his readers, setting the benchmark for what would become a recurring ritualistic element of the genre. See Athanasius, *Life of Antony*.
50 Sarah Thomas, "Celebrity in the 'Twitterverse,'" 246. See also McKenna, "Aging Film Actor," 494.
51 Scholar Robert Orsi remarks that for mid-twentieth-century American Catholics, suffering was seen as a "thrilling" mark of divine favour, of being chosen by God. Orsi, *Between Heaven and Earth*, 22–4.
52 According to Aviad Kleinberg, stories recounting the ongoing suffering of the saints and Christian martyrs serve as "memory and example" to the Christian community. He remarked that "each generation had the moral obligation [that]… the martyrs must not be forgotten." Kleinberg, *Flesh Made Word*, 24, 25. See also Orsi, *Between Heaven and Earth*, 24.
53 Sheen, *Treasure in Clay*, 9.
54 Sheen, *Treasure in Clay*, 20.
55 Among twentieth-century saints and saintly men and women, numerous childhood sufferers come to mind. The Venerable Arcangelo Biasi, a confident to Saint Maximilian Kolbe, was born to a poor rural family and contracted tuberculosis yet managed to overcome his illness so that he could be ordained as a priest in 1922. And perhaps most famously, the young Italian saint Maria Gemma Umberta Galgani (known more simply as "Gemma Galgani"), who passed away in 1903, perfectly epitomized the suffering child saint. Consistently sickly, she developed spinal meningitis as a teenager and later succumbed to tuberculosis at the age of twenty-five. Even the previously mentioned Thérèse of Lisieux died of tuberculosis.
56 Moments of suffering and ascetic discipline in hagiography inevitably serve as reminders of ideal Christian behaviour to the faithful. See Weinstein and Bell, *Saints and Society*, 85.
57 Aviad Kleinberg remarks that, in his suffering and death, Jesus became for future Christians the "ultimate, the one true model." Kleinberg, *Flesh Made Word*, 15.

58 During times when there are relatively few martyrs, Christians have historically found new ways to "change the present to make it more like the past." Kleinberg, *Flesh Made Word*, 34.

59 Orsi, *Between Heaven and Earth*, 22.

60 In the conclusion to his lengthy study on hagiography, David Williams ponders the question of ancient precedents being remade in the twenty-first century. As he remarks, "It is the essence of tradition to minimize change. Faith communities by the nature of their shared beliefs … are capable of transcending the differences that the historical process introduces without, however, needing to negate them." Williams, *Saints Alive*, 200.

61 Sheen, *Treasure in Clay*, 44.

62 According to Fulton Sheen, the rector of the university – Bishop Shahan – met with the faculty to discuss whether they should open undergraduate courses to complement their graduate offerings. Apparently, there were few grad students, and, in Sheen's own words, the faculty was "not sufficiently occupied and challenged." Sheen proposed instead to expand their graduate offerings and seek prospective students and priests from across the country to come study. The immediate reaction was apparently one of open hostility from both his peers and the bishop, resulting in a quick end to their meeting. See *Treasure in Clay*, 43–4. While Sheen is overall sparse and selective with his details, other biographers provide a more detailed account of his tenure at the CUA – see Reeves, *America's Bishop*; and Riley, *Fulton J. Sheen*.

63 The matter of the Doctor of Divinity (DD) requirement at the CUA is likely more complex and nuanced – perhaps even embarrassing – than what Fulton Sheen is suggesting took place. While Sheen has earned himself a Doctor of Sacred Theology, he, too, had not acquired a DD. However, in his biography of Sheen, Thomas C. Reeves notes that Sheen may have claimed to have been awarded such a degree as, for a time, a DD would appear (either through falsification or clerical error) on his résumé. Reeve's conclusion is not that Sheen necessarily sought to mislead people of his credentials, but rather that he couldn't bear being also being singled out for having different credentials to his name. See Reeves, *America's Bishop*, 66–9.

64 Fulton Sheen details, in his oft-grandiose fashion, the extent to which these rumours apparently spread. At some unspecified point Sheen's name was floated to be the rector of the university, but he was blocked by Archbishop McNicholas, who stated that after what he did to Ryan he would "not let Sheen in charge of a doghouse." The rumours flew so high up the chain of command that apparently even Cardinal Pacelli – the future Pius XII – asked Sheen for details of the situation during a meeting. Sheen, *Treasure in Clay*, 46–7.

65 Thomas C. Reeves provides a detailed exposition of Fulton Sheen's troubled time in Rochester. See Reeves, *America's Bishop*, 291–327.

66 Lynch, *Selling Catholicism*, 28.

67 Reeves, *America's Bishop*, 307.

68 Sheen, *Treasure in Clay*, 178. Here, Fulton Sheen also remarks in an off-handed manner that once the plan was devised, it came up that the local press had an existing contract that locked them into previous obligations for two more years. That no one raised this earlier in the months of investigative work into the project points to a remarkable oversight.

69 Sheen, *Treasure in Clay*, 178. Again, this was another plan that Fulton Sheen worked hard to implement without consulting any of the hospitals beforehand.

70 Sheen, *Treasure in Clay*, 178.

71 Sheen, *Treasure in Clay*, 178.

72 The land was valued at $680,000 and included a church, a rectory, and a school that would be demolished or refurbished as needed. See Noonan, *Passion of Fulton Sheen*, 163.

73 *Treasure in Clay* includes verbatim a letter that Fulton Sheen apparently wrote the Secretary. In his letter Sheen uses very Vatican II–inspired language, declaring the church's responsibility in the world and outlining his plan to provide a gift of church property to be used for housing for the poor. See *Treasure in Clay*, 179.

74 Sheen, *Treasure in Clay*, 180.

75 It should be noted that it wasn't just the parishioners who opposed the idea. A letter of protest was drafted and signed by 130 of his priests, declaring that the parish already served the poor through its outreach and sermons. One of his closest allies during the early months of his posting – a parish priest named Father Finks, who was known for his eager social activism and earlier support of Sheen – turned against him and led the call urging Sheen to backtrack. Sheen eventually retracted his offer, but by then it was too late to make amends with his clerics and community, and he resigned shortly afterward. See Reeves, *America's Bishop*, 301–20; Lynch, *Selling Catholicism*, 29–30; Noonan, *Passion of Fulton Sheen*, 166.

76 Sheen, *Treasure in Clay*, 180–1. In this excerpt, Fulton Sheen is referring to several passages from Jeremiah 18. In the biblical story, Jeremiah is sent by God to visit a potter. There, the prophet witnesses how the craftsman can tear down and remake his pots when they do not fit his expectations. God then informs Jeremiah that he does the same thing to kingdoms when its people refuse to listen to listen.

77 If Fulton Sheen's posting at Rochester was meant to be a litmus test for the applicability and viability of Vatican II's reforms and new approach to bringing the church into the world, his failures and resignation from his posting can only be read as foreshadowing what would become ongoing issues of disconnect between the church and its parishioners that continue to this day.

78 Sheen, *Treasure in Clay*, 181.
79 As mentioned previously, Fulton Sheen's time in Rochester has been unanimously referred to as a failure by biographers and commentators. See Reeves, *America's Bishop*; Lynch, *Selling Catholicism*; Noonan, *Passion of Fulton Sheen*.
80 Kleinberg, *Flesh Made Word*, 13. See also Orsi, *Between Heaven and Earth*, 22.
81 Sheen, *Treasure in Clay*, 3.
82 Sheen, *Treasure in Clay*, 309–10. Here, Fulton Sheen clearly references Jesus in the garden of Gethsemane, and his approaching passion. See also Luke 22.
83 Rochester has been referred to as a "Diocesan Siberia" owing to its relative remoteness and cold weather. After Sheen's resignation, Thomas C. Reeves remarks that he had the appearance of a "broken man." Reeves, *America's Bishop*, 321.
84 Noonan, *Passion of Fulton Sheen*, 161. Even if their relationship was not as strained as sources suggest, in all of *Treasure in Clay*, Francis Spellman is mentioned by name less than a handful of times – despite having a personal and working relationship with Fulton Sheen of over twenty years – and the cardinal's face was also conveniently cropped out of a publicity photo of Sheen that was used to grace the cover of his 2004 critical biography by Riley. The original photo can be viewed in the photograph section of Noonan's *The Passion of Fulton Sheen*.
85 Noonan, *Passion of Fulton Sheen*, 161.
86 Fulton Sheen was certainly given the opportunity to voice his concerns about his experiences. When asked by Mike Wallace during an interview on *Sixty Minutes* why he was never offered a cardinal's hat, Sheen replied, in a rare moment of disagreement, that he would have gladly moved up within the church but that he refused to "pay the price" demanded of him. Noonan, *Passion of Fulton Sheen*, 67. Sheen further remarked that it was "God who made certain people throw stones at me" and that "the curious would like me to open healed wounds; the media, in particular, would relish a chapter which would pass judgement on others." Sheen, *Treasure in Clay*, 314, 310. Again, rather than seize upon a controversial moment that would be worth more than its weight in gold in any celebrity biographical account, Sheen is conspicuously silent, reminding his reader instead that "any discussion of conflicts within the Church diminishes the content of the Christ … as the hand excessively rubbing the eye diminishes vision." Sheen, *Treasure in Clay*, 312.
87 Fulton Sheen's relationship with Cardinal Spellman over the years seems to have had two sides. Publicly, the two men put on a pleasant face and spoke politely of each other. In New York, Sheen was feted as the successor to the cardinal for a time and saw his career flourish. However, all that initial goodwill seems to have crumbled shortly after Sheen's program hit its peak.

Between 1950 and 1966, Sheen acted as the national director for the SPOF, placing Sheen in yet another position under Spellman's direct authority. While Sheen's natural charisma lent itself well to his fundraising efforts – he managed to secure $200 million in sixteen years, double what the rest of the world had raised during that same period – this success opened the door for Spellman to dip into Society funds for his other "pet charities," as with the infamous "milk incident." In 1957 Spellman used the Society to distribute a surplus of milk donated by the federal government, later insisting that he had paid the government for the surplus and that he was owed a refund from the Society. Sheen, knowing Spellman had received the milk for free, refused. In the end Pope Pius XII had to personally intervene, settling the "milk incident" in Sheen's favour and trapping Spellman in a lie. This would mark the first and only time Sheen could claim a victory over his superior, and Spellman, for his part, would have none of it. Sheen's show was soon taken off the air, and he was removed as director for the SPOF. Not long after, Spellman had Sheen assigned to Rochester. See Lynch, *Selling Catholicism*, 22; Noonan, *Passion of Fulton Sheen*, 82.

88 Sheen, *Treasure in Clay*, 312.

89 Sheen, *Treasure in Clay*, 309–10.

90 Donald Weinstein and Rudolph M. Bell have outlined how, since Urban VIII's reforms to the canonization process in the seventeenth century, the ideal candidate for sainthood will often have moments of prophecy attached to themselves in their hagiographies. Weinstein and Bell, *Saints and Society*, 147.

91 Sheen, *Treasure in Clay*, 12; Lynch, *Selling Catholicism*, 15.

92 Bishop Spalding oversaw the founding of numerous schools and had a role to play in the establishment of the Catholic University of America. Fulton Sheen would indeed attend the Spalding Institute in Peoria and later the CUA; Lynch, *Selling Catholicism*, 16. See also Dolan, *In Search of American Catholicism*.

93 Sheen, *Treasure in Clay*, 12; Riley, *Fulton Sheen*, 2.

94 It has also been observed that childhood encounters with holy figures who serve as models for the protagonist are a common element of hagiography. Weinstein and Bell, *Saints and Society*, 56.

95 Sheen, *Treasure in Clay*, 44.

96 Weinstein and Bell, *Saints and Society*, 147.

97 Lee, "Reading Celebrity Autobiographies," 87.

98 In discussing the autobiography of St Ignatius of Loyola, itself an early modern precedent for auto-hagiography, Ulrike Strasser echoes this observation, remarking how the act of interpreting such works hinge on the reader and their familiarity with or expectations of the genre. See Strasser, *German Jesuits and Pacific*, 50.

99 See Krueger, *Hagiography*, 221.

100 I would note that due to the brevity of the nature of this study, I was not able to touch upon other aspects of the text that support the central arguments of this chapter. In *Treasure in Clay* there remain numerous elements of auto-hagiography waiting be explored in future studies, such as his focus on ascetic disciplines, the ongoing emphasis on his humility and obedience to church hierarchy and orthodoxy, and the telling of his numerous (and typically successful) attempts as a convert-maker and missionary in the vein of the apostles.

101 See Krueger, *Hagiography*, 221.

## Chapter Two

1 Fulton Sheen's ambiguous relationship with his celebrity is discussed in chapter 1, while a closer look into his time in New York is discussed in more detail in chapter 3.

2 Alphonse Gallegos was the Auxiliary Bishop of Sacramento from 1981 until his death from being struck by an automobile in 1991. His remains were initially interred at St Mary's Cemetery in Sacramento, before being moved to the nearby Our Lady of Guadalupe Church. For more information on his cause, see [Home page], Bishop Alphonse, OAR, accessed 7 March 2025, https://bishopgallegos.org/. For her part, Sister Wilhelmina Lancaster was the founder of the Benedictines of Mary, Queen of the Apostles religious order. She was initially interred in a burial plot on the property of the monastery she founded, before her remains were exhumed in 2023 and transferred to a chapel inside the monastery proper. Kelsey Wicks, "Who Was Sister Wilhelmina Lancaster, Whose Body Is Now the Center of Attention in Missouri?," *Catholic News Agency*, 24 May 2023, www.catholicnewsagency.com/news/254413/who-was-sister-wilhelmina-lancaster-the-african-american-whose-body-is-potentially-incorrupt.

3 Classic works such as John Tracy Ellis's *American Catholicism* (1965) set the stage for approaches like this, while with more recent ones such as John McGreevy's *Parish Boundaries* (1996), Robert Orsi's *Madonna of 115th Street* (1985) and even James M. O'Toole's annotated collection *The Faithful* (2008) have perhaps inadvertently helped reinforce the perception that American Catholicism is primarily rooted in urban neighbourhoods rather than the remote and often sparsely populated farmlands of the American Midwest and South. See also Marlett, "Strangers in Our Midst"; Marlett, "Harvesting an Overlooked Freedom"; Bovée, "Middle Way"; Bovée, *Church and the Land*; Smith, "Implementing Vatican II"; Avella, "Catholicism in the Twentieth-Century American West."

4 Bovée, "Middle Way," 766; Andrews, "Rural Ministry Collegium," 231.

5 Numerous scholars have commented on the influence of urban parishes on not only American Catholic culture but also academia. Of this, scholar

Timothy Matovina has commented how Catholic historians and historians of Catholicism have tended to focus on urban centres and primarily immigrant stories, particularly in Boston, Chicago, and New York City, while ignoring other Catholics farther afield in the peripheries. See Matovina, "Remapping American Catholicism."

6 "Home," The Archbishop Fulton J. Sheen Foundation, accessed 7 March 2025, www.archbishopsheencause.org/the-cause/about-the-cause/history (defunct).

7 Bishop Jenky continues to be, at the time of this writing, the prelate of Peoria. Interestingly, he was appointed to his current posting in 2002, making the opening of Fulton Sheen's cause one of his first official acts. While the history on the foundation website makes it appear as if he was approached without any awareness of the foundation's actions, as they refer to his involvement only as a "possibility" before coming onboard, his rapid petitioning for the cause makes it seems unlikely that he would not have been a proponent of the foundation's work before his appointment.

8 Haley Stewart, "She Prayed to Fulton Sheen and Her Baby Was Saved. Meet Boonie Engstrom," *America*, 28 July 2019, www.americamagazine.org/faith/2019/07/28/she-prayed-fulton-sheen-and-her-baby-was-saved-meet-bonnie-engstrom.

9 The miracle would later be officially recognized by Pope Francis on 6 July 2019.

10 That Fulton Sheen was ordained in Peoria would become a major fact in the diocese's case for housing his remains and shrine, as well as play a role in the diocese's own self-perception and relation to the would-be saint. More on this is elaborated later in the chapter.

11 The press release stated that "the bishop is heartbroken not only for his flock in Peoria, but also for the many supporters of the Sheen cause from throughout the world who have so generously supported Peoria's efforts." The original document was previously available through the Diocese of Peoria's website (https://cdop.org/post/PostFeatured.aspx?ID=3490, last accessed 14 October 2019) and the Fulton Sheen Foundation website (www.archbishopsheencause.org/, last accessed 3 February 2019) but it has since been removed in both locations. See Peter Jesserer, "New York Archdiocese Stalls Fulton Sheen Canonization Process," *National Catholic Register*, accessed 24 June 2020, www.ncregister.com/daily-news/new-york-archdiocese-stalls-fulton-sheen-canonization-process (defunct).

12 It appears that the Archdiocese of New York may have also reached out to the Vatican beforehand to confirm that their refusal to move Fulton Sheen's remains would in no way impede the beatification ceremony.

13 Though both the remains of Fulton Sheen and Francis Spellman reside in the same crypt, they were carefully interred at opposite ends so as not to rest next to each other in the afterlife. Reeves, *America's Bishop*, 361.

14 While the ceremony of beatification is normally held at the saint's "home" diocese (in this case Peoria), there is no requirement that their body be present in the diocese at the time of the ceremony. For more information on the technicalities of the canonization process, see Msgr Robert Sarno, "Saints," *United States Conference of Catholic Bishops*, accessed 11 February 2021, www.usccb.org/offices/public-affairs/saints.

15 See Bartlett, *Why Can the Dead?*, especially 239–324; and Freeman, *Holy Bones, Holy Dust*.

16 For a foundational discussion on the cult of saints and their connection to space, power, and sanctity, see Brown, *Cult of the Saints*.

17 In situating these concerns within the modern era – and also within the geography that constitutes present-day America – one can draw certain parallels from Emma Anderson and her 2013 monograph *The Death and Afterlife of the North American Martyrs*, as well as Kathleen Sprows Cummings's' 2019 monograph *A Saint of Our Own: How the Quest for a Holy Hero Helped Catholics Become American*. Anderson's work – which explores how the identities of saints are tied to the identities of the people revering them – showcases how the cultural, historical and religious meanings of sainthood are as fluid as they are contentious, particularly when the legacy of the saint is claimed by multiple parishes or dioceses, across regional or national boundaries. Anderson thus highlights how sanctity acts as a point of reference, a tool to make possible the formulation and reimagining of specific cultural identities and differences. Referencing the long-standing drive American Catholics have had for finding and making saints of their own, Cummings's work elucidates the ways in which these figures can act as a reflection and validation of American culture and values. See Anderson, *Martyrs*, particularly 214–54. See also Cummings, *A Saint of Our Own*, particularly 1–14.

18 James T. Keane "What is to be done with the body of Fulton Sheen?," *America*, 11 October 2017, www.americamagazine.org/faith/2017/10/11/what-be-done-body-archbishop-fulton-sheen.

19 One would be hard pressed to find occasions of Catholics referring to the collection of relics negatively as "dismemberment." However, it seems hardly a coincidence that New York would use such harsh language in their public rebuke against Peoria. As the quote was picked up by mainstream American news outlets, I would surmise that it was a means of smearing Peoria's request among wider American audiences who may be unfamiliar (and hence more uncomfortable) with Catholic practices around dead bodies. See "New York and Peoria in Tug of War Over Archbishop Fulton Sheen's Body," *NBC News*, 5 September 2014, www.nbcnews.com/news/us-news/new-york-peoria-tug-war-over-archbishop-fulton-sheens-body-n196721.

20 It bears repeating that even in the modern world, relics continue to remain multivalent sources of sacred power, political charisma, and fiscal profit, whether it be in explicitly religious settings or religious-like settings (such as Soviet-era devotion-like activities pertaining to the body of Lenin). Hardly a medieval phenomenon, dead bodies exert a fascination for modern people who continue to recognize the power inherent in them. See Walsham, "Introduction."

21 Dye, "Irish America's Rural Man of Letters," 22–3; see also Avella, "Next Frontier."

22 Of particular note is the fiery John Hughes, who fought tooth and nail against nineteenth-century nativism for Irish immigrants and American-born Irish – earning him the moniker "Dagger John." His influence would continue to exert itself through his successor, John McClosky, who would go on to become the first American cardinal. For more on John Hughes, see Shelley, "Founding Father"; William J. Stern, "How Dagger John Saved New York's Irish," *City Journal* (Spring 1997), accessed 18 January 2025, www.city-journal.org/html/how-dagger-john-saved-new-york%E2%80%99s-irish-11934.html.

23 Francis Spellman was, after all, made Apostolic Vicar for the US Armed Forces during World War II and later founded the annual Al Smith Dinner charity that even today continues to be frequented by sitting presidents of the United States. Spellman was also one of the main campaigners pushing for Elizabeth Ann Seton's canonization, who became the first American-born saint. See Cummings, *Saint of Our Own*, 126.

24 See Matovina, "Remapping American Catholicism."

25 While many of the Catholics to settle in rural America were of German origin – and many of whom arrived more well-off than other nationalities – there were nevertheless a number of Irish family units that opted for the Midwest over the more well-known urban centres. Though small, these communities formed tight-knit bonds with their peers and the land. Dye, "Irish America's Rural Man of Letters," 22–5.

26 Bovée, "Middle Way," 777; Bovée, *Church and the Land*, 358.

27 Bieter, "'Lay People Can Teach,'" 54.

28 Jay P. Dolan, "Catholics in the Midwest," University of Notre Dame, accessed 28 July 2020, https://www3.nd.edu/~jdolan/midwest.html (defunct).

29 Dolan, *American Catholic*, 130–6; Dye, "Leo R. Ward," 22–5.

30 According to the Pew Research Center, in 2014, Catholics made up approximately 28 per cent of the state's population, compared with 43 per cent for all Protestant denominations. Pew Research Center, "Religious Landscapes Study," accessed 28 July 2020, www.pewforum.org/religious-landscape-study/state/illinois/.

31 Marlett, "Strangers in Our Midst," 86.

32 Bieter, "Lay People Can," 63.
33 Dye, "Irish America's Rural Man of Letters," 24.
34 Pastoral motifs appear to have featured prominently in the rural Catholic imaginary, with rather direct parallels in the life of Christ to Midwesterners' own labours. Such imagery was also often gendered, focusing on male physicality and the authority of the male body over the land itself. As historian J.L. Anderson observes, rural imagery has the tendency to show physically capable and sturdy men whose masculinity is rooted in their body and the practices they perform on the land. Sociologist Katie Holmes also remarks that a quintessential feature of rural imagery "position[s] men as dominating nature and conquering the landscape" and that "the entangled relationships between men's bodies, animals, machines, and the land they worked are in turn connected to broader understandings about nationhood, settlement, and the Judeo-Christian imperative to subdue the wilderness." See Marlett, "Strangers in Our Midst," 98; Anderson, "'You're a Bigger Man'"; Holmes, "Making Masculinity."
35 Marlett, "Harvesting an Overlooked Freedom," 102.
36 The NCRLC also sought to "ruralize" the wider church in America, imprinting what it saw were the superior values of the countryside on urban centres, albeit to little success. For a scholarly, historical analysis of the NCRLC and its anti-urbanism, see Bovée, *Church and The Land*; and Marlett, "Harvesting an Overlooked Freedom." Additionally, as historian Geneviève Zubrzycki remarks, similar sentiments were also seen farther north in Quebec. Quoting an oft-repeated proverb in favour of Catholic ruralism and against urbanization that reads "church steeples will always be higher than factory chimneys," she remarks that late nineteenth and early twentieth-century French Canadians were keen to "renounce the luxuries of city life and the lure of industry for a simple but enlightened life on the land … locating heavenly virtue in the simple act of tilling the soil." Zubrzycki, *Beheading the Saint*, 62, 56.
37 Hamlin and McGreevy, "Greening of America," 466.
38 Marlett, "Strangers in Our Midst," 96.
39 Marlett, "Harvesting an Overlooked Freedom," 102.
40 Marlett, "Harvesting an Overlooked Freedom," 89.
41 While the NCRLC's influence quickly faded post–World War II along with much of the earlier anti-urbanism, awareness of rural differences continues to permeate in rural parishes and dioceses. See Bovée, *Church and the Land*, 258–366; Marlett, "Harvesting an Overlooked Freedom"; Smith, "Implementing Vatican II."
42 For instance, Indigenous Peoples of North America, Australia, and New Zealand have sought to reclaim the bones and material possessions of their ancestors confiscated and placed in foreign museums. In reclaiming their relics,

they effectively reclaim some of their lost agency and identity. See Walsham, "Relics and Remains."

43 Catholic News Service, "New York State Court Rules Sheen Remains Should Be Transferred to Peoria," *America*, 18 November 2016, www.americamagazine.org/faith/2016/11/18/new-york-state-court-rules-sheen-remains-should-be-transferred-peoria.

44 Sharon Otterman, "Tug of war for Archbishop Fulton Sheen's body, or Its Parts, Delays Sainthood," *Seattle Times*, 13 September 2014, www.seattletimes.com/nation-world/tug-of-war-for-archbishop-fulton-sheenrsquos-body-or-its-parts-delays-sainthood/.

45 James T. Keane, "What Is to Be Done with the Body of Archbishop Fulton Sheen?," *America*, 11 October 2017, www.americamagazine.org/faith/2017/10/11/what-be-done-body-archbishop-fulton-sheen.

46 Keane, "What Is to Be Done with the Body of Archbishop Fulton Sheen?"

47 Despite the tense atmosphere at the proceedings, the hearing wasn't without some lighter moments that Fulton Sheen himself might have approved of. When arguing his final point, Mr Callagy, the principal attorney for the Archdiocese of New York, argued that it would be a shame for Sheen to be removed from the high altar of St Patrick's Cathedral and brought all the way to distant Peoria for no good reason. "'Eh,' interrupted Justice Dianne Renwick, who was overseeing the case, 'Peoria's not that bad.'" See Keane, "What Is to Be Done with the Body of Archbishop Fulton Sheen?" See also "New York's Highest Court Dismisses Legal Appeal, Says Sheen's Body Can Go to Peoria," *National Catholic Register*, 7 May 2019, www.ncregister.com/daily-news/civil-appeals-court-dismisses-legal-challenge-says-sheens-body-can-go-to-pe.

48 It is perhaps worth noting that of the twelve recognized American saints, at least half of them featured New York prominently in their hagiographical materials.

49 Following the reopening of Maryland to Catholics and the end to the penal laws in 1774, Elizabeth Ann Seton founded Saint Joseph's Academy and Free School, an academy for girls, followed by Sisters of Charity of St Joseph's, the first religious congregation founded in the United States. For more on the penal laws of Maryland and the Catholic exclusionary policies, see Farrelly, *Papist Patriots*.

50 Cummings, *Saint of our Own*, 126.

51 Cummings, *Saint of our Own*, 109.

52 Most of Francis Cabrini's body would be interred first at a chapel in Mother Cabrini High School, and then moved in 1959 to their current resting place at the St Francis Xavier Cabrini Shrine in Upper Manhattan. Her head, however, was sent back to the motherhouse in Rome, and her heart to Codogno, Italy, where she founded her order. Michael T. Luongo, "In Upper Manhattan, Restoring the Golden Halo of Mother Cabrini," *New York Times*, 6 February

2015, www.nytimes.com/2015/02/08/nyregion/in-upper-manhattan-restoring-the-golden-halo-of-mother-cabrini.html.

53 Luongo, "Restoring the Golden Halo of Mother Cabrini."

54 It seems that after her death, Francis Cabrini's American devotees saw in her narrative an affirmation of her Americanness and an embrace of her immigrant origins, whereas her Italian devotees saw her as a devout Italian working amid a foreign culture. Differences such as this showcase how devotees seem themselves in the figures they revere while simultaneously affirming their own identities and positionality. Cummings, *Saint of Our Own*, 110.

55 Cummings, *Saint of Our Own*, 119.

56 While devotees are quick to declare that Mother Cabrini saw something in American life that mirrored her own Catholic devotionalism, hence moving her to seek citizenship, the historical rational behind her move towards citizenship was quite possibly much more mundane. To facilitate her constant border crossings and to help secure the funding and construction permits to plant numerous institutions of the Missionary Sisters of the Sacred Heart of Jesus across the country, US citizenship was likely the means to expediting what might otherwise amount to larger legal issues for a foreigner. Cummings, *Saint of Our Own*, 109.

57 The eight Jesuit missionaries grouped together were martyred during the mid-seventeenth century among the Iroquois people in what was at the time part of colonial Canada, but which now encompasses areas located in both Ontario and upstate New York.

58 Anderson, *Martyrs*, 104.

59 As Emma Anderson remarks, shrines not only establish geographic markers in the holy landscape of a given nation, they also establish the identity of that location and its people within the larger patchwork of the nation. Accordingly, "French Canadians utilized the martyrs to symbolize their cultural distinctiveness," as the suffering and tragedy of the martyrs mirrored their own self-perception as French Canadians whose identity was (and continues to be) tied to the trauma of the eighteenth-century conquest and annexation by the British. As a result of this strong French-Canadian identification with the martyrs, the saints, though still rooted to New York via their hagiographical traditions, had their identity with the United States diminished. Anderson, *Martyrs*, 104.

60 Cummings, *Saint of Our Own*, 2.

61 On the Sheen foundation's website, it suggests that one of the major contributing factors for Bishop Jenky's decision to spearhead the cause was because he "[recognized] Sheen's mid-west roots." See "History," The Archbishop Fulton John Sheen Foundation.

62 Fulton Sheen dedicates a lengthy chapter of his autobiographical *Treasure in Clay* to his travels. See Sheen, *Treasure in Clay*, 127–68.

63 While there is no hard reason to doubt Msgr Franco's testimony, it does seem oddly convenient for New York that Futon Sheen should have expressed such personal wishes in confidence to a single source who then went public. Meaghan M. McDermott, "Bishop Fulton Sheen's Bones at Center of Raging Court Case," *Democrat and Chronicle*, 11 February 2018, www.democratandchronicle.com/story/news/2018/02/11/bishops-bones-center-raging-court-case/3271 74002/

64 New York was technically correct in this assertion, as mentioned previously in this chapter. "Case on Transfer of Archbishop's Body Is Returned to Original N.Y. Court," *National Catholic Reporter*, 13 February 2018, www.ncronline.org/news/people/case-transfer-archbishops-body-returned-original-ny-court.

65 "Appeals Court Says Fulton Sheen's Body Should Go to Peoria," *Catholic News Agency*, 5 March 2019, www.catholicnewsagency.com/news/appeals-court-says-fulton-sheens-body-should-go-to-peoria-71875.

66 "New York's Highest Court Dismisses Legal Appeal, Says Sheen's Body Can Go to Peoria," *National Catholic Register*, 7 May 2019, www.ncregister.com/daily-news/civil appeals-court-dismisses-legal-challenge-says-sheens-body-can-go-to-pe.

67 Phil Luciano, "New York Archdiocese Files Another Appeal to Keep Fulton Sheen's Remains," *Peoria Journal Star*, 20 May 2019, www.pjstar.com/news/20190520/new-york-archdiocese-files-another-appeal-to-keep-fulton-sheens-remains.

68 More lengthy discussions on the uneasy balance of Fulton Sheen's celebrity are found in chapters 1 and 3.

69 Andrew Apostoli, like many of the members of the cause, had been friends with Fulton Sheen and knew the man before his death. He first came into acquaintance with Sheen in the 1960s and was ordained as a priest by the then-archbishop shortly before his death. "Founding Member of CFRS and EWTN Host Father Andrew Apostoli Dies at Age 75," *Crux*, 15 December 2017, https://cruxnow.com/obituary/2017/12/founding-member-cfrs-ewtn-host-father-andrew-apostoli-dies-age-75/.

70 It bears noting that images of this sort –imagining the saints during their youths and depicting them in idealized and gendered manner, in this case masculine, with accompanying setting and activities – are hardly unique in terms of resources and visual media aimed specifically for children and adolescents, particularly in the modern era. After all, in American Catholicism, we have witnessed the creation of baseball cards, comic books, and even feature-length animated movies recounting the lives of saints for younger audiences. Fulton Sheen's masculinity is discussed in more detail in chapters 4 and 5.

71 While not necessarily at the same level of biblical woodcuts, audiovisual resources such as these can be seen as a modern, if somewhat diverse, continuation of the prominent use of pastoral motifs among rural Catholics looking to lionize their spiritual identity and sacred connection to the land.

72 Illustrations such as this depicting Fulton Sheen as a cheerful and able farmhand contradict the way he depicted himself in his autobiography. He remarks that while his brothers enjoyed working the fields, he "suffered" it and felt "ashamed … at having to wear overalls." As well, in a colourful anecdote, he remarks how a friend of his father's, upon noticing young Sheen struggling in the fields, remarked, "Newt, that boy of yours, Fulton, will never be worth a damn." Sheen, *Treasure in Clay*, 18.

73 "Fulton Sheen's Remains Arrive in Peoria; Sainthood Cause Resumes," *Catholic News Agency*, 27 June 2019, www.catholicnewsagency.com/news/fulton-sheens-remains-arrive-in-peoria-sainthood-cause-resumes-40990.

74 See Jennifer Willems, "Miracle Confirmed in Fulton Sheen Cause for Beatification," *Catholic Register*, 8 July 2019, www.catholicregister.org/faith/item/29868-miracle-confirmed-in-fulton-sheen-cause-for-beatification.

75 "Beatification for Archbishop Sheen Postponed," *National Catholic Reporter*, 3 December 2019, www.ncronline.org/news/people/beatification-archbishop-sheen-postponed.

76 Nick Vlahos, "Rochester Diocese Blocked Fulton Sheen Beatification More Than Once, Peoria Claims," *Peoria Journal Star*, 12 December 2019, www.democratandchronicle.com/story/news/2019/12/10/rochester-bishop-matano-blocked-sheen-beatification-process-more-than-once/4382895002/.

77 David Crary, "Two Catholic Dioceses in Public Spat over Sheen Sainthood," *Crux*, 13 December 2019, https://cruxnow.com/church-in-the-usa/2019/12/two-catholic-dioceses-in-public-spat-over-sheen-sainthood/.

78 David Crary, "Catholic Dioceses Spar Over Archbishop Sheen Sainthood," *ABC News*, 12 December 2019, https://abcnews.go.com/US/wireStory/catholic-dioceses-public-dispute-sheen-sainthood-67697541.

79 John L. Allen Jr., "Church Now faces 'Sheen Dilemma' in Evaluating Saints and Their Halos," *Crux*, 8 December 2019, https://cruxnow.com/news-analysis/2019/12/church-now-faces-sheen-dilemma-in-evaluating-saints-and-their-halos/.

80 It perhaps bears repeating that during his tenure at Rochester – specifically during the fiasco with the parish donation – Fulton Sheen faced a nearly full-fledged revolt of his parish priests, some of whom had notably less than kind things to say about him on the public record. For more on his tumultuous tenure in Rochester, see Reeves, *America's Bishop*, especially 291–327.

81 Pope John Paul II removed the longstanding norm of keeping a five-year period of wait between a person's death and the initiation of their canonization process in 1999. During his lengthy tenure, it is well affirmed that he encouraged and approved the canonization of 482 saints across 110 causes – roughly as many as his predecessors combined over several centuries prior. For comparison of his proficiency when it came to canonization, all the previous

popes of the twentieth century canonized a combined total of 98 figures. His successor Benedict XVI thought less prolific, nevertheless canonized 45 saints in his 8-year reign before retirement. The death of Mary Teresa Bojaxhiu, more commonly known as Mother Teresa and herself quite the celebrity figure, in 1997, seems to have been the impetus for John Paul II to make the changes to the convention. That she was canonized in 2003, a mere six years after her death, makes her cause the emblem of holy expediency. Stadick. "Saint Patrons," 123. See also Gertz, "John Paul II's 'Canonization Cannon,'" *Christianity Today*, 8 August 2008, www.christianitytoday.com/history/2008/august/john-paul-iis-canonization-cannon.html.

82 Allen, "Church Now Faces 'Sheen Dilemma.'"

83 While in Peoria, I was given the chance to read the testimonies prepared by his cause but was asked to refrain from directly quoting any of the material. However, I can relate broadly that a recurring theme of the questions asked were to ensure that there would be no embarrassing details that could be brought to light. For instance, witnesses were questioned about Sheen's feelings toward Cardinal Spellman, potential instances of Fulton Sheen succumbing to pride or vanity, his feelings for his family (including his Protestant grandparents), and how he behaved around his own wealth and that of the charities he ran. That his cause has been proceeding suggests that no improprieties were discovered.

84 Anderson, *Martyrs*, 8.

85 Cummings, *Saint of our Own, 3*.

86 Cummings, *Saint of Our Own*, 5.

87 Stadick, "Saint Patrons," 136.

88 Cummings, *Saint of Our Own*, 10.

## Chapter Three

1 *What's My Line?*, Produced by Mark Goodson and Bill Todman, CBS, 21 October 1956, accessed 11 January 2025, as "What's My Line? – Lerner & Loewe; Bishop Sheen; David Niven [panel] (Oct 21, 1956)," 26:14, YouTube video, www.youtube.com/watch?v=T74qnT7WFZw&ab_channel=What%27sMyLine%3F.

2 See Slide, *Television Industry*, 121. For examples of Hollywood veterans "descending" to television, some were purely promotional, such as James Cagney appearing on *The Ed Sullivan Show* to tout an upcoming film, while others were indeed celebrities engaged in a sort of migration from one medium to another, such as James Mason hosting NBC's *Lux Video Theatre* and Loretta Young with *The Loretta Young Show.* Such a popular misconception, however, obscures the fact that the majority of the medium's celebrities were figures who came with a prior celebrity standing and fan base, many of them having

established themselves as vaudeville-style performers, nightclub singers, or stand-up comedians. Many of the most popular prime-time television programs during the 1950s were thus adaptations of their charismatic hosts' earlier stage productions or club routines. And so it wasn't uncommon for a successful Broadway star or club performer to count themselves among not only the first generation of television personalities but also among the more successful. While Sheen was hardly a vaudevillian performer, he can nevertheless be included in this category to some extent, as his television routine was markedly similar to the way he approached his radio program as well as his lectures at the CUA. See Becker, "Televising Film Stardom in the 1950s," 5; Calvert, "Similar Hats on Similar Heads," 4.

3 America in the 1950s was widely perceived to be a time of "crisis" – both geopolitically and bodily. This topic is discussed in more detail in chapter 5.

4 Technically, Billy Graham made his first forays into television in the late 1940s but only became a regular program host in the 1950s.

5 In describing the format of Fulton Sheen's delivery during his episodes, scholar Timothy Sherwood uses the word "talks." While I find this an appealing way of describing the accessible approach Sheen took with his audience, I do not feel that it fully conveys the purpose and intent of their messaging as much as preaching does – albeit, bearing in mind the qualifiers discussed. Sherwood, *Age of Extremes*, 15.

6 Additionally, like numerous Catholic celebrities involved in Hollywood, both Danny Thomas and Loretta Young were members of the Church of the Good Shepherd in Beverly Hills. See Mervyn Rothstein, "Danny Thomas, 79, the TV Star of 'Make Room for Daddy,' Dies," *New York Times*, 7 February 1991, www.nytimes.com/1991/02/07/obituaries/danny-thomas-79-the-tv-star-of-make-room-for-daddy-dies.html. See also Jay Horning, "Loretta Young Works for Charity," *Tampa Bay Times*, 8 September 1991, www.tampabay.com/archive/1991/09/08/loretta-young-works-for-charity/.

7 Curiously, the *Time* magazine article that proclaimed Fulton Sheen as the first televangelist did little to connect his program to any evangelization efforts on Sheen's part, commenting instead on his credentials as the director for the nation's Society for the Propagation of the Faith (SPOF). "Bishop Fulton Sheen: The First 'Televangelist,'" *Time*, 14 April 1952, https://time.com/archive/6794617/bishop-fulton-sheen-the-first-televangelist/.

8 Concerning the purpose of *Life Is Worth Living*, scholar Timothy Sherwood remarks that "the [program] was never designed or intended to be a preaching ministry." Sherwood, *Age of Extremes*, 2.

9 Sherwood, *Age of Extremes*, 14.

10 *Texaco Star Theater* was previously broadcast on radio, running from 1939 to 1949.

11 Prime time is typically designated as taking place from 8:00 p.m. to 11:00 p.m. on weeknights. Cantor, *Prime-Time Television,* 12.

12 While often considered the first variety show program, the weekly *Kraft Television Theatre* beat *Texaco Star Theater* to the screen by several months, first airing in 1947. However, it was *Texaco Star Theater* that dominated the early ratings, and the popularity of host Milton Berle helped television become the "national medium" for entertainment in America. See Cantor, *Prime-Time Television,* 15.

13 Numerous programs – such as *The Jackie Gleason Show, Cavalcade of Stars, The Morey Amsterdam Show,* and *Broadway Open House,* among others – came and went as audiences acclimatized themselves to the formats being offered and the expectations they created. Few programs survived longer than a handful of seasons (one notable exception being *The Red Skelton Show,* which endured until the 1970s).

14 For a detailed survey of early FCC requirements, trade slots, and the emergence of religious programming, see Horsfield, "'And Now a Word from Our Sponsor.'"

15 Notably, NBC broadcast over sixty hours of religious programming, composed largely of Catholic and Protestant worship services, to coincide with Easter in 1940. Horsfield, "And Now a Word from Our Sponsor," 259. For more information about the changing mandate, see also Rosenthal, "'This Nation Under God,'" 38.

16 Weinstein, *Forgotten Network,* 162.

17 Horsfield, "And Now a Word from Our Sponsor," 262

18 Rosenthal, "'This Nation Under God,'" 47.

19 Christopher Lynch observes that many would have found Fulton Sheen's performances both intimate and compelling, being that he, a member of the clergy, was talking to them as one might a friend, rather than as a distant, almost untouchable figure meant to be viewed with awe. It's also worth mentioning that whenever he addressed the audience, he referred to his viewers simply as "friends." Lynch, *Selling Catholicism,* 133.

20 Of the many jokes Sheen told, one of the more memorable comes from the episode "Angels." Here, Fulton Sheen begins with a story of a child asking her mother why there are no angels with beards or moustaches, wondering if men could even make it into Heaven. The mother responded with "Yes, child, but they get in by a close shave." There's then a perceptible moment where the audience bursts into laughter as Sheen, himself a clean-shaved man, smiles like a co-conspirator. See *Life Is Worth Living,* "Angels," DuMont Network, Written by Fulton Sheen, 1953.

21 Milton Berle's ego and narcissism has been long documented by those close to him, and even by casual observers, such as was the case with his infamous and seemingly final variety show appearance in 1979 on *Saturday Night Live.* See, e.g., Lewis and Berle, *My Father, Uncle Miltie.* For more details about his stint

on *Saturday Night Live*, see Megan Hemenway, "Saturday Night True Story: Why Was Milton Berle Banned From SNL?," *Screen Rant*, 16 October 2024. https://screenrant.com/saturday-night-live-milton-berle-banned-true-story/.

22 As an alternative reading, Christopher Lynch suggests that economic factors and ratings might have been contributing factors in the decision to end his show. By 1957 television had evolved and audiences were perhaps expecting more from a half hour of entertainment than an elderly man with a piece of chalk. By that time Sheen's old rival, Milton Berle, had also fallen to relative obscurity, a slew of similar programs had been cancelled, and advertisers were seeking new ways of increasing revenues, including returning to Hollywood in search of sponsorship. Lynch, *Selling Catholicism*, 158; Cantor, *Prime-Time Television*, 27.

23 The clipping in question was located in an uncategorized box from archives at the Diocese of Peoria. Unfortunately, most of the article is missing and all that remains is a small scrap with the text in question but missing the byline and the title of the piece: *Democrat and Chronicle*, 20 September 1969.

24 Vincent J. Nugent, "He Strikes from the Pulpit," *Catholic Post*, 2 October 1977. News Clippings, 1970–79, Catholic University of American Archives, Washington, DC.

25 The *Washington Star*'s obituary of Fulton Sheen, e.g., reminds readers that "many industry experts predicted a short run when Archbishop Fulton J. Sheen first decided to go on television in 1952." In addition, ten years after his funeral, Vintage released a retrospective remarking that Sheen's biggest "triumph was … when he began television's 'Life is Worth Living.'" See "Archbishop Sheen Dies at Home in New York," *Washington Star*, 10 December 1979, News Clippings, 1970–79, Catholic University of American Archives, Washington, DC; Bill Adams, "Milton Berle Took a Back Seat to Bishop Sheen," *Vintage*, 18 September 1989, uncategorized box, Fulton Sheen Museum Archives, Peoria, Illinois.

26 See also William McFadden and George James, "Bishop Sheen Dead at 84," *Daily News*, 10 December 1979, uncategorized box, Fulton Sheen Museum Archives, Peoria, Illinois; "The World Says Goodbye to Uncle Fultie," *Tablet*, 13 December 1979.

27 *Twin Circle*, 23 December 1979, uncategorized box, Fulton Sheen Museum Archives, Peoria, Illinois.

28 "Archbishop Fulton J Sheen Dead at 84," *Wanderer*, 1979, uncategorized box, Fulton Sheen Museum Archives, Peoria, Illinois; Adams, "Milton Berle Took Back Seat to Bishop Sheen," *Vantage Point*, 18 September 1989, uncategorized box, Fulton Sheen Museum Archives, Peoria, Illinois.

29 Claudia McDonnell, "Sheen Remembered, Celebrated," *Catholic Post*, 20 December 2009, uncategorized box, Fulton Sheen Museum Archives, Peoria, Illinois.

30 A study referenced by Christopher Lynch indicates that of his audiences, 75 per cent of households tuning in were Catholic, roughly 13 per cent were Protestant, 7.9 per cent were of mixed affiliation, and 2.2 per cent were Jewish. See Parker et al., *Television-Radio Audience*, 211; Lynch, *Selling Catholicism*, 8. Studies citing Fulton Sheen's denominationally inclusive base would later assist the proponents of his cause for canonization, who enjoyed highlighting the importance Sheen held, not just for Catholics but for all Americans, too. One notable example of this comes from Father Andrew Apostoli (the vice-postulator for Sheen's cause until his death in 2017), who once stated – somewhat optimistically, albeit cryptically – to a local Peoria publication that Sheen's audience was mostly "Jewish, with Protestants second and Catholics third." See "Process Could Take Decades, Centuries," *Peoria Journal Star*, 24 November 2002, uncategorized box, Fulton Sheen Museum Archives, Peoria, Illinois.

31 One also wonders if this humourous nickname for the Virgin Mother was also a way to make the distinctly Catholic and typically magnanimous figure more approachable, as well as less alien, to regular audiences. Lynch, *Selling Catholicism*, 87.

32 Protestant America's suspicions and unease about its Catholic minority is a central part of our discussion in the following chapter.

33 Massa, *Catholics and American Culture*, 84.

34 Lynch, *Selling Catholicism*, 63–4; Sherwood, *Age of Extremes*, 15.

35 *Life Is Worth Living*, "Signs of Our Times."

36 In the 1950s, belief in God was at an all-time high in the United States, peaking at an estimated 96–98 per cent. This suggests that viewers would have very much agreed in the importance of the spiritual, if not necessarily been at risk of drifting away from it. See Hudnut-Beulmer, *Looking for God in the Suburbs*, 41, 71–8. See also The Short Answer, "How Many Americans Believe in God?," *Gallup*, 24 June 2022, https://news.gallup.com/poll/268205/americans-believe-god.aspx. See also *Life Is Worth Living*, "Angels."

37 *Life Is Worth Living*, "How to Compare World Religion."

38 *Life Is Worth Living*, "How to Compare World Religion."

39 Concerns for pre–Vatican II ecumenism appear to have largely been concentrated in the United States as a multicultural society where Catholics were but one denomination among many. While Fulton Sheen's views on ecumenism are limited in the way he conceptualizes the category of "world religions" – he valorizes the primacy of the Abrahamic faiths while largely excluding any mention of non-Abrahamic faiths – Sheen's take on the uniqueness of Catholicism and its relationship to other world religions can nevertheless be read as part of a wider progressive stance witnessed in pre–Vatican American Catholicism. For further discussion on pre– and post–Vatican II Catholic understandings of religious pluralism, see Carey,

"American Catholic Ecumenism"; and Radano, "Contributions of Americans to Vatican II."

40 Becker, "Televising Film Stardom in the 1950s," 5.

41 Hudnut-Beulmer, *Looking for God in the Suburbs*, 16.

42 Becker, "Televising Film Stardom in the 1950s," 6.

43 Nathalie Heinich also adds fans to the list of those who played a role in shaping the identity of celebrities during this time. See Heinich, "Consommation de la Célébrité," 112.

44 Becker, "Televising Film Stardom in the 1950s," 6–7.

45 Moldea, *Dark Victory*, 150.

46 Lynch, *Selling Catholicism*, 10.

47 At the cinema, individual strangers gather together quietly in a darkened room where they refrain from talking or disturbing those around them, whereas television is primarily viewed at one's home or in the home of one's friends or family. As Tony Wilson remarks, "The subject interpolated by television has been always already familiar." See Wilson, *Watching Television*, 24.

48 Wilson, *Watching Television*, 24. See also Cantor, *Prime-Time Television*, 49.

49 Wilson's theory of television as applied to this period is thus at odds with structuralist understandings of television from within communication studies, which portray it as being a medium of "pure conveyance." For Wilson, viewers cannot be understood as passive vessels who simply receive whatever message is being broadcast. Rather, a viewer's decision to tune into a program is an active and even reciprocal process, in that the viewer's choice to watch or not watch a particular show affects both the viewer and the show itself (its ratings, renewals, etc.).

50 This feeling of familial recognition is communicated well in the fact that both Milton Berle and Fulton Sheen were popularly referred to as "Uncle Miltie" and "Uncle Fultie" – nicknames which highlighted their familiarity and regular presence in the intimate space of America's living rooms. Additionally, many of the early television stars, and the celebrity preachers among them, had a recurring stable of jokes, anecdotes, and stories that they would frequently reuse – not unlike an uncle who tells the same joke at every family gathering.

51 Wilson, *Watching Television*, 28.

52 Wilson, 24.

53 Wilson, 26.

54 See Massa, "Catholic for President," 300.

55 Smith, *What Would Jesus Read?*, 136.

56 Smith, *What Would Jesus Read?*, 145.

57 The so-called Red Scare and Joseph McCarthy's personal crusades is a subject of discussion in chapter 5.

58 See Hudnut-Beulmer, *Looking for God in the Suburbs*, 41, 71–8.

59 Some notable examples include Fulton Sheen's *Peace of Soul*, rabbi Joshua Loth Liebman's *Peace of Mind*, and even Trappist monk Thomas Merton's *The Seven Story Mountain*, each of which was published in the preceding years but saw ongoing demand well into the 1950s. See also Smith, *What Would Jesus Read?*, 135; Weinstein, *Forgotten Network*, 168.

60 See Ellwood quoted in Weinstein, *Forgotten Network*, 167. See also Ellwood, *Fifties Spiritual Marketplace*.

61 Riley points to the increased material presence of religion in the form of bookstores packed with bestsellers and new churches being built as a sign of a society-wide change of attitude in religion. See Riley, *Fulton J. Sheen*, 187.

62 In his seminal work, *Revivals, Awakenings, and Reforms*, historian William G. McLoughlin argued that the 1950s set the stage for a "Fourth Great Awakening" that began in earnest by 1960 – effectively placing this outpouring of religious expression on par with earlier revivals, such as the more well-known awakening of the mid-eighteenth century centred around evangelicals such as George Whitfield. As a counterpoint, Hudnut-Beulmer contends that some critics have questioned the nature of the apparent upswing in American religiosity, suggesting that the actual situation may not have been as remarkable as painted by the polls, nor even measurably different than attitudes a decade prior. See McLoughlin, *Revivals, Awakenings, and Reforms*, 41, 71–8.

63 See Patterson, "Cross or the Double Cross," 49.

64 Reeves, *America's Bishop*, 126.

65 Massa, *Catholics and American Culture*, 85.

66 The spiritual opposition between America and the Soviet Union is discussed further in chapter 5. See also Patterson, "Cross or the Double Cross."

67 Lynch, *Selling Catholicism*, 24. Of course, it bears qualifying that while Sheen's audiences were not entirely Catholic, Catholics nevertheless made up roughly three-quarters of his viewers.

68 Sherwood, *Age of Extremes*, 49.

69 Sherwood, 54.

70 Russell Chandler, "Norman Vincent Peale, 'Minister to Millions,' Dies: Religion: Mixing Faith and Psychology, Author of 'The Power of Positive Thinking,' Spread Inspiration Worldwide," *Los Angeles Times*, 26 December 1993, www.latimes.com/archives/la-xpm-1993-12-26-mn-5771-story.html.

71 Orwig, "Business Ethics and the Protestant Spirit," 82. Italics in original.

72 Similar remarks could be made about Fulton Sheen's program, which Christopher Sheen describes as being focused on "people's problems" – a sentiment echoed by David Weinstein, who observes that Sheen primarily spoke about the "everyday problems" of Americans. See Orwig, "Business Ethics and the Protestant Spirit," 84; Lynch, *Selling Catholicism*, 124; Weinstein, *Forgotten Network*, 166.

73 Emphasis mine. Weinstein, *Forgotten Network*, 168.

74 For a comprehensive biography of Billy Graham, see Wacker, *America's Pastor.*

75 "Ruth Bell Graham and Peace With God," *Voices from Wheaton Archives & Special Collections*, 28 November 2014, https://fromthevault.wheaton.edu/2018/11/28/ruth-bell-graham-on-peace-with-god/.

76 Wacker, "Billy Graham's America," 489.

77 Unlike Fulton Sheen and Vincent Norman Peale, whose popularity may have peaked in the mid-to-late 1950s, Billy Graham's star continued to rise in the decades that followed. He was so prolific as a preacher and speaker, that biographer Grant Wacker estimates Graham addressed more people face to face than anyone else in history save for Pope John Paul II. Wacker, "Billy Graham's America," 490. See also Whitfield and Bourguinon, "Billy Graham," 211. Seemingly as a tongue-in-cheek response to John Paul II's prolific reach with audiences, Graham is quoted as once claiming that he could reach more people in a single night on television than John Paul II did in his entire lifetime. Abelman and Neuendorf, "Themes and Topics,"152.

78 Billy Graham owed much of his crusade format and presentation style to the earlier, and highly animated, evangelist Billy Sunday. Diekema, "Televangelism," 144–6.

79 An often-repeated story of Billy Graham's was how a woman in a restaurant once stopped to ask him if he was aware that he had an uncanny resemblance to Billy Graham. Another, was how a man sharing an elevator ride with him first excitedly recognized him, but then once he sized him up sighed with disappointment, muttering "My, what an anticlimax." Wacker, *America's Pastor*, 56.

80 Wacker, *America's Pastor*, 40.

81 It would become routine for televangelists by the 1970s and especially the 1980s to argue not just for the necessity of the Evangelical message, but even sometimes the superiority of their own message against all others. See Krohn, "Language of Television Preachers," 501.

82 Wacker, "Billy Graham's America," 505.

83 Wacker, *America's Pastor*, 14.

84 Billy Graham's approach and openness would continue to make him something of an outlier among Protestant television preachers, sometimes in remarkable ways. For instance, in 1979, Graham supported the founding of the Evangelical Council for Financial Accountability, which would have created an opt-in code of ethics and transparency that televangelists could follow. Among the tenets of the council were stipulations that forbade unethical fundraising tactics and made the financial affairs of the participating evangelists public. However, Graham was the sole televangelist to participate. See Hughey, "Internal Contradictions of Televangelism," 44.

85 To say that Catholics and mainlines had little interest in using television to acquire monetary donations is perhaps an understatement. Historian Jeffrey K. Hadden suggests that both groups saw the Evangelical habit of requesting donations as being beneath the stature of their institutions, bordering on the repugnant. Hadden, "Rise and Fall of American Televangelism," 117. An additional hindrance for any Evangelicals hoping to work with the government-mandated time slots was the requirement that the broadcaster justify how each program in this category acted in the public interests, which would be difficult to square with their fundraising. See Horsfield, "'And Now a Word from Our Sponsor,'" 262.

86 In effect, this created in the Evangelicals a much more symbiotic relationship between themselves, their programs, and their audience than any of the preachers giving talks on the public service slots that would only grow more pronounced in the decades that followed and further distance the latter televangelists from the ecumenism and openness of this early period. Horsfield, "And Now a Word from Our Sponsor," 260.

87 As a far cry of the early free spot offered to public service religious broadcasting, by the 1980s, Protestant televangelists Jimmy Swaggert, Jerry Fallwell, Jim Bakker, Oral Roberts, and Pat Robertson together were estimated to be spending a combined quarter billion annually on media acquisition. Hughey, "Internal Contradictions of Televangelism," 33.

88 A well-known scandal related to the excess of funds and their misappropriation was in 1986 when televangelist Rex Humbard was found to have been using proceeds from his mission to purchase homes and condos in Florida, together amounting to a small real estate empire. This is not to say that it is the nature of the televangelist to lean toward financial misdeeds, but the symbiosis between their audience numbers and fundraising efforts would nevertheless seem to create ripe atmospheres for misbehaviour. See Hughey, "Internal Contradictions of Televangelism," 35.

89 Smith, *What Would Jesus Read?*, 140

90 Christopher Lynch comments on the double nature of Fulton Sheen, both as a television host and as a member of the clergy. As a host, he inevitably acted as a familiar, intimate figure, and yet owing to his stature within the church, he was at the same time a figure of authority. Lynch, *Selling Catholicism*, 155.

91 See Jade Scipioni, "How This 1950s Self-Help Guru shaped Donald Trump's Attitude Towards Life and Business," *CNBC*, 10 July 2020, www.cnbc.com/2020/07/10/how-self-help-author-norman-vincent-peale-influenced-donald-trump.html.

92 Smith, *What Would Jesus Read?*, 139.

93 This fear was perhaps compounded by the belief that if religious figures utilized television as a means to accessibly engage with their audiences, then Americans

might be more inclined to skip out on more traditional avenues of engagement and encounter – such as attending their local church on Sundays. While the data don't suggest that this was the case, the fear that America was leaning toward "invisible" religious participation detached from public life would persist – particularly when traditional televangelists like Rex Humbard started drawing tens of millions of viewers. See Abelman and Neuendorf, "Themes and Topics." See also Krohn, "Language of Television Preachers," 51–3.

94 While Fulton Sheen was criticized for delivering a more individualistic faith than pre–Vatican I Catholics may have been expecting, he was not accused of equating wealth with happiness and spirituality the way Norman Vincent Peale did.

95 The prosperity gospel, also called prosperity theology, is the belief that God will grant the faithful financial abundance and good health, or contrarily that the accrual of material wealth is a sign of God's good fortunes. For a critical study addressing this topic, see Bowler, *Blessed*.

96 Sherwood, *Age of Extremes*, 5; 70.

97 A *Politico* piece from 2015 reports that Fred and Mary Trump were particularly attracted to Norman Vincent Peale's message and would attend the Marble Collegiate Church where he preached on Sundays. Donald himself had one of his weddings held there, and both his parents their funerals. Gwenda Blair, "How Norman Vincent Peale Taught Donald Trump to Worship Himself," *Politico*, 6 October 2015, www.politico.com/magazine/story/2015/10/donald-trump-2016-norman-vincent-peale-213220.

98 While commentators, especially those from the mainline churches, had many more issues with Graham's 1940s output than from the following decade, "the public heard enough factual blunders to sink lesser [pastors]." Wacker, *America's Bishop*, 26.

99 Whitfield and Bourguinon, "Billy Graham," 217.

100 Billy Graham was close to virtually every American president following Harry S. Truman, whose impression of the preacher never warmed up after a chilly first meeting. Wacker, "Billy Graham's America," 494.

101 It is worth mentioning that while Norman Vincent Peale was pastor at Marble Collegiate Church, a Reformed Church in America, a congregation lacking a formal institutionalized hierarchy and run instead by a council of elders, Sheen was a bishop at an institution that thrived – and continues to thrive – on hierarchy and the mysteries of the Eucharist.

102 Krohn, "Language of Television Preachers," 51.

103 Smith, *What Would Jesus Read?*, 140.

104 According to David Weinstein, one reviewer remorsefully described his issues with the sponsorship as follows: "*Life is Worth Living* was a half-hour oasis that afforded a pause and a moment for individual contemplation free from all the desperately urgent salesmanship so common on TV. It was an invitation to the

spiritual plane that allowed a personal re-examination of one's heart and mind. That experience is not something to be made to serve as a cue for a typical, hard-selling commercial." Quoted in Weinstein, *Forgotten Network*, 166.

105 Fulton Sheen's program was perhaps the only such public service broadcast of the time to have a major sponsor like Admiral, pointing to the experimental and yet to be fully understood nature of television's relationships between sponsor and program. Hadden, "Rise and Fall of American Televangelism," 117–18.

106 Bekkering, *American Televangelism*, 3.

107 Lest the corporation become more intrusive, he limited Admiral's direct pitching to two segments – once before the beginning of his lecture and again immediately following its conclusion. This had the effect of giving him an uninterrupted twenty-plus minutes for his lecture, letting his viewers focus on the message at hand and likely also satisfying his own perfectionist trends for controlling his program. Weinstein, *Forgotten Network*, 167.

108 As host of *Life Is Worth Living*, he was paid a salary by Admiral, the show's sponsor, of $10,000 per episode in 1952 and later $16,000 per episode in 1956 that he donated entirely to the SPOF. Noonan, *Missionary with a Mike*, 71.

109 This act of divine thievery did not go unnoticed in the wider press. Speaking to this phenomenon, an obituary in *The Tablet* commented on the competition between the two stars, with the author proudly observing that Fulton Sheen "attracted former devotees of the Milton Berle show." The choice of the word "devotee" here is of course interesting in that it points toward the ways in which fans can become fixated on television programs and the celebrities who host them – not unlike that of religious devotion. As such it also takes on the connotation of conversion, highlighting Sheen's prowess as an evangelist – a prowess that was able to attract the Jewish comedian Berle's viewership toward Sheen's own Catholic programming. *Tablet*, 13 December 1979, uncategorized box, Fulton Sheen Museum Archives, Peoria, Illinois.

110 As mentioned in chapter 1, Sheen barely discussed his celebrity and the activities that made him famous, skimming over his tenure as the host for *The Catholic Hour* and for *Life Is Worth Living*. While there were strategic reasons for omitting these elements from his late-life autobiography and focusing the reader's attention elsewhere, his similarly disparaging attitude toward celebrity can be traced much earlier in his career.

111 Sheen, *Treasure in Clay*, 12

112 Speaking in what would be considered a foreign language to American audiences was a means of putting up a barrier between Fulton Sheen the celebrity and the viewing audience, his fans, and in doing so distancing himself from the very fame of his being proclaimed by the people around him.

113 Reeves, *America's Bishop*, 370.

114 Noonan, *Passion of Fulton Sheen*, 54

115 Daniel Noonan states that Fulton Sheen personally requested this sort of lighting so that his eyes "would look like dark, glowing coals." Noonan, *Missionary with a Mike*, 81. See also Reeves, *America's Bishop*, 217.

116 Conniff, *Bishop Sheen Story*, 26. According to Thomas C. Reeves, Fulton Sheen eventually began to fear being seen in public with young actresses, after the husband of one saw the photos of them circulating in the press and accused him of having an affair with his wife. Reeves, *America's Bishop*, 137.

117 Conniff, *Bishop Sheen Story*, 28.

118 Conniff, *Bishop Sheen Story*, 28. One cannot help but notice the way his home is described here is very much the way his eyes often are.

119 Conniff, *Bishop Sheen Story*, 28.

120 For more on this, refer to my discussions in chapter 2.

121 Cantor, *Prime-Time Television*, 131.

122 Lynch, *Selling Catholicism*, 139.

123 Lynch, *Selling Catholicism*, 147.

124 Den Berg and ter Hoeven, "Madonna as Symbol of Reflexive Modernisation," 150.

125 Fulton Sheen's niece, Joan Sheen Cunningham, also once remarked that her uncle associated good looks with morality. Sheen himself appears to have said as much when he reportedly told fellow Catholic Loretta Young that "we dress for God, we are his representatives" Curiously, such comments seem to mirror certain Protestant social ethics and some elements of the early twentieth-century "muscular Christianity" movement, which equated the physical beauty of athletes with morality and godliness (of which we will discuss in more detail in chapter 5). That is not to say that Sheen was either directly or indirectly influenced by muscular Christianity, but rather that there are interesting parallels between religious celebrity and religious bodybuilding concerning the emphasis on the body. See Reeves, *America's Bishop*, 137, 272. For more on muscular Christianity, see Putney, *Muscular Christianity*.

126 Hall, "What Is This 'Black'?" 113.

127 Bacheci, "Our Icons," 167.

128 Sherwood, *Age of Extremes*, 4.

129 Smith, *What Would Jesus Read?*, 158.

130 Erin Smith cites this concept from Will Herberg. Smith, *What Would Jesus Read?*, 162. See also Patterson, "Cross or the Double-Cross," 49. The three elements of the melting pot refer to the Protestant, Catholic, and Jewish immigrants who together make up the nation.

131 In some cases, their messages also acted in contrast to those provided by learned members of society, such as psychiatrists. Smith, *What Would Jesus Read?*, 160.

132 Becker, "Televising Film Stardom in the 1950s," 17.

133 Of course, there are caveats to authenticity. In "Televising Film Stardom in the 1950s," Becker observes that "even television's claims to authenticity and the ordinary … could increasingly be recognized as constructed ideals" Becker, "Televising Film Stardom in the 1950s," 11. Celebrity historian Will Scheibel has made a similar observation, remarking how the "authenticity" of the celebrity is every bit as constructed as their fame. See Scheibel, "Marilyn Monroe," 12. It would seem that the normalcy and familiarity conveyed by television stars, while perhaps closer to their "real" selves or rather their private selves than what was the case with Hollywood celebrities, was nevertheless itself a performance, and perhaps one that followed them off screen into their own private lives.

134 In *Catholics and American Culture*, Mark S. Massa, for one, has argues that Fulton Sheen was in some part personally responsible for changing these norms and creating the demand itself.

135 Krohn, "Language of Television Preachers," 60.

136 Krohn, "Language of Television Preachers," 42.

137 While Fulton Sheen's choice to dress in full ceremonial regalia made him visually remarkable, he nevertheless chose to downplay the distinctiveness of Catholic doctrine in his messaging. One can certainly contrast these with his Protestant peers. Norman Vincent Peale and Billy Graham alike both dressed visually "normal" and familiar in two-piece flannel suits, and yet their respective messaging emphasized the distinctiveness of their teachings – with Peale on his pseudo–prosperity gospel and Graham with his revivalist crusades.

138 Massa, *Catholics and American Culture*, 86.

139 Weinstein, *Forgotten Network*, 168.

140 Lynch, *Selling Catholicism*, 7; Weinstein, *Forgotten Network*, 169.

141 Then-contemporary articles and proclamations about Fulton Sheen's wide-reaching and universal appeal consistently focused on his ability to reach audiences of other ecumenical backgrounds – and notably, Jews. One television critic remarked that Sheen "talked of life and philosophy and God, all pretty large subjects, with such charm and humor and assurance that many people, Catholic and Protestant and Jew alike, began listening to him." True, Sheen had among his supporters a number of Jewish voices: Saul Abraham – the manager of the Adelphi Theatre where *Life Is Worth Living* was filmed – was open about his praise for Sheen, as was Jewish magazine *The Tablet*, which ran a number of stories on him over the years, including a favourable obituary. However, media historian David Weinstein argues that "of the five religious television programs polled, *Life is Worth Living* … was [but] one of several programs that attracted viewers of all faiths," and, moreover, when the data were considered, the actual percentage of Sheen's extra-denominational viewers was likely never more than a minority among his audiences. Weinstein, *Forgotten Network*, 167.

142 David Weinstein makes a similar observation, arguing that "articles about Sheen's far-reaching appeal reflected a popular pride that Americans were becoming more religious and more tolerant." In other words, whether the far-reaching appeal was grounded in the data or not, Americans were nevertheless proud about the possibility of it being true. Weinstein, *Forgotten Network*, 167.

143 In the 1928 US presidential election, the Democratic Party chose four-term New York mayor Al Smith as their candidate. Smith, a Roman Catholic, came to be on the receiving end of massive and widespread anti-Catholic nativism and fearmongering that sank any chance he might had at winning the election. Smith and his presidential aspirations are discussed further in chapter 4.

144 As mentioned in the note above, to bring one example of the previous generation's inability to imagine a Catholic minority leading and uniting Americans of all stripes, one needs only look to the 1928 landslide defeat of Al Smith's presidential campaign.

## Chapter Four

1 As film critic Tim Brayton observes in a 2020 retrospective on the movie, the plot of *On the Waterfront* – with its emphasis on removing the stigma of testifying – in many ways mirrors the real-life decision of Elia Kazan to testify against his peers at the House Un-American Activities Committee. Tim Brayton, "On the Waterfront," *Alternate Ending*, 24 May 2020, www.alternateending.com/2020/05/on-the-waterfront-1954.html.

2 Allen Almachar, "An Appreciation – On the Waterfront," *Macguffin*, 5 December 2011, https://macguff.in/macguffin-spotlight/an-appreciation-on-the-waterfront/.

3 The hard-boiled genre emerged in the post–World War I era of changing social and political realities, further framed against the background of the Great Depression. The individualist protagonists of these stories were invariably men who defined themselves and their masculinity through opposition and competition, often embracing both stoicism and toughness. See *Nyman*, *Men Alone*, 41, 90.

4 Fulton Sheen won his Emmy for Most Outstanding Personality in 1953 and was nominated for the award a second time in 1954 (losing it to Jack Webb for his portrayal of Sgt Friday on *Dragnet*). Sheen would receive a third nod at the Emmy's in 1957 for Best Male Personality Continuing Performance, losing to Leonard Bernstein, who was then the director of the New York Philharmonic orchestra.

5 Within the Catholic Church, Monsignor is an honorific title dispensed by the Pope to individuals who have rendered invaluable services to the church. As a member of an inner church aristocracy, monsignors were allowed to wear

special dress and colours particular to their station. Sheen was made monsignor in 1934 by Pope Pius XI while he was a professor at the CUA in Washington, coinciding with his being selected as the speaker for the institution's 150th anniversary.

6 The changing depiction of priests in Hollywood can be witnessed in other films of the era. In Alfred Hitchcock's thriller *I Confess* (1953), Montgomery Clift plays Father Michael Logan, a World War II veteran who becomes a priest and finds himself embroiled in a murder mystery – with the climactic scene going so far as having the villain fire a pistol at him. Through the film, Logan embodies elements of hard masculinity while retaining his moral and spiritual edge. The pulpy *Edge of Doom* (1950) goes arguably further in its depiction of priests, having the disturbed Martin Lynn (played by Farley Granger) beat a priest to death with a crucifix after refusing to acknowledge the wrongs he had done to his father. The protagonist, Father Thomas Roth (played by Dana Andrews), then solves the mystery and confronts Lynn in the climactic scene, showing no fear and acting as his voice of conscience. Like *On the Waterfront*, both films employ priests as leading characters in hard-boiled crime dramas, as opposed to the softer "feel good" movies of the 1930s and 1940s.

7 For an insightful discussion on these films, and more details on their relationship with combating early twentieth-century nativism, see Shannon's *Bowery to Broadway*.

8 That was arguably the central thesis of his 1965 work, *American Catholicism*.

9 Dearinger, *Filth of Progress*, 29. For a slightly different tally, see O'Toole, *Faithful*, 97–8. Ryan Dearinger emphasizes that this wave of immigration didn't just cause famine and political unrest: the success of the generation who moved during the famine was also a motivating factor.

10 In 1840 there were seventeen dioceses in the country, a number that would jump to sixty by 1880. While Catholics made up the largest denomination, they were still considerably outnumbered by Protestants as a whole. O'Toole, *Faithful*, 101.

11 Indeed, since before the War of Independence, Catholics in America were viewed with suspicion by their Protestant neighbours. While the eighteenth and early nineteenth centuries saw legislation effectively banning their religious practice, the situation deteriorated further at the turn of the twentieth century, when militant nativist organizations – such as the Ku Klux Klan – gathered strength and numbers through anti-immigrant and notably anti-Catholic messaging. See Robert Curran, *Shaping American Catholicism*, 3–7; and Farrelly, *Papist Patriots*, 135. See also Baker, *Gospel According to the Klan*.

12 Haden, "Anti-Catholicism in U.S. History," 27. See also Baker, *Gospel According to the Klan*, 34–69.

13 Kyle E. Haden writes that through much of American history, widespread social and political paranoia rooted itself in the belief that "foreign nations

were … sending subservices under the pretense of legitimate immigration." Haden, "Anti-Catholicism in U.S. History," 28.

14 McGreevy, *Catholicism and American Freedom*, 176.

15 English colonization was cemented into the nation's foreign policy during the sixteenth century under the Tudor monarchy. Historian Nicholas P. Canny remarks that the English colonists were not only "hypercritical" of Catholicism on the island, but that Irish culture – and particularly Irish Catholic culture – was deemed to be so brutish that they were essentially infidel barbarians in need of utter civilizing and subjugation. Canny, "Ideology of English Colonization."

16 See Dearinger, *Filth of Progress*, 29.

17 Kelleher, "Class and Irish Catholic Masculinity," 11–12.

18 Irish Catholics were largely responsible for handling the toughest, most gruelling, and lowest-wage positions, positions that literally laid the foundations for America's future. While native-born workers were increasingly becoming mythologized and romanticized as noble artisans, the contributions of the Irish were largely undervalued. Dearinger, *Filth of Progress*, 16–17.

19 Dowd, *Irish and the Origins*, 11.

20 Ryan Dearinger remarks that one major impediment to Irish Catholic acceptance, apart from their religion, was that "though visibly white in the social category of color, Irish immigrants were depicted as nonwhite in the nation's dominant racial system." It was only at the end of the nineteenth century – when African American freedmen migrated to the Northern industrial states en masse – when attitudes toward the Irish by their peers began to shift. In other words, as anxiety surrounding the blackness of freedmen heightened, the social currency attached to having any sort of European identity – even an Irish one – began to grow. See Dearinger, *Filth of Progress*, 76; Dowd, *Irish and the Origins*, 21. For more on the topic of the Irish, race, and "whiteness," see Ignatiev, *How the Irish Became White*; and Roediger, *Wages of Whiteness*.

21 That is not to say that Al Smith's only fault was his religion, as it would have been an uphill battle nationally against his opponent Herbert Hoover. For an in-depth, if dated, study of the bigotry Smith's campaign generated see Moore, *Catholic Runs for President*. See also Goldway, *Machine Made*.

22 After critic Charles Marshall published an open letter declaring that several of Pope Leo XIII's encyclicals made it clear that no Catholic could ever be fit to become president of the United States, Al Smith is popularly reported to have said "What the hell is an encyclical?" See Shelley, "'What the Hell Is an Encyclical?,'" 88. See also McGreevy, *Catholicism and American Freedom*, 149.

23 Shannon, *Bowery to Broadway*, xxvi.

24 Shannon, xii.

25 Shannon, xxxi.

26 The Know Nothings were members of a nativist political movement that existed for roughly twenty years in the mid-nineteenth century. It was largely anti-Catholic, anti-Irish, and anti-immigration, finding its membership among those who traced or claimed descent from the earlier British colonists and settlers. They were propagators of the "fifth column" conspiracy that suggested all Roman Catholics, owing to their religious allegiance to Rome, were also politically aligned with the foreign power, rather than with America. McGreevy, *Catholicism and American Freedom*, 148.

27 Thomas Edison's use and control of patents was notorious, and "Hollywood was the ideal place to produce movies since filmmakers couldn't be sued there for infringing on motion picture patents." See "Hollywood," *History*, 21 August 2018, www.history.com/topics/roaring-twenties/hollywood.

28 It should be noted that certain scholars disagree with the idea that Hollywood was the predominant force in shaping American visual culture. Regarding the representation of masculinity in American visual culture specifically, John Beynon suggests that the influence of films must be placed alongside the influence of television, advertising, and pop music. In other words, Beynon argues that the visual culture surrounding masculinity was constructed by this larger aggregate, and that film did not play a disproportionally larger role. See Beynon, *Masculinities and Culture*, 63–5.

29 To name a few: women such as Helen Kane, Helen Hayes, and Maureen O'Sullivan gave highly acclaimed performances, while American-born Irish men such as James Cagney, Spencer Tracy, and Pat O'Brien became prominent leading men in some of the highest grossing pictures of the early decades of American cinema.

30 While largely lost save for a few preserved clips, *The Callahans and the Murphys* was widely seen at the time of its release to have been catering to negative and stereotypical portrayals of the Irish as being rowdy and uncivilized. Irish magazines in America such as the *Gaelic American* received thousands of letters decrying the film. See Rhodes, "Irish-American Film Audience." Commenting on the prominence of Irish actors in more positive films from early Hollywood, film historian Kevin Brownlow remarks that even as far back as the silent picture era, the common Hollywood stereotype that the "Jews ran the business, [and] the Irish made the pictures" wasn't far from the reality. He also remarks that during the first few decades of the twentieth century, Irish prominence in American films was ironic given that Ireland had "no film industry" of its own worthy of mention. Brownlow, "When the Irish Ruled Hollywood," 97.

31 Rhodes, "Irish-American Film Audience," 70.

32 See Dowd, *Irish and the Origins*, 120. Christopher Shannon argues that the Irish American characters and actors who portrayed them called attention to both their differences and similarities, becoming both recognizably American

and subtly other – with priests as the most visible and recognizable symbol of their difference and shared values. See Shannon, *Bowery to Broadway*, xxxiv; see also Fisher, *On the Irish Waterfront*, ix.

33 See Doherty's, *Pre-Code Hollywood*, 9; and Doherty, *Hollywood's Censor*, 11–14.

34 The voluntary and unenforceable nature of the pre-code era of Hollywood can be directly contrasted with the post-code era. Pre-code movies were largely informed by depression era consumer habits, in large part catering to the masses of unemployed men seeking entertainment. As such, they toyed with riskier depictions of sexual themes and notably women's bodies. While studios were generally unafraid of showing slightly more on screen than might otherwise be permissible in American society (such as a woman's exposed legs in stockings), advertisements such as posters or trailers emphasized or hinted at lewder themes than might have been present in the films. See Doherty, *Pre-Code Hollywood*, 1999.

35 Fisher, *On the Irish Waterfront*, x.

36 Michael Curtiz, dir. (1938: Warner Bros.). The real-life Father Flanagan's decision to focus on wayward youth was likely less dramatic but more pragmatic. According to one story, after working with the poor among his Omaha parish, he apparently chose to focus his attention on uplifting the area's youth to prevent them from following the same path as adults. It is also likely that Flanagan saw opportunity in the lack of available housing and resources for youth. See "Mercy! Mercy!," *Time*, 7 December 1931, accessed 1 January 2025, https://web.archive.org/web/20081215023207/http://www.time.com/time/magazine/article/0,9171,930396,00.html.

37 See Haden, "Anti-Catholicism in U.S. History," 28.

38 Shannon, *Bowery to Broadway*, 119.

39 Rotundo, *American Manhood*, 201. See also Pehl, "Remaking of the Catholic Working Class," 39.

40 Dearinger, *Filth of Progress*, 75. See also Meyer, *Manhood on The Line*, 1–5; Shannon, *Bowery to Broadway* 29.

41 Ryan Dearinger observes an irony in the stereotypes surrounding the apparent propensity to drink among the Irish, noting that many of the same people promoting these stereotypes were also involved in ensuring their working men never had want for alcohol. It wasn't uncommon for labourers to find part of their wages paid in rations of alcohol or even to have foremen supply their workers with a daily stipend of alcohol to both raise morale and push the men to work harder, and often more dangerously, than otherwise. See Dearinger, *Filth of Progress*, 66–74.

42 Besnier and Brownell, "Sport, Modernity, and the Body," 449. See also Dearinger, *Filth of Progress*, 77; Meyer, *Manhood on the Line*, 199.

43 Shannon, *Bowery to Broadway*, 24. One prominent real-life example of a Catholic leader embracing sports, and boxing in particular, was Chicago's

Auxiliary Bishop Bernard Sheil who founded the Catholic Youth Organization in 1930 that emphasized participation in sports and athleticism as a means to combat secular temptations in the city. Among the many activities they promoted, boxing attracted the most attention from working-class youth in the urban centre and elsewhere. For more on Sheil, see Neary, *Crossing Parish Boundaries*.

44 John Beynon echoes this sentiment, commenting on the sexual and racial nature of boxing as a pastime: victory emphasizes not just the physical superiority of the fighter but also of the entire nation from which he sprang. Beynon, *Masculinities and Culture*, 46. See also Kelleher, "Class and Irish Catholic Masculinity," 26; Dowd, *Irish and the Origins*, 47.

45 Niko Besnier and Susan Brownell observe how particularly in migrant or transnational communities, local athletes become the embodiment of the pride of those same communities. Besnier and Brownell, "Sport, Modernity, and the Body," 453. Pierre Bourdieu also refers to boxing as a bodily expression of the working class through sport. See Bourdieu, "How Can One Be a Sports Fan."

46 Dowd, *Irish and the Origins*, 46.

47 Kelleher, "Class and Irish Catholic Masculinity," 29. It is worth remarking, however, that Catholic men's identities and "spaces" are not necessarily as clear-cut as Christopher Dowd and Patricia Kelleher seem to be suggesting. *Lifeblood of the Parish*, by religious studies scholar Alyssa Maldonado-Estrada, helps showcase the complexity of Catholic male spaces owing to their devotional lives. She remarks that while often overlooked, churches and devotional communities are no less "male spaces" than stadiums or boxing rings, owing to the capacity for men to enact "manly" patterns of behaviour there, including lending their labour, artisanal skills, and so forth.

48 Dowd, *Irish and the Origins*, 17; Maldonado-Estrada, *Lifeblood of the Parish*, 9–13.

49 Kelleher, "Class and Irish Catholic Masculinity," 23.

50 Irish studies scholars Rebecca Anne Barr, Sean Brady, and Jane McGaughey remark in the introduction to their edited collection *Ireland and Masculinities in History* (2019), that Irish masculinities were religiously oriented and "inflected [with] social conservatism." Barr, Brady and McGaughey, "Ireland and Masculinities in History," 4.

51 Nugent, "Sword and the Prayerbook," 597.

52 Nugent, "Sword and the Prayerbook," 592, 609.

53 Rotundo, *American Manhood*, 5.

54 Beynon, *Masculinities and Culture*, 56.

55 Shannon, *Bowery to Broadway*, 109.

56 While this message was implicit in the film, it hasn't gone unnoticed by reviewers and Catholic commentators. E.g., a piece from Catholic publication *Word on Fire* discussing a recent Father Flanagan documentary discussed the

impact of the film *Boys Town* and the centrality of this theme in the film. Thomas Salerno, "'Heart of a Servant' Shows Us a Saint for Our Time," *Word On Fire*, 1 October 2024, www.wordonfire.org/articles/heart-of-a-servant-shows-us-a-saint-for-our-time/.

57 Jospeh Nugent remarks that in the early twentieth century Irish Catholic priests ceased emphasizing the earlier superhuman and martial models of ideal masculinity, replacing them with an emphasis on the bodies of priests as ordinary people capable of ordinary acts of sanctity, effectively suggesting that the most positive role model for the young weren't figures from the distant past, but those in their immediate, everyday life. Nugent, "Sword and the Prayerbook," 609.

58 "Mercy! Mercy!," *Time*, 7 December 1931, accessed 1 January 2025, web.archive.org/web/20081215023207/http://www.time.com/time/magazine/article/0,9171,930396,00.html.

59 John Fay, "On This Day: The Founder of Boys Town Father Flanagan Passed Away," *Irish Central*, 15 May 2024, www.irishcentral.com/roots/history/father-flanagan-boys-town-founder.

60 Michael Curtiz, dir., *Angels with Dirty Faces* (1938: Warner Bros).

61 As John McGreevy notes, until the 1950s, Catholics primarily associated their sense of self with their parish neighbourhood, a situation made more pronounced by the catastrophic economic conditions of the 1920s that led many communities to turn inward into ethnic enclaves and stasis. See McGreevy, *Parish Boundaries*, especially chapter 4.

62 Nyman, *Men Alone*, 90.

63 Shannon, *From Bowery to Broadway*, 19.

64 Perhaps unsurprisingly, proponents of Pat O'Brien seem to have felt the same way about the kinds of roles he played in Hollywood. During a tribute to his storied career when he was named man of the year by the Catholic Actors Guild in 1973, the tribute highlighted how numerous roles of his involved O'Brien portraying "great Americans," and then listed Catholic characters he played as examples of this, among them several of his roles as priests. See C. Gerald Fraser, "Pat O'Brien, Movies' All-American, Is Dead," *New York Times*, 16 October 1983, www.nytimes.com/1983/10/16/obituaries/pat-obrien-movies-allam, accessed 4 January 2025. Curiously, the headline of this obituary in the *New York Times* felt the need to highlight that the man who built a career out of playing Catholic characters on screen was in fact "All-American."

65 Leo McCary, dir. *Going My Way* (1944: Paramount).

66 Though Father O'Malley disappears at the film's end, he nevertheless returned the following year in the sequel to the film, titled *The Bells of St. Mary's*, which sees the character attempt to save a inner-city school in his parish that's about to be shut down.

67 Shafer, "From Crooner to American Icon," 131.
68 See Kurt Jensen, "New Bing Crosby Bio Paints Picture of Crooner and His Priest Alter-Ego," *America*, 26 October 2018, www.americamagazine.org/faith/2018/10/26/new-bing-crosby-bio-paints-picture-crooner-and-his-priest-alter-ego.
69 The box office tracking website *The Numbers* lists the total theatrical run of the film at just over $16,000, 000 in 1944. Adjusted for inflation, as of this writing, it amounts to roughly $280,000,000. See "Going My Way (1944)," The Numbers, www.the-numbers.com/movie/Going-My-Way#tab=summary, accessed 6 January 2025.
70 To give one example, when Bing Crosby was considering divorcing his wife due to her alcoholism, he approached Francis Spellman for advice and support. The cardinal's response was blunt, stating that "Bing, you are Father O'Malley and under no circumstances can Father O'Malley get a divorce." Giddins, *Bing Crosby*, chapter 24.
71 Leo McCary, dir. *Going My Way* (1944: Paramount).
72 Leo McCary, dir. *Going My Way* (1944: Paramount).
73 Catholic comics from the 1940s and 1950s frequently featured parish priests as protagonists or mentor figures in sometimes adventurous stories aimed at teenage readers. For a brief overview of Catholic comic books, see Joel Fernandez, "A Brief History of Catholic Comic Books," *Damn Catholic*, 21 October 2019, https://damncatholic.com /2019/10/21/a-brief-history-of-catholic-comic-books/.
74 Of the apparent danger of secular comics, Robert Orsi quotes Jesuit scholar Robert Southard's remarks about comic book superheroes representing "a kind of duplicate of the Christian ideal [but] with pagan overtones." Orsi, *History and Presence*, 157. As discussed in chapter 2, Fulton Sheen himself was also the subject of a children's colouring book that emphasized his connection to the land and his capacity for manual (and manly) labour.
75 See Holt, "Between Warrior and Priest."
76 While this season would be Fulton Sheen's last on the DuMont Network – which had been in financial trouble for some years, owing in part to poor business decisions and bad luck – it would continue on for three more seasons after being picked up by ABC shortly following the dissolution of DuMont.
77 See, e.g., his comment referenced in chapter 3 about how "there are not one hundred people in the United States who hate the Catholic Church, but there are millions who hate what they wrongly perceive the Catholic Church to be." *Life Is Worth Living*, "Signs of Our Times."
78 One notable televised appearance of Fulton Sheen without his regalia was his appearance on *What's My Line?*, as discussed in chapter 3.
79 *Life Is Worth Living*, "Signs of our Times."

80 *Life Is Worth Living*, "Training of Children."
81 *Life Is Worth Living*, "Three Greatest Confessions in History."
82 As referred to in the previous chapter, Sheen's "Uncle Fultie" nickname can be read as more than just a play on words with Milton Berle's similar "Uncle Miltie" nickname – it demonstrates the extent to which he was effective in endearing himself to audiences as a safe wholesome figure and family-viewing choice.
83 Doherty, *Cold War*, 153.
84 Doherty, *Cold War*, 153–4.
85 James Martin, S.J., "Fr Corridan: Karl Malden's 'Waterfront' Inspiration," *America*, 1 July 2009, www.americamagazine.org/content/all-things/fr-corridan-karl-maldens-waterfront-inspiration.
86 Nyman, *Men Alone*, 33.
87 Chicago-born Karl Malden was of Serbian and Czech ancestry. For the line quoted, see Elia Kazan, dir., *On the Waterfront* (1954: Horizon Pictures).
88 Kazan, dir., *On the Waterfront.*
89 Kazan, dir., *On the Waterfront.*
90 Nyman, *Men Alone*, 35.
91 Kazan, dir., *On the Waterfront.*
92 Kazan, dir., *On the Waterfront.*
93 Martin, "Fr Corridan."
94 Much has been written about how transformative World War II was in reshaping America's ethnic and religious landscape, pushing it from one of division toward one where unity was possible. For examples of studies examining this current, the trends that made it possible, and those who pushed for it, see A. Bruscino, *Nation Forged in War*; and Fleegler, "'Forget All Differences.'"
95 Martin, "Fr Corridan."
96 Rotten Tomatoes Classic Trailers, "On the Waterfront (154) Trailer #1 | Movieclips Classic Trailers,", YouTube video, 2;32, accessed 16 January 2025, www.youtube.com/watch?v=vOdYAXOfLMc.
97 See Roger Ebert, "On the Waterfront," RogerEbert.com, 21 March 1999, www.rogerebert.com/reviews/great-movie-on-the-waterfront-1954, accessed 4 January 2025. For a review highlighting and discussing the film's perceived realism, see London Film Critic, "On the Waterfront Review: 'Self-Assured Realism' - Archive, 1954," *Guardian*, 11 September 1954, www.theguardian.com/film/article/2024/sep/11/on-the-waterfront-review-self-assured-realism-brando-1954.
98 Martin, "Fr Corridan."
99 Giddins, *Bing Crosby*, chapter 24.
100 Giddins, *Bing Crosby*, chapter 24.
101 Doherty, *Cold War*, 153.
102 Shannon, *Bowery to Broadway*, 120.
103 Dowd, *Irish and the Origins*, 2.

104 Dowd, *Irish and the Origins*, 13.
105 Some scholars also point to the widespread Irish American participation in the military forces in World War II as a final test of their "Americanness." A similar thing occurred for post-Famine immigrants who were swiftly encouraged to join the Union army during the Civil War. See Mosse, *Image of Man*.
106 Shannon, *Bowery to Broadway*, xxxi.

## Chapter Five

1 Not to be confused with *The Bishop Sheen Story* (1953) by C.G. Conniff, which was published by Fawcett as a stand-alone magazine at the height of his popularity. Francis Sugrue, "The Bishop Sheen Story: Part Five" *New York Herald Tribune*, 1959, News Clippings, 1950–59, Catholic University of American Archives, Washington, DC.
2 Though based in New York City at the time of the article, Fulton Sheen had previously resided in Washington, DC, where he taught at the CUA from 1927 to 1950.
3 Sugrue, "Bishop Sheen Story."
4 The concept of "crisis" is discussed later in this chapter.
5 Bavel and Reher, "Baby Boom," 264–5.
6 Advertising in the 1950s frequently emphasized the outdoors as man's domain, while also refiguring certain household tasks – i.e., those that involved tools and hard work – as being suitably manly responsibilities around the house. Moss, *Media*, 30.
7 For a scholarly discussion of David Reisman's and Sloan Wilson's work, see Gilbert, *Men in the Middle*; for Arthur Schlesinger's and William Whyte's work, see Cuordileone, "Age of Anxiety." It is perhaps ironic that while men in the 1950s and 1960s saw the immediate postwar decade as one of decay and estrangement from masculinity, Robert Bly of the later mythopoetic men's movement saw it in quite the opposite vein, writing "the Fifties male had a clear vision of what a man was … each liked football, [was] aggressive, [could] stick up for the United States, never [cried]." This perhaps goes to show the cyclical and often contradictory nature of men's anxieties. Bly, *Iron John*, 1–2.
8 Numerous scholars have noted this perceived trend and society's reaction toward it, among them, Cuordileone, "Age of Anxiety"; Friedman, "Smearing of Joe McCarthy"; Rausch, "'All Man, All Priest'"; and Tunc, "'Mad Men' of Nutrition."
9 Jeffords, *Hard Bodies*, 25.
10 See Connell, *Masculinities*.
11 Susan Jeffords argues that in this binary system, soft men were understood to lack the gall needed to make the right and often difficult decisions for the good

of the nation while hard men were able to stand up to and withstand such adversity. See Jeffords, *Hard Bodies*, 38–52. Tanfer Emin Tunc also comments on how the popular and political culture of the 1950s linked hardness with patriotism and the strength of national institutions. Tunc, "'Mad Men' of Nutrition," 190–2.

12 There do exist certain caveats when discussing the crisis of masculinity of the 1950s. In reviewing then-contemporary literature, scholar James Gilbert argues that talk of crisis is "so pervasive and convincing" that historians may be inclined to take the term at face value, a move which risks allowing the narrative of crisis to obscure the fact that men during this period had a diversity of lived experiences. Additionally, while some men may well have felt their masculinity to be in crisis, an equal number carried on without experiencing anxiety at all. See Gilbert, *Men in the Middle*, 11, 1. Historian Marko Dumančić comments on this diversity, noting how crisis literature inevitably focuses on the experiences of white, Anglo-Saxon, and heterosexual men while overshadowing and silencing men of colour, gay men, and others who fall outside the normative assumptions about race and sexuality. Dumančić, "Hidden in Plain Sight," 1–11.

13 It is worth noting that this was not the first perceived crisis of masculinity of which history, or even America, was to endure. This idea was first postulated by Michael S. Kimmel, in1987, when he articulated two disparate historical contexts (late seventeenth-century England and late nineteenth-century America) as having both experienced apparent moments of male crisis, each of which coincided with times of social change and women's upward social mobility. See Kimmel, "Contemporary 'Crisis,'" 121–54. Considering this cyclical pattern of repetition, cultural studies scholars Kathleen Starck and Russel Luyt also question the usefulness of the term "crisis" in scholarly works. Bearing this in mind, male-specific anxieties appear to be deeply rooted in the male experience of their own bodies, gender, and sexuality in contrast to femininity and otherness in any given historical context.

14 The longer-lasting and more military-focused successor to the Truman Doctrine, NATO would be signed into existence in 1949 by America along with thirty other nations. See Merrill, "Truman Doctrine"; and McNamara "McCarthy and McCarthyism."

15 Though principally economic in its clauses, the Marshall Plan was also ideologically driven, as American financial backing encouraged closer ties with the regimes of Western Europe while limiting potential Soviet influence. See Hogan, *Marshall Plan*; and Milward, *Reconstruction of Western Europe*.

16 See "President's Council on Sports, Fitness & Nutrition," OASH Office of Disease Prevention and Health Promotion," accessed 9 March 2025, www.hhs.gov/fitness/about-pcsfn/our-history/index.html (defunct).

17 Hunt, "American Sport," 274; Cuordileone, "Age of Anxiety," 527–8.
18 Rausch, "'All Man, All Priest,'" 63.
19 The program would eventually coalesce into the Presidential Youth Testing Program. See "President's Council on Sports, Fitness & Nutrition."
20 Anxieties surrounding the bodies of boys and the young men who would one day grow into the nation's able-bodied men can be found in literature immediately following the conclusion of World War II. One notable book lamenting the loss of vigour in the nation and connecting physical and moral patriotism was Catholic ex-marine John Cross's *Let's Take the Hard Road.*
21 Hunt, "American Sport Policy," 274.
22 The Soviets were invited to attend the 1948 Olympics, despite some protest from the United States. Nevertheless, they declined to send any athletes, opting instead to send observers and prepare for the coming Games in Helsinki. Even then, the chair of the Soviet Sports Committee, Nikolai Romanov, was initially hesitant about sending athletes to the event as he equated sporting competitions with "bourgeois" excess and dangerous capitalist influences. Stalin, however, pushed his minister, all but accusing him of "cowardice" and unmanly behaviour. Stalin saw the Olympics as an opportunity to showcase the vigour of Soviet athletes, and, by extension, the vitality of their nation. The Soviets therefore approached each successive Olympics – along with any other international athletic competition – with the sole intention of winning as many events as possible. This marked a notable shift in Soviet ideology concerning sports, as, in the early post-revolutionary years, what was emphasized was *fitzkultura* – athleticism framed as a benign and non-competitive way to benefit the health of its citizens internally. See Coates, "Weaponization of Sports"; and Emiliantseva, "Russian Sport."
23 Coates, "Weaponization of Sports," 219.
24 Emiliantseva, "Russian Sport," 363–4.
25 Jeffords, *Hard Bodies*, 6.
26 Facing a fresh wave of anti-Catholic propaganda during his presidential bid, John F. Kennedy, too, flexed his own hardness when he famously declared "I am not the Catholic candidate for president. I am the Democratic Party's candidate for president, who happens to be a Catholic." For a more detailed discussion of his run and the implications of his Catholicism, see Casey, *Making of a Catholic President*; and Dawidowicz, "Religion in the 1960 Presidential Campaign." See also Matusow, *Joseph R. McCarthy*, 107.
27 John F. Kennedy, "The Soft American," *Sports Illustrated*, 26 December 1960; "Council on Youth Fitness: 'The Soft American,' John F. Kennedy Presidential Library and Museum, Boston, Massachusetts, accessed 18 January 2025, www.jfklibrary.org/asset-viewer/archives/jfkpof-094-003.
28 Tunc, "'Mad Men' of Nutrition," 190.

29 While the definition of "hard masculinity" I will be employing in this chapter is largely in accordance with Jefford's, it is worth stating that the imperative of hardness has been variously theorized and understood by both scholars and the public. See, for instance, Lafrance, "Building a Body, Building a Life," 348.
30 R. Brannon, "Male Sex Role," 12.
31 See Cross, *Let's Take the Hard Road*, 57–84; 117–38; 147–59.
32 See Connell, "Hegemonic Masculinity and Emphasized Femininity"; Connell, *Masculinities*; and Connell and Messerschmidt, "Hegemonic Masculinity: Rethinking the Concept."
33 Connell, *Masculinities*, 75.
34 See Rotundo, *American Manhood*; Meyer, *Manhood on The Line*. As scholar Hoon Choi remarks, hegemonic sentiments have a tendency to grow during times of perceived national turmoil and when there is a strong impression that a nation and its ideologies are under attack. Though Choi's research deals with hegemonic and military masculinity in 1950s South Korea, his observation that citizens seek a stronger nation through stronger bodies would appear to ring true in the American context as well. Choi "Brothers in Arms and Brothers in Christ."
35 Besnier and Brownell, "Sport, Modernity, and the Body," 446.
36 Putney, *Muscular Christianity*, 1. See also McGrath, *Christianity's Dangerous Idea*, 368.
37 Putney, *Muscular Christianity*, 5.
38 Besnier and Brownell, "Sport, Modernity, and the Body," 447; McGrath, *Christianity's Dangerous Idea*.
39 Theodore Roosevelt is perhaps the most emblematic of America's muscular Christianity, proving himself through a love of boxing and big game hunting, doing everything he could to contrast himself with the asthmatic, sickly child he had once been. That he would become president further reified this posture to wider America. See Putney, *Muscular Christianity*, 26.
40 Du Mez, *Jesus and John Wayne*, 10.
41 Du Mez, *Jesus and John Wayne*, 11. In a curious twist on the Protestant adoration of the figure, John Wayne converted to Catholicism shortly before his death.
42 Wacker, *America's Pastor*, 82–4.
43 Wacker, *America's Pastor*, 86.
44 See Kelleher, "Class and Irish Catholic Masculinity"; and Dearinger, *Filth of Progress*.
45 See Nugent, "Sword and the Prayer Book."
46 Scholar Ulrike Stasser remarks that "biological reproduction and fatherhood [have] long been mainstays for men in the secular world … Catholics asserted the superiority of chastity to marriage by insisting on the sexual purity of

priests … this uncompromising emphasis on purity, more than ever cast Catholic clerics as unlike other men." Strasser, *German Jesuits*, 57. For a deeper discussion of the earlier medieval response of these questions about clerical masculinity, see Andrew Holt, "Between Warrior and Priest." See also Karras, *From Boys to Men*.

47 See Maldonado-Estrada, *Lifeblood of the Parish*.

48 McGrath, *Christianity's Dangerous Idea*, 371.

49 Tomothy Neary suggests that one of Bernard Sheil's personal heroes and inspirations was none other than the "muscular" early twentieth-century Protestant preacher Billy Sunday. Neary, *Crossing Parish Boundaries*, 77–8.

50 Neary, *Crossing Parish Boundaries*, 9.

51 Neary, 71–2.

52 Neary, 78.

53 Papal encyclicals dating back to 1848 declared communism to be atheistic, materialistic, and evil, and American Catholics had enthusiastically embraced anti-communism since the 1930s as a way to point their loyalty to the larger institutions of the church. Notably, Pius XI strongly warned against communism in *Quadrageimo anno* in 1931 and later denounced it outright in *Divini Redemptoris* in 1937.

54 Rausch, "'All Man, All Priest,'" 62.

55 As John Seitz remarks, scenes of preaching during wartime "could offer reassurance that US fighting men had not grown deaf to the elevating word of God." Seitz, "Altars of Ammo," 414.

56 McNamara, "Russia, Rome, and Recognition," 87.

57 McNamara, 75–6.

58 Seitz, "Mass-Clock," 927.

59 See McNamara, "Russia, Rome, and Recognition"; NcMamara, "'Argument of Strength,'" especially 71–2.

60 According to a largely anecdotal story from journalist Drew Pearson, Edmund Walsh apparently approached Joseph McCarthy at a celebrity dinner in the early 1950s and appointed him as the man who could make anti-communism the mainstay of his political career. Though Walsh challenged Pearson to prove his story, he steadfastly refused to ever address any questions concerning his relationship and influence with McCarthy, leading McNamara to remark that his silence on the topic led many to believe it to be true. McNamara, "McCarthy and McCarthyism," 85–8.

61 Joseph McCarthy was one of several guests invited to speak at the dinner, and of those was likely the least well known at the time. As few papers expected anything memorable to come from the event, there was but a single reporter from the Associated Press in attendance. See Berinsky and Lenz, "Red Scare?"; and Kercher, "Joseph McCarthy," 27.

62 Matusow, *Joseph R. McCarthy*, 1. Additionally, scholar Anthony Lewis argues that McCarthy's political power and influence was so great that Eisenhower was held virtually captive by his posturing and, despite the president's dislike for the senator, was unable to intervene so long as his position was secure. Glazer et al., "'Have You No Sense of Decency?,'" 25.

63 Joseph McCarthy's fiery persona had already been well established by Republican Party insiders due to his previous stint as a judge of the Wisconsin tenth circuit. It has been suggested that in their haste to mollify him and keep him out of the limelight, his party had sought to put him in charge of an unassuming committee, and that initially the Senate Committee on Government Operations seemed the most likely to do. See Matusow, *Joseph R. McCarthy*.

64 That his charges were likely trumped up mattered little as "many prominent politicians at the time knew McCarthy had fabricated his explosive allegations, they feared him and failed to stand up to him … many cowed in silence." However, in 1952, aging Democratic Senator Herbert Lehman of New York demanded to see the evidence for McCarthy's claims of widespread communist infiltration, only to have McCarthy loudly retort, "Go back to your seat old man." Berinsky and Lenz, "Red Scare?," 372, 388.

65 Joseph McCarthy also went so far as to equate sexual suspicion with political suspicion, arguing that just as soft-bodied men were more susceptible to communism, so, too, were they susceptible to homosexual tendencies. While not the first to do so, as the current linking softness with unmanliness was already current – with the logical extension that homosexuality was demasculinization at its fullest extent. Ironically, when journalists such as Edward R. Murrow and Drew Pearson were able to highlight cracks in McCarthy's life and entourage, by raising suspicions about his bachelorhood and the seemingly homoerotic relationship between his associates Roy Cohn and Gerard Schine that he was unable to defend, it suggested to audiences that McCarthy was perhaps not quite as hard as he seemed, and, and more importantly, that if he wasn't, then perhaps he wasn't the hard-bodied man needed to defend the nation. Cuordileone, "Age of Anxiety," 520. See also Friedman, "Smearing of Joe McCarthy."

66 Matusow, *Joseph R. McCarthy*, 110, 46.

67 Matusow, 37; 45, 48.

68 Andrea Friedman remarks that parallel to the Red Scare was also the often overlooked "Lavender Scare" that saw the vilification of men who had sex with men, and anyone suspected of non-normative sexuality. Friedman, "Smearing of Joe McCarthy," 1109.

69 Crosby, "Catholic Bishops and Senator Joseph McCarthy," 138.

70 Doherty, *Cold War, Cool Medium*, 13.

71 Matusow, *Joseph R. McCarthy*, 111, 113.

72 Friedman, "Smearing of Joe McCarthy," 1109. It has been suggested that McCarthy's drinking and eating habits greatly contributed to his early death in 1957 at the age of forty-eight.

73 Friedman, "Smearing of Joe McCarthy," 1108.

74 Matusow points out that Joseph McCarthy seemed to genuinely believe that communism, as a sort of cosmic force, was out to get him – that the press, government agents, everyone were working together and singing praises of committees that moved against him, and by that association, against the interest of America. Matusow, *Joseph R. McCarthy*, 100–1.

75 Bernard J. Sheil, Auxiliary Bishop of Chicago, was one prominent anti-communist and hard-bodied Catholic who saw the conflict with communism being primarily rooted in morality – something which he felt had gotten overlooked in the wider conflict. Though he was also a proponent of "tough" activities, himself an avid promoter of boxing, he had little love for the brash senator from Wisconsin. Crosby, "Catholic Bishops and Senator Joseph McCarthy," 140 1.

76 Oshinsky, *Conspiracy so Immense*, 11.

77 Helen William, "Never Sound Retreat!," *Catholic World* 176 (Nov. 1952): 88–9, quoted and abridged in Genzel, "Pride, Wrath, Glee, and Fear," 38.

78 *Time*, 22 October 1951, 22, quoted and abridged in Genzel, "Pride, Wrath, Glee, and Fear," 37.

79 Joseph McCarthy' spiritual hardness wasn't lost on his Catholic supporters. Despite his crude tactics, he was widely seen among Catholic conservatives as a "defender of the faith." Genzel, "Pride, Wrath, Glee, and Fear," 28.

80 Italics mine. US Congress, Senate, Congressional Record, 81st Cong., 2d sess., 1950, 96, referenced in Matusow, *Joseph R. McCarthy*, 20.

81 McCarthy further embraced the persona of the Cold Warrior, claiming (quite falsely) to have flown dozens of dangerous volunteer combat missions during World War II where he acquired for himself the nickname "Tail Gunner Joe." Rather than having true, bona fide credentials as a hardened man, the more important thing, it would seem, was the perception of having them. His claims would eventually be revealed as utter fabrication as, in reality, he worked behind a desk during the war and the only times he found himself in the air was during training runs in friendly airspace. James T. Keane and Jim McDermott, "Cold Warrior: America's Battle Against Joe McCarthy," *America*, 9 February 2009, www.americamagazine.org/politics-society/2009/02/09/cold-warrior-americas-battle-against-joe-mccarthy.

82 I should note that this is not to suggest that Fulton Sheen and Jospeh McCarthy ever colluded, or, for that matter, even saw eye to eye. It was

once erroneously believed that Bishop Sheen had approved and sided with McCarthy's public discourse, however the historical record reveals a substantial divide between the two men. While Sheen was notoriously tight-lipped about the senator, he was once quoted as having dismissed McCarthy's campaigns owing to the fact that McCarthy was "not an authority on communism in any case." See Crosby, "Catholic Bishops and Senator Joseph McCarthy," 132; see also Patterson, "Cross or the Double-Cross."

83 A similar sentiment would be echoed by Donald F. Crosby, who referred to Fulton Sheen as the nation's foremost "prophet and philosopher" where anti-communism was concerned. See Crosby, *God, Church, and Flag*, 1; see also Noonan, *Missionary with a Mike*, 15–17.

84 Fields, "Anti-Communism and Social Justice," 84.

85 Daniel Noonan tends to aggrandize Fulton Sheen (for better or worse) while ignoring the larger context. Anti-communism was hardly novel in Catholicism, as the church itself had already taken a stance against communism, such as with Pius XI's encyclicals. In America, the popular and prolific radio priest Father Coughlin stands out as being the most vocal Catholic anti-communist of his era until being censured in 1942. Though Noonan does concede that Father Coughlin was a prominent figure, he suggests (largely without evidence) that his influence paled in comparison to Sheen's, and that much of his fiery vitriol was meant to be taken "tongue in cheek." See Noonan, *Missionary with a Mike*, 24–5.

86 Sherwood, *Age of Extremes*, 57.

87 Fields, "Anti-Communism and Social Justice," 85–6.

88 Seitz, "Mass-Clock," 929.

89 Timothy Sherwood sums up Pius XI's arguments against communism as being based on spiritual and moral factors, namely that in the ideology of the Soviet Union there was no place for God, and that atheism was effectively promoted like a state religion. Sherwood, *Age of Extremes*, 58. See also Noonan, *Passion of Fulton Sheen*, 51.

90 Crosby, *God, Church, and Flag*, 15.

91 Sherwood, *Age of Extremes*, 55; see also Sherwood, *Age of Extremes*, 62.

92 Sherwood, *Age of Extremes*, 63.

93 See Sheen, *Communism and the Conscience of the West*.

94 *The Observer*, 1 June 1947, uncategorized box, Fulton Sheen Museum Archives, Peoria, Illinois.

95 *The Observer*, 1 June 1947.

96 *Life Is Worth Living*, "Comparison of the Soviet and American Constitution."

97 Patterson, "Cross or the Double-Cross," 47. Similar fears about the potential moral decay of the nation and its vulnerabilities were held by American Catholics during World War II; as John Seitz remarks, "The enemy was not

Germany or Japan, not Nazism or totalitarianism, nor even the lurking menace of communism. The enemy was a [spiritually] wayward America." Seitz, "Mass-Clock," 928.

98 *Life Is Worth Living*, "The Role of Communism and the Role of America."

99 *Life Is Worth Living*, "The Philosophy of Communism."

100 A similar mentality was gradually espoused by Catholic leaders during World War II, where they "framed the problem of [the conflict] not as a matter of geo-politics or justice, but as a challenge to the moral and spiritual authority of the church" all the while "[cherishing] the idea that their tradition offered the country its best hope against a perilous future." Seitz, "Mass-Clock," 929, 938.

101 *Life Is Worth Living*, "The Philosophy of Communism."

102 *Life Is Worth Living*, "Pain and Suffering."

103 David Morgan devotes an entire monograph to reading the works of Warner Sallman, focusing on Sallman's hale and hearty depictions of Christ. Scholars Edward J. Blum and Paul Harvey also notably discuss how Protestant figurations of Christ similarly emphasized images of a healthy and stoic Christ that can be contrasted with Catholic images of presence brought into the nation by the Irish in the nineteenth century. See Morgan, *Icons of American Protestantism*; and Blum and Harvey, *Color of Christ*.

104 *Time*, 14 April 1953, uncategorized box, Fulton Sheen Museum Archives, Peoria, Illinois; see also McNamara, "Argument of Strength," 67.

105 *Life Is Worth Living*, "On the Death of Stalin."

106 *Life Is Worth Living*, "On the Death of Stalin."

107 Numerous Catholic commentators (and more recently, bloggers) have framed Sheen's pronouncement as "prophetic" and taken this as further proof of his saintly character. See, e.g., Charles F. Harvey, "The Virtually Venerable Fulton J Sheen," *Ignatius Insights*, accessed 24 December 2019, www.ignatiusinsight.com /features2006/fultonsheen_bio_nov06.asp (defunct), and Michael Cunningham "Living the Worthy Life – The Devil in the Details," *Catholic365.com*, accessed 24 December 2019, www.catholic365.com/article/10646/living-the-worthy-life-the-devil-is-in-the-details.html.

108 Jeffords, *Hard Bodies*, 5.

109 Jeffords, *Hard Bodies*, 25.

110 For a lengthier study on Hollywood, politics, and in particular Ronald Reagan's intersection between the two, see Vaughn, *Ronald Reagan in Hollywood*.

111 "The Seven Deadly Sins of Our Time." *News Weekly*, 20 October 1952, uncategorized box, Fulton Sheen Museum Archives, Peoria, Illinois.

112 "The New Bishop of Rochester" by Father Henry Atwell, uncategorized box, Fulton Sheen Museum Archives, Peoria, Illinois.

113 Sugrue, "Bishop Sheen Story."

114 Sugrue, "Bishop Sheen Story." For more on the rural/urban divide and narratives emphasizing Sheen as a "farm boy," see chapter 2.

115 There is something to be said about a hardened anti-communist appearing each night on television wearing, for all intents and purposes, a dress made for men. As John Seitz remarks, clerical vestments have the capacity to bring a touch of delicacy to cold or rough environments - but not necessarily in a detrimentally "soft" manner for Catholics. In one of his studies on World War II military chaplains, he observes how Catholic clerical garbs can signal moral hardness through the "imprint of austerity, solemnity, and historical depth" these vestments carry. I would also add that seeing Fulton Sheen in full clerical garb had the capacity to reinforce an aesthetic association between the visual culture of American Catholicism and America's Cold war ideologies. Seitz, "Altars of Ammo," especially 413–16.

116 See chapter 1.

117 Fulton Sheen played golf and tennis in Manhattan's Upper East Side. He also drove an imposing black Cadillac and lived in a gaudy home that was then valued at half a million dollars. He enjoyed what would have might otherwise been a normal existence for a wealthy, young New York City playboy, except for the fact he was a celibate bishop. He was also a scholar and an academic, two things which were far flung from typical conceptions of hard bodily masculinity, but which nevertheless suited his approach emphasizing spiritual and intellectual hardness.

118 Angela Canade and Paul Fisher, "Archbishop Fulton J, Sheen: A Life Crowned by Love," *Twin Circle*, Sunday, 4 June 1978, uncategorized box, Fulton Sheen Museum Archives, Peoria, Illinois.

119 *Twin Circle*, 23 December 1979, uncategorized box, Fulton Sheen Museum Archives, Peoria, Illinois.

120 Paul Hoffman, "Bishop Sheen's Vitality Startles and Delights Rochester," *New York Times*, 6 August 1967, uncategorized box, Fulton Sheen Museum Archives, Peoria, Illinois.

121 George Murphy, *Democrat and Chronicle*, Rochester, 1 December 1969, uncategorized box, Fulton Sheen Museum Archives, Peoria, Illinois.

122 Dumančić, "Hidden in Plain Sight," 5.

123 Patterson, "Cross or the Double-Cross," 52.

124 Sherwood, *Age of Extremes*, 105.

125 Father Emil Kapaun was captured after refusing to retreat, choosing instead to remain with the wounded. His spiritual and bodily hardness led him to become a role model and father figure to his men until he died in a POW camp in 1951 before the war's end. Rausch, "'All Man, All Priest,'" 88–9. For similar observations about World War II military chaplains, see also Seitz "Mass-Clock"; and Seitz, "Altars of Ammo."

126 Jeffords, *Hard Bodies*, 193.

127 Franklin Rausch observes that while anti-communism enabled a space for men to harden themselves against soft enemies, it was not the sole factor leading to this need for hardness. The rising status of women, African Americans, changes in the workplace, and the corporatization of American life were equally guilty of apparently sapping men's vitality. Rausch, "'All Man, All Priest,'" 63.

128 See Kimmel, "Contemporary 'Crisis.'"

## Conclusion

1 Michael R. Heinlein, "A Year Later, Still No Answers on the Delay of Fulton Sheen's Beatification," *Our Sunday Visitor*, 2 December 2020, www.osvnews.com/2020/12/02/a-year-later-still-no-answers-on-the-delay-of-fulton-sheens-beatification/.

2 Tom Dermody, "Naming Street Near Cathedral for Archbishop Sheen Called 'Wonderful Tribute,'" *Boston Pilot*, 10 February 2021, www.thebostonpilot.com/article.asp?ID=189365.

3 See Rausch, "'All Man, All Priest.'"

4 Kevin J. Jones, "Medal of Honor Chaplain Fr. Emil Kapaun's Body Identified as Sainthood Inquiry Continues," *Catholic News Agency*, 5 March 2021, www.catholicnewsagency.com/news/medal-of-honor-chaplain-fr-emil-kapauns-body-identified-as-sainthood-inquiry-continues-46493.

5 Both Dorothy Day and Thomas Merton have open canonization causes. In 2012 Day was elevated to Servant of God, while Merton's cause has yet to make any significant inroads. For Pope Francis's remarks, see Dan Zak, Abby Ohlheiser, and Sarah Pulliam Bailey, "Pope Francis Praised Dorothy Day and Thomas Merton. Here's Who They Were," *Washington Post*, 24 September 2015, www.washingtonpost.com/news/acts-of-faith/wp/2015/09/24/pope-francis-praised-dorothy-day-and-thomas-merton-heres-who-they-were/.

6 See Michelle Boorstein, "Dorothy Day Was A Radical. Now Many People Want the Vatican to Make Her A Saint," *Washington Post*, 28 January 2020, www.washingtonpost.com/religion/2020/01/28/being-communist-socialist-anarchist-sympathizer-once-made-dorothy-day-radical-now-many-want-vatican-make-her-saint/. See also Klejment, "Dorothy Day and César Chávez."

7 See Clooney, "Thomas Merton's Deep Chrisian Learning"; and Gleeson, "'Meditation with Fireflies.'"

8 As discussed in chapter 1, my use of the term *auto-hagiography* differs from its classical usages. Please see chapter 1 for the full discussion.

9 Vatican II and the period since have seen an increased interest in "normal" saints by the popes canonizing them. The cause for John Neumann, a Redemptorist priest and bishop of Philadelphia, had stalled somewhat before

the council owing to the difficulties in showing that he had lived a life of "heroic" rather than ordinary virtues. However, with the changes in the air, what had once been a liability soon became a quality and he was canonized in 1977. Cummings, *Saint of Our Own*, 173–5. A similar mood can perhaps be read in Sheen's autobiography, with his emphasis on his own ordinariness, as discussed in chapter 1.

10 Typically, and historically, to be canonized as a saint, the candidate is required to have performed at least two miracles demonstrated to have been such by the cause and investigators at the Congregation. However, candidates who have become beatified may only require a single miracle, depending on the reasons for which they were beatified. This could include the founding of a religious order or other acts deemed to have been greatly meritorious by either the Sacred College of Cardinals or the Congregation.

# Bibliography

## Archival Collections

Digital Archive, Papers of John F. Kennedy. Presidential Papers. President's Office Files. John F. Kennedy Presidential Library and Museum, Boston, Massachusetts.

From the Vault. Voices from Wheaton Archives & Special Collections, Wheaton, Illinois.

Fulton J. Sheen Collection. News Clippings, 1950–59. Catholic University of America, Washington, District of Columbia.

Fulton J. Sheen Collection. News Clippings, 1970–79. Catholic University of America, Washington, District of Columbia.

Uncategorized box. Fulton Sheen Museum Archives, Peoria, Illinois.

## Periodicals and Magazines

*ABC News*. New York City, New York.

*Alternate Ending*. www.alternateending.com/.

*America*. New York City, New York.

*Boston Pilot*. Braintree, Massachusetts.

*Catholic News Agency*. Denver, Colorado.

*Catholic Post*. Peoria, Illinois.

*Catholic Register*. Toronto, Ontario.

*Catholic365*. www.catholic365.com/.

*Christianity Today*. Carol Stream, Illinois.

*City Journal*. New York City, New York.

*CNBC*. Englewood Cliffs, New Jersey.

*Crux*. Boston, Massachusetts.

*Damn Catholic*. https://damncatholic.com/.

*Democrat and Chronicle*. Rockaway, New Jersey.

*Irish Central*. New York City, New York.
*Los Angeles Times*. Los Angeles, California.
*MacGuffin*. https://macguff.in/.
*Mel Magazine*. Marina del Ray, California.
*National Catholic Register*. Irondale, Alabama.
*National Catholic Reporter*. Kansas City, Missouri.
*NBC News*. New York City, New York.
*New York Times*. New York City, New York.
*Numbers*. www.the-numbers.com/.
*Our Sunday Visitor*. Huntingdon, Indiana.
*Peoria Journal Star*. Peoria, Illinois.
*Politico*. Arlington County, Virginia.
*Screen Rant*. Montreal, Quebec.
*Seattle Times*. Seattle, Washington.
*Tampa Bay Times*. St Petersburg, Florida.
*Time*. New York City, New York.
*Wanderer*. White Bear Lake, Minnesota.
*Washington Post*. Washington, District of Columbia.

## Secondary Scholarship

Abelman, Robert, and Kimberly Neuendorf. "Themes and Topics in Religious Television Programming." *Review of Religious Research* 29, no. 2 (December 1987): 152–74.

Alpion, Gëzim. *Mother Teresa: Saint or Celebrity*. London: Routledge, 2006.

Alpion, Gëzim. *Mother Teresa: The Saint and Her Nation*. New Deli: Bloomsbury India, 2020.

Alpion, Gëzim. "Why Are Modern Spiritual Icons Absent in Celebrity Studies? The Role of Intermediaries in Enhancing Mother Teresa's Advocacy in India and Australia Prior to the 1979 Nobel Peace Prize." *Celebrity Studies* 11, no. 2 (2020): 221–36.

Anderson, Emma. *The Death and Afterlife of the North American Martyrs*. Cambridge, MA: Harvard University Press, 2013.

Anderson, Eric. *Inclusive Masculinity: The Changing Nature of Masculinities*. London: Routledge, 2009.

Anderson, J.L. "'You're a Bigger Man': Technology and Agrarian Masculinity in Postwar America." *Agricultural History* 94, no. 1 (Winter 2020): 1–23.

Athanasius. *Life of Antony*. Translated by Carolinne White. London: Penguin Books, 1998.

Atkinson, Clarissa W. *Mystic and Pilgrim: The Book and the World of Margery Kempe*. Ithaca, NY: Cornell University Press, 1983.

Augustine of Hippo. *Confessions*. Translated by J.G. Pilkington. Edinburgh: T. & T. Clark, 1886.

Avella, Steven M. "Catholicism in the Twentieth-Century American West: The Next Frontier." *Catholic Historical Review* 97, no. 2 (April 2011): 219–49.

Bacheci, Kimberly. "Our Icons: Ourselves. Britney Spears, Justin Timberlake, Kevin Federline, and the Construction of Whiteness in a Post-Race America." *Celebrity Studies* 6, no. 2 (2015): 164–77.

Baker, Kelly J. *Gospel According to the Klan: The KKK's Appeal to Protestant American, 1915–1930*. Lawrence: University of Kansas Press, 2011.

Bartlett, Robert. *Why Can the Dead Do Such Great Things? Saints and Worshippers from the Martyrs to the Reformation*. Princeton, NJ: Princeton University Press, 2013.

Barr, Rebecca Anne, Sean Brady, and Jane McGaughey. "Ireland and Masculinities in History: An Introduction." In *Ireland and Masculinities in History*, edited by Rebecca Anne Barr, Sean Brady, and Jane McGaughey, 1–18. Cham, Switzerland: Palgrave Macmillan, 2019.

Becker, Christine. "Televising Film Stardom in the 1950s." *Framework: The Journal of Cinema and Media* 26, no. 2 (Fall 2005): 5–21.

Bekkering, Denis J. *American Televangelism and Participatory Cultures: Fans, Brands, and Play with Religious "Fakes*." Cham, Switzerland: Palgrave Macmillan, 2018.

Berinsky, Adam J., and Gabriel S. Lenz. "Red Scare? Revisiting McCarthy's Influence on 1950s Elections." *Public Opinion Quarterly* 78, no. 2 (Summer 2014): 369–91.

Besnier, Niko, and Susan Brownell. "Sport, Modernity, and the Body." *Annual Review of Anthropology* 41 (2012): 443–59.

Beynon, John. *Masculinities and Culture*. Buckingham, UK: Open University Press, 2002.

Bianchi, Eugene C. "John XIII, Vatican II, and American Catholicism." *Annals of the American Academy of Political and Social Science* 480 (July 1985): 63–74.

Bieter, John. "'Lay People Can Teach': Rural Life, Edwin O'Hara, and the Confraternity of Christian Doctrine, 1920–1960." *American Catholic Studies* 120, no. 2 (Summer, 2009): 53–69.

Blum, Edward J., and Paul Harvey. *The Color of Christ: The Son of God and the Saga of Race in America*. Chapel Hill: University of North Carolina Press, 2012.

Bly, Robert. *Iron John: A Book About Men*. Reading, MA: Addison-Wesely, 1990.

Bolton, Lucy. "Beautiful Penitent Whore: The Desecrated Celebrity of Mary Magdalene." *Celebrity Studies* 11, no. 1 (2020); 25–42.

Boone, Joseph A., and Nancy J. Vickers. "Celebrity Rites." *PMLA* 126, no. 4 (October 2011): 900–11.

Bourdieu, Pierre. "How Can One Be a Sports Fan?" In *The Cultural Studies Reader*, edited by S. During, 427–40. London: Routledge, 1999.

Bovée, David S. *The Church and the Land: The National Catholic Rural Life Conference and American Society, 1923–2007*. Washington, DC: Catholic University of America Press, 2010.

Bovée, David S. "The Middle Way: The National Catholic Rural Life Conference and Rural Issues of the 20th and 21st Centuries." *American Journal of Economics and Sociology* 75, no. 3 (May 2016): 762–808.

Bowler, Kate. *Blessed: A History of the American Prosperity Gospel.* Oxford: Oxford University Press, 2013.

Brannon, Robert. "The Male Sex Role: Our Culture's Blueprint of Manhood and What It's Done for Us Lately." In *The Forty-Nine Percent Majority: The Male Sex Role*, edited by Deborah Sarah David and Robert Brannon, 1–45. Reading, MA: Addington-Wesley, 1977.

Brinkley, Douglas, and Julie M. Fenster. *Parish Priest: Father Michael McGivney and American Catholicism*. New York: HarperCollins, 2006.

Brook, Eric. "Writing the Holy Image: The Relationship Between Hagiography and Iconography." *International Journal of the Image* 1, no. 1 (2011): 13–20.

Brown, Peter. *The Cult of the Saints: Its Rise and Function in Latin Christianity.* Chicago: University of Chicago Press, 1981.

Brownlow, Kevin. "When the Irish Ruled Hollywood." *Post-Script* 32, no. 3 (Summer 2013): 97–102.

Bruscino, Thomas A. *A Nation Forged in War: How World War II Taught Americans to Get Along*. Knoxville: University of Tennessee Press, 2014.

Calvert, Dave. "Similar Hats on Similar Heads: Uniformity and Alienation at the Rat Pack's Summit Conference of Cool." *Popular Music* 24, no. 1 (2015): 1–21.

Canny, Nicholas P. "The Ideology of English Colonization: From Ireland to America." *William and Mary Quarterly* 30, no. 4 (October 1973): 575–98.

Cantor, Muriel G. *Prime-Time Television Content and Control.* London: SAGE Publications, 1980.

Casey, Shaun A. *The Making of a Catholic President: Kennedy vs. Nixon 1960*. Oxford University Press, 2009.

Carey, Patrick W. "American Catholic Ecumenism on the Eve of Vatican II, 1940–1962." *U.S. Catholic Historian* 28, no. 2 (Spring 2010): 1–17.

Carrigan, T., B. Connell, and J. Lee, "Towards A New Sociology of Masculinity." *Theory and Society* 14, no. 5 (1985): 551–604.

Choi, Hoon. "Brothers in Arms and Brothers in Christ? The Military and the Catholic Church as Sources for Modern Korean Masculinity." *Journal of the Society of Christian Ethics* 32, no. 2 (Fall–Winter 2012): 75–92.

Clooney, Francis X. "Thomas Merton's Deep Christian Learning Across Religious Borders." *Buddhist-Christian Studies* 37 (2017): 49–64.

Coates, Dennis C. "Weaponization of Sports: The Battle for World Influence Through Sporting Success." *Independent Review* 22, no. 2 (Fall 2017): 215–21.

Connell, R.W. "Hegemonic Masculinity and Emphasized Femininity." In *Gender and Power: Society, the Person, and Sexual Politics*, 183–88. London: Allen and Unwin, 1987.

Connell, R.W. *Masculinities*. Oakland: University of California Press, 1993.

Connell, R.W., and James W. Messerschmidt. "Hegemonic Masculinity: Rethinking the Concept." *Gender and Society* 19, no. 6 (December 2005): 829–59.

Conniff, C.G. *The Bishop Sheen Story*. London: Fawcett, 1953.

Cooper, Jerry C. *To Bataan and Back: The World War II Diary of Major Thomas Dooley*. College Station: Texas A&M University Press, 2016.

Cressler, Matthew J. "Black Catholic Conversion and the Burden of Black Religion." *Journal of Africana Religions* 2, no. 2 (2014): 280–87.

Cressler, Matthew J. "Black Power, Vatican II, and the Emergence of Black Catholic Liturgies." *U.S. Catholic Historian* 32, no. 4 (Fall 2014): 99–119.

Crosby, Donald F. "The Catholic Bishops and Senator Joseph McCarthy." *Records of the American Catholic Historical Society of Philadelphia* 86, nos 1–4 (March–December 1975): 132–48.

Crosby, Donald F. *God, Church, and Flag*. Chapel Hill: University of North Carolina Press, 1978.

Cross, John. *Let's Take the Hard Road: A Book on Strength for Young Men*. Kenosha, WI: Cross, 1946.

Crotty, Ken. "Bishop Sheen's Devotions Recalled." *Boston Post*, 9 May 1953. News Clippings, 1950–59, Catholic University of American Archives, Washington, DC.

Cummings, Kathleen Sprows. *A Saint of Our Own: How the Quest for a Holy Hero Helped Catholics Become American*. Chapel Hill: University of North Carolina Press, 2019.

Cuordileone, K. A. "'Politics in an Age of Anxiety': Cold War Political Culture and the Crisis in American Masculinity, 1949–1960." *Journal of American History* 87, no. 2 (September 2000): 515–45.

Curran, Emmett. *Shaping American Catholicism: Maryland and New York, 1850–1915*. Washington, DC: Catholic University of America Press, 2012.

Curtiz, Michael, dir. *Angels with Dirty Faces*. Burbank, CA: Warner Bros., 1938.

Dawidowicz, Lucy S. "Religion in the 1960 Presidential Campaign." *American Jewish Year Book* 63 (1961): 111–28.

DeAngelis, Michael, and Mary Desjardins. "Introduction." *Celebrity Studies* 8, no. 4 (2017): 489–92.

Dearinger, Ryan. *The Filth of Progress: Immigrants, Americans, and the Building of Canals and Railroads in the West*. Oakland: University of California Press, 2015.

den Berg, Marguerite, and Claartje L. ter Hoeven. "Madonna as Symbol of Reflexive Modernisation." *Celebrity Studies* 4, no. 2 (2013): 144–52.

Diekema, David A. "Televangelism and the Mediated Charismatic Relationship." *Social Science Journal* 28, no. 2 (1991): 143–62.

Doherty, Thomas. *Cold War, Cool Medium*. New York: Columbia University Press, 2005.

Doherty, Thomas. *Hollywood's Censor: Joseph I. Breen and the Production Code Administration*. New York: Columbia University Press, 2009.

Doherty, Thomas. *Pre-Code Hollywood: Sex, Immorality, and Insurrection in American Cinema, 1930–1934*. New York: Columbia University Press, 1999.

Dolan, Jay P. *The American Catholic Experience: A History from Colonial Times to the Present*. New York: Image Books, 1985.

Dolan, Jay P. "Catholics in the Midwest." University of Notre Dame. https://www3.nd.edu/~jdolan/midwest.html (defunct). Accessed 28 July 2020.

Dolan, Jay P. *In Search of American Catholicism*. Oxford: Oxford University Press, 2002.

Dowd, Christopher. *The Irish and the Origins of American Popular Culture*. New York: Routledge, 2018.

Du Mez, Kristin Kobes. *Jesus and John Wayne: How White Evangelicals Corrupted a Faith and Fractured a Nation*. New York: Liveright, 2020.

Dumančić, Marko. "Hidden in Plain Sight: The Histories of Gender and Sexuality During the Cold War." In *Sexuality, Gender, and the Cold War: A Global Perspective*, edited by Philip E. Muehlenbeck, 1–11. Nashville: Vanderbilt University Press, 2017.

Duvall, Spring-Serenity, and Nicole Heckemeyer. "#BlackLivesMatter: Black Celebrity Hashtag Activism and the Discursive Formation of a Social Movement." *Celebrity Studies* 9, no. 3 (2018): 391–408.

Dye, Ryan D. "Leo R. Ward, C.S.C.: Irish America's Rural Man of Letters." *American Catholic Studies* 118, no. 4 (Winter 2007): 19–35.

Ellis, John Tracy. *American Catholicism*. Chicago: University of Chicago Press, 1965.

Ellwood, Robert S. *The Fifties Spiritual Marketplace: American Religion in a Decade of Conflict*. New Brunswick, NJ: Rutgers University Press, 1997.

Emiliantseva, Ekaterina. "Russian Sport and the Challenges of Its Recent Historiography." *Journal of Sport History* 38, no. 3 (Fall 2011): 361–72.

Farrelly, Maura Jane. *Papist Patriots: The Making of an American Catholic Identity*. New York: Oxford University Press, 2011.

Fields, Kathleen Riley. "Anti-Communism and Social Justice: The Double-Edged Sword of Fulton Sheen." *Records of the American Catholic Historical Society of Philadelphia* 96, nos 1–4 (March–December 1985): 83–91.

Fisher, James T. *The Catholic Counterculture in America, 1933–1962*. Chapel Hill: University of North Carolina Press, 1989

Fisher, James T. *Dr. America: The Lives of Thomas A. Dooley, 1927–1961.* Amherst: University of Massachusetts Press, 1997.

Fisher, James T. *On the Irish Waterfront: The Crusader, the Movie, and the Soul of the Port of New York.* Ithaca, NY: Cornell University Press, 2009.

Fleegler, Robert L. "'Forget All Differences Until the Forces of Freedom Are Triumphant': The World War II-Era Quest for Ethnic and Religious Tolerance." *Journal of American Ethnic History* 27, no. 2 (Winter 2008): 59–84.

Forsthoefel, Thomas. "Merton and the Axes of Dialogue." *Buddhist-Christian Studies* 37 (2017): 65–72.

Freeman, Charles. *Holy Bones, Holy Dust: How Relics Shaped the History of Medieval Europe.* New Haven, CT: Yale University Press, 2011.

Friedman, Andrea. "The Smearing of Joe McCarthy: The Lavender Scare, Gossip, and Cold War Politics." *American Quarterly* 57, no. 4 (December 2005): 1105–29.

Genzel, Glen. "Pride, Wrath, Glee, and Fear: Emotional Responses to Senator Joseph McCarthy in the Catholic Press, 1950–1954." *American Catholic Studies* 120, no. 2 (2009): 27 52.

Giddins, Gary. *Bing Crosby: Swinging on a Star: The War Years, 1940–1946.* Little, Brown, 2018). Kindle.

Gilbert, James. *Men in the Middle: Searching for Masculinity in the 1950s.* Chicago: University of Chicago Press, 2005.

Gleeson, Denis "'Meditation with Fireflies': An Introduction to Thomas Merton." *Studies: An Irish Quarterly Review* 102, no. 405 (Spring 2013): 43–52.

Glazer, Nathan, Anthony Lewis, and Sam Tanenhaus. "'Have You No Sense of Decency?': McCarthyism 50 Years Later." *Bulletin of the American Academy of Arts and Sciences* 57, no. 3 (Spring 2004): 21–7.

Goldway, Terry. *Machine Made: Tammany Hall and The Creation of Modern American Politics.* New York: Liveright, 2014.

Graus, Andrea. "A Visit to Remember: Stigmata and Celebrity at the Turn of the Twentieth Century." *Journal of the Social History Society* 14, no. 1 (2017): 55–72.

Greenspan, Kate. "The Autohagiographical Traditional in Medieval Women's Devotional Writing." *Biography Studies* 6, no 2 (1991): 157–68.

Hadden, Jeffrey K. "The Rise and Fall of American Televangelism." *Annals of the American Academy of Political and Social Science* 527 (May 1993): 113–30.

Haden, Kyle E. "Anti-Catholicism in U.S. History: A Proposal for a New Methodology." *American Catholic Studies* 124, no. 4 (Winter 2013): 27–45.

Hall, Stuart. "What Is This 'Black' in Black Popular Culture?" *Social Justice* 20, no. 1 (Spring–Summer 1993): 104–14.

Hamlin, Christopher, and John T. McGreevy. "The Greening of America, Catholic Style, 1930–1950. *Environmental History* 11, no.3 (July 2006): 464–99.

Harris, Daniel. "Celebrity Clothing." *Salmagundi* 168–9 (Fall 2010–Winter 2011): 233–47.

Heinich, Nathalie. "La consommation de la célébrité." *L'Année sociologique* 61, no. 1 (2011): 103–23.

Heinich, Nathalie. "Des limites de l'analogie religieuse: L'exemple de la célébrité." *Archives de sciences sociales des religions* 57, no. 158 (April–June 2012): 157–77.

Henderson, Amy. "Media and the Rise of Celebrity Culture." OAH *Magazine of History* 6, no. 4 (Spring 1992): 49–54.

Hendrickson, Brett. *Border Medicine: A Transcultural History of Mexican American* Curanderismo. New York: NYU Press, 2014.

Hitchcock, Alfred, dir. *I Confess*. Burbank, CA: Warner Bros., 1953.

Hill, George W., dir. *The Callahans and the Murphys*. Beverly Hills: Metro-Goldwyn-Mayer, 1927.

Hogan, Michael J. *The Marshall Plan: America, Britain, and the Reconstruction of Western Europe, 1947–1952*. Cambridge: Cambridge University Press, 1987.

Holmes, Katie. "Making Masculinity: Land, Body, Image in Australia's Mallee Country." RCC *Perspectives* 2, no. 2 (2017): 39–48.

Holt, Andrew. "Between Warrior and Priest: The Creation of a New Masculine Identity During the Crusades." In *Negotiating Clerical Identities: Priests, Monks and Masculinity in the Middle Ages*, edited by Jennifer D. Thibodeaux, 182–203. London: Palgrave Macmillian, 2010.

Horrocks, Roger. *Male Myths and Icons: Masculinity in Popular Culture*. New York: St Martin's Press, 1995.

Horsfield, Peter G. "'And Now a Word from Our Sponsor': Religious Programs on American Television." *Revue française d'études américaines*, no. 12 (Octobre 1981): 259–74.

Hudnut-Beulmer, James. *Looking for God in the Suburbs: The Religion of the American Dream and Its Critics, 1945–1965*. New Brunswick, NJ: Rutgers University Press, 1994.

Hughey, Michael W. "Internal Contradictions of Televangelism: Ethical Quandaries of That Old Time Religion in a Brave New World." *International Journal of Politics, Culture, and Society* 4, no. 1 (1990): 31–47.

Hunt, Thomas M. "American Sport Policy and the Cultural Cold War: The Lyndon B. Johnson Presidential Years." *Journal of Sport History* 33, no. 3 (Fall 2006): 273–97.

Ignatiev, Noel. *How the Irish Became White*. New York: Routledge, 1995.

Jeffords, Susan. *Hard Bodies: Hollywood Masculinity in the Reagan Era*. New Brunswick, NJ: Rutgers University Press, 1994.

Jerslev, Anne, and Line Nybro Petersen, "Introduction: Ageing Celebrities,

Ageing Fans, and Ageing Narratives in Popular Media Culture." *Celebrity Studies* 9, no. 2 (2018): 157–65.
Karras, Ruth Mazo. *From Boys to Men: Formations of Masculinity in Late Medieval Europe*. Philadelphia: University of Pennsylvania Press, 2003.
Kazan, Elia, dir. *On the Waterfront*. New York: Horizon Pictures. 1954.
Kelleher, Patricia. "Class and Irish Catholic Masculinity in Antebellum America: Young Men on the Make in Chicago." *Journal of American Ethnic History* 28, no.5 (Summer 2009): 7–42.
Kercher, Stephen E. "Joseph McCarthy: A Modern Tragedy." *History News* 58, no. 2 (Spring 2003): 27–8.
Kimmel, M. "The Contemporary 'Crisis' of Masculinity in Historical Perspective." In *The Making of Masculinities: The New Men's Studies*, edited by Harry Brody, 121–54. London: Allen and Unwin, 1987.
Kimmel, M. *Manhood in America: A Cultural History*. Oxford: Oxford University Press, 2006.
Kitchen, John. *Saints' Lives and the Rhetoric of Gender*. Oxford: Oxford University Press, 1998.
Kleinberg, Aviad. *Flesh Made Word: Saints' Stories and the Western Imagination*. Cambridge, MA: Belknap Press, 2008.
Klejment, Anne, "Dorothy Day and César Chávez: American Catholic Lives in Nonviolence." *U.S. Catholic Historian* 29, no. 3 (Summer 2011): 67–90.
Krohn, Franklin B. "The Language of Television Preachers: The Marketing of Religion." *ETC: A Review of General Semantics* 38, no. 1 (Spring 1981): 51–63.
Krueger, Derek. "Hagiography as an Ascetic Practice in the Early Christian East." *Journal of Religion* 79, no. 2 (1999): 216–33.
Lafrance, Marc. "Building a Body, Building a Life: Men, Masculinity and the Birth of Bodybuilding Magazines in Montreal." In *Canadian Men and Masculinities: Historical and Contemporary Perspectives*, edited by C.J. Greig and W.J. Martino, 345–60. Toronto: Canadian Scholars' Press, 2012.
Lee, Katja. "Reading Celebrity Autobiographies." *Celebrity Studies* 5, nos 1–2 (2014): 87–89.
Lewis, Bradley and William Berle. *My Father, Uncle Miltie*. Fort Lee, NJ: Barricade Books, 1999.
*Life Is Worth Living*. "Angels." DuMont Network. Written by Fulton Sheen, 1953.
*Life Is Worth Living*. "Comparison of the Soviet and American Constitution." DuMont Network Written by Fulton J. Sheen, 1953.
*Life Is Worth Living*. "How to Compare World Religion." DuMont Network. Written by Fulton Sheen, 1953.

*Life Is Worth Living*. "On the Death of Stalin." DuMont Network. Written by Fulton J. Sheen, 1953.

*Life Is Worth Living*. "Pain and Suffering." DuMont Network. Written by Fulton J. Sheen, 1954.

*Life Is Worth Living*. "The Philosophy of Communism." DuMont Network. Written by Fulton J. Sheen, 1953.

*Life Is Worth Living*. "The Role of Communism and the Role of America." DuMont Network. Written by Fulton J. Sheen, 1953.

*Life Is Worth Living*. "Signs of our Times." DuMont Network. Written by Fulton Sheen, 1954.

*Life Is Worth Living*. "Three Greatest Confessions in History." ABC. Written by Fulton Sheen, 1957.

*Life Is Worth Living*. "The Training of Children." ABC. Written by Fulton Sheen, 1956.

Lynch, Christopher. *Selling Catholicism: Bishop Sheen and the Power of Television*. Lexington: University Press of Kentucky, 1998.

Maldonado-Estrada, Alyssa. *Lifeblood of the Parish: Men and Catholic Devotion in Williamsburg, Brooklyn*. New York: NYU Press, 2020.

Marcus, Sheldon. *Father Coughlin: The Tumultuous Life of the Priest of the Little Flower*. Boston: Little, Brown, 1973.

Marlett, Jeffrey. "Harvesting an Overlooked Freedom: The Anti-Urban Vision of American Catholic Agrarianism, 1920–1950." *U.S. Catholic Historian* 16, no. 4 (Fall 1998): 88–108.

Marlett, Jeffrey. "Strangers in Our Midst: Catholics in Rural America." In *Roman Catholicism in the United States*, edited by Margaret M. McGuiness and James T. Fisher, 86–107. New York: Fordham University Press, 2019.

Marshall, P. David. "The Promotion and Presentation of the Self: Celebrity as Market of Presentational Media." *Celebrity Studies* 1, no. 1 (2010): 35–48.

Martinez, Anne M. *Catholic Borderlands: Mapping Catholicism onto American Empire, 1905–1935*. Lincoln: University of Nebraska Press, 2014.

Massa, Mark S. "A Catholic for President? John F. Kennedy and the 'Secular' Theology of the Houston Speech, 1960." *Journal of Church and State* 39, no. 2 (Spring 1997): 297–317.

Massa, Mark S. *Catholics and American Culture: Fulton Sheen, Dorothy Day, and the Notre Dame Football Team*. New York: Herder and Herder, 1999.

Matovina, Timothy. "Remapping American Catholicism." *U.S. Catholic Historian* 28, no. 4 (Fall 2010): 31–72.

Matovina, Timothy. *Latino Catholicism: Transformation in America's Largest Church*. Princeton, NJ: Princeton University Press, 2012.

Matusow, Allen J. *Joseph R. McCarthy*. Inglewood, CA: Prentice-Hall, 1970.

McAvoy, Thomas T. "American Catholicism and the *Aggiornamento*." *Review of Politics* 30, no. 3 (July 1968): 27–91.

McCarraher, Eugene D. "The Saint in the Gray Flannel Suit: The Professional-Managerial Class, 'The Layman,' and America-Catholic-Religious Culture, 1945–1965." *U.S. Catholic Historian* 15, no. 3 (Summer 1997): 99–118.

McCarey, Leo, dir. *Going My Way*. Los Angeles: Paramount, 1944.

McCarey, Leo, dir. *The Bells of St. Mary's*. New York City: Rainbow Productions, 1945.

McGreevy, John. *Parish Boundaries: Catholic Encounters with Race*. Chicago: University of Chicago Press, 1998.

McGreevy, John. *Catholicism and American Freedom*. New York: Norton, 2004.

McKenna, Mark. "Sylvester Stallone and The Economics of the Aging Film Actor." *Celebrity Studies* 10, no. 4 (2019): 489–503.

McLoughlin, William G. *Revivals, Awakenings, and Reforms*. Chicago: Chicago University Press, 1980.

McNamara, Patrick J. "'The Argument of Strength Justly and Righteously Employed': Edmund A. Walsh, Catholic Anticommunism, and American Foreign Policy, 1945–1952." *U.S. Catholic Historian* 22, no. 4 (Fall 2004): 57–77.

McNamara, Patrick J. "McCarthy and McCarthyism." *American Catholic Studies* 116, no. 2 (Summer 2005): 85–88.

McNamara, Patrick J. "Russia, Rome, and Recognition: American Catholics and Anticommunism in the 1920s." *U.S. Catholic Historian* 24, no. 2 (Spring 2006): 71–88.

Merrill, Dennis. "The Truman Doctrine: Containing Communism and Modernity." *Presidential Studies Quarterly* 36, no. 1 (2006): 27–37.

Meyer, Stephen. *Manhood On the Line: Working-Class Masculinities in the American Heartland*. Urbana: University of Illinois Press, 2016.

Milward, Alan S. *The Reconstruction of Western Europe, 1945–1951*. Berkeley: University of California Press, 2006.

Miscamble, Wilson D. *American Priest: The Ambitious Life and Conflicted Legacy of Notre Dame's Father Ted Hesburgh*. New York: Image Books, 2019.

Moldea, Dan. *Dark Victory: Ronald Reagan, MCA and the Mob*. New York: Viking Press, 1986.

Moller, Michael. "Exploiting Patterns: A Critique of Hegemonic Masculinity." *Journal of Gender Studies* 16, no. 3. (2007): 263–76.

Moore, Emund A. *A Catholic Runs for President: The Campaign of 1928*. New York: Ronald Press, 1956.

Morgan, David. *Icons of American Protestantism: The Art of Warner Sallman*. New Haven, CT: Yale University Press, 1996.

Moss, Mark. *The Media and Models of Masculinity*. Lanham, MD: Lexington Books, 2012.

Mosse, George L. *The Image of Man*. Oxford: Oxford University Press, 1996.

Murphy, George. *Democrat and Chronicle*. Rochester, 11 December 1969, uncategorized box, Fulton Sheen Museum Archives, Peoria, Illinois.

Neary, Timothy B. *Crossing Parish Boundaries: Race, Sports, and Catholic Youth in Chicago, 1914–1954*. Chicago: University of Chicago Press, 2016.

Newman, Mark. "The Marching Priest: The Civil Rights and Labor Activism of Father Sherril Smith During the 1950s and 1960s." *Southwestern Historical Quarterly* 124, no. 3 (January 2021): 300–24.

Noonan, Daniel P. *Missionary with a Mike: The Bishop Sheen Story*. New York: Pageant Press, 1968.

Noonan, Daniel P. *The Passion of Fulton Sheen*. New York: Dodd Mead, 1972.

Nugent, Joseph. "The Sword and the Prayerbook: Ideals of Authentic Irish Manliness." *Victorian Studies* 50, no. 4 (Summer 2008): 587–613.

Nugent, Vincent J. "He Strikes from the Pulpit." *Catholic Post*, 2 October 1977. News Clippings, 1970–79, Catholic University of American Archives, Washington, DC.

Nyman, Jopi. *Men Alone: Masculinity, Individualism, and Hard-Boiled Fiction*. Amsterdam: Brill, 1997.

O'Brien, David J. *The Renewal of American Catholicism*. Mahwah, NJ: Paulist Press, 1974.

Orsi, Robert A. *Between Heaven and Earth: The Religious Worlds People Make and the Scholars Who Study Them*. Princeton, NJ: Princeton University Press, 2005.

Orsi, Robert A. *History and Presence*. Cambridge, MA: The Belknap Press of Harvard University Press, 2016.

Orsi, Robert A. *The Madonna of 115th Street: Faith and Community in Italian Harlem, 1880–1950*. New Haven, CT: Yale University Press, 1985.

Orsi, Robert A. *Thank You, St. Jude: Women's Devotion to the Patron Saint of Hopeless Causes*. New Haven, CT: Yale University Press, 1996.

Orwig, Sarah Forbes. "Business Ethics and the Protestant Spirit: How Norman Vincent Peale Shaped the Religious Values of American Business Leaders." *Journal of Business Ethics* 38, nos 1–2 (June 2002): 81–89.

Oshinsky, David. *A Conspiracy So Immense: The World of Joe McCarthy*. Oxford: Oxford University Press, 2005.

O'Toole, James M. *The Faithful: A History of Catholics in America*. Cambridge, MA: Belknap Press, 2008.

Parker, Everett C, David W. Barr, and Dallas W. Smythe. *The Television-Radio Audience and Religion*. New York City: Harper, 1955.

Patterson, James M. "The Cross or the Double Cross: Roman Catholicism, Anti-Communist and the Political Theology of Venerable Fulton Sheen." *Perspectives on Political Science* 45, no. 1 (2016): 47–58.

Payne, Robert. *The Fathers of the Western Church*. New York: Viking Press, 1951.

Pehl, Matthew. "The Remaking of the Catholic Working Class: Detroit, 1919–1945." *Religion and American Culture: A Journal of Interpretation* 19, no. 1 (Winter 2009): 37–67.

Pelzer, Danté L. "Creating a New Narrative: Reframing Black Masculinity for College Men." *Journal of Negro Education*, 85, no. 1 (Winter 2016): 16–27.

Pope, Barbara Corrado. "A Heroine Without Heroics: The Little Flower of Jesus and Her Times." *Church History* 57, no. 1 (March 1988): 46–60.

Putney, Clifford. *Muscular Christianity: Manhood and Sports in Protestant America, 1880–1920*. Cambridge, MA: Harvard University Press, 2009.

Radano, John A. "Contributions of Americans to Vatican Ecumenism: The Critical Period, 1960–1978." *U.S. Catholic Historian* 28, no. 2 (Spring 2010): 19–38.

Rausch, Franklin. "'All Man, All Priest': Father Emil Kapaun, Religion, Masculinity, and the Korean War." *Journal of Korean Religions* 6, no. 2 (October 2015): 61–92.

Reeves, Thomas C. *America's Bishop: The Life and Times of Fulton J. Sheen*. New York: Encounter Books, 2002.

Rhodes, Gary D. "Irish-American Film Audience, 1915–1930." *Post-Script* 32, no. 3 (Summer 2013): 70–96.

Riley, Kathleen L. *Fulton J. Sheen: An American Catholic Response to the Twentieth Century*. New York: Alba House, 2004.

Robson, Mark, dir. *Edge of Doom*. New York City: RKO, 1950.

Roediger, David. *The Wages of Whiteness: Race and the Making of the American Working Class*. New York: Verso Books, 1991.

Rosenthal, Michele. "'This Nation Under God': The Broadcast and Film Commission of the National Council of Churches and the New Medium of Television." *Communication Review* 18 (May 2009): 347–71.

Rotundo, E. Anthony. *American Manhood: Transformations in Masculinity from the Revolution to the Modern Era*. New York: Basic Books, 1993.

Scheibel, Will. "Marilyn Monroe, 'Sex Symbol': Film Performance, Gender Politics and 1950s Hollywood Celebrity." *Celebrity Studies* 4, no. 1 (2013): 4–13.

Schrock, Douglas, and Michael Schwalbe. "Men, Masculinity, and Manhood Acts." *Annual Review of Sociology* 25 (2009): 277–95.

Seitz, John C. "Altars of Ammo: Catholic Material and the Visual Culture of World War II." *Material Religion: The Journal of Objects, Art and Belief* 15, no. 4 (2019): 401–32.

Seitz, John C. "The Lives of Priests." *American Catholic Studies* 127, no. 2 (Summer 2016): 18–23.

Seitz, John C. "The Mass-Clock and the Spy: The Catholicization of World War II." *Church History* 83, no. 4 (December 2014): 924–56.

Seitz, John C. "'What better place?': Refiguring Priesthood at St. John's Seminary, Boston, 1965–1970." *U.S. Catholic Historian* 33, no. 2 (January 2015): 49–82.

Shafer, Stephen C. "From Crooner to American Icon: Caricatures of Bing Crosby from the 1930s to the 1950s." In *Going My Way: Bing Crosby and American Culture*, edited by Ruth Prigozy and Walter Raubicheck, 123–32. Rochester, NY: University of Rochester Press, 2007.

Shannon, Christopher. *Bowery to Broadway: The Irish in Classic Hollywood Cinema*. Scranton, PA: University of Scranton Press, 2010.

Sheen, Fulton J. *Communism and the Conscience of the West*. Indianapolis: Refugee of Sinners Publishing, 1948.

Sheen, Fulton J. *Peace of Soul*. New York: McGraw-Hill, 1949.

Sheen, Fulton J. *Treasure in Clay*. New York: Image Books, 1982.

Shelley, Thomas J. *Fordham, A History of the Jesuit University of New York: 1841–2003*. New York: Fordham University Press, 2016.

Shelley, Thomas J. "'What the Hell Is an Encyclical?': Governor Alfred E. Smith, Charles C. Marshall, Esq., and Father Francis P. Duffy." *U.S. Catholic Historian* 15, no. 2 (Spring 1997): 87–107.

Sherwood, Timothy H. *The Rhetorical Leadership of Fulton J. Sheen, Norman Vincent Peale, and Billy Graham in the Age of Extremes*. Lanham, MD: Lexington Books, 2013.

Slide, Anthony, ed., *The Television Industry: A Historical Dictionary*. New York: Greenwood Press, 1991.

Smith, Erin A. *What Would Jesus Read? Popular Religious Books and Everyday Life in Twentieth-Century America*. Durham, NC: University of North Carolina Press, 2015.

Smith, Seth. "Implementing Vatican II in Two Rural, Southern Parishes." *U.S. Catholic Historian* 30, no. 3 (Summer 2012): 93–114.

Stadick, Anna. "Saint Patrons: The Role of Archives in the Roman Catholic Process of Canonization." *Archival Issues* 24, no. 2 (1999): 123–43.

Starck, Kathleen, and Russell Luyt. "Political Masculinities, Crisis Tendencies, and Social Transition: Toward an Understanding of Change." *Men and Masculinities* 22, no. 13 (June 2018): 431–43.

Strasser, Ulrike. *German Jesuits and Pacific Journeys*. Amsterdam: Amsterdam University Press, 2020.

Sugrue, Francis. "The Bishop Sheen Story." *New York Herald Tribune*, 1959. News Clippings, 1950–59, Catholic University of American Archives, Washington, DC.

Sutton, Matthew Avery. *Aime Semple McPherson and the Resurrection of Christian America*. Cambridge, MA: Harvard University Press, 2007.

Sweedler, Milo. "Autohagiography: The Écrits de Laure." *Dalhousie French Studies* 7 (Summer 2005): 65–73.

Taurog, Norman, dir. *Boys Town*. Burbank, CA: Warner Bros., 1938.

Tentler, Leslie Woodcock. "'God's Representative in Our Midst': Toward a History of the Catholic Diocesan Clergy in the United States." *Church History* (June 1998): 326–49.

Thomas, Sarah. "Celebrity in the 'Twitterverse': History, Authenticity and the Multiplicity of Stardom Situating the 'Newness' of Twitter." *Celebrity Studies* 5, no. 3 (2014): 242–55.

Tunc, Tanfer Emin. "The 'Mad Men' of Nutrition: The Drinking Man's Diet and Mid-Twentieth-Century American Masculinity." *Global Food History* 4, no. 2 (2018): 189–206.

Van Bavel, Jan, and David S. Reher. "The Baby Boom and Its Causes: What We Know and What We Need to Know." *Population and Development Review* 39, no. 2 (2013): 258–88.

Vaugh, Stephen. *Ronald Reagan in Hollywood: Movies and Politics.* Cambridge: Cambridge University Press, 1994.

Wacker, Grant. *America's Pastor: Billy Graham and the Shaping of a Nation.* Cambridge, MA: Belknap Press of Harvard University Press, 2015.

Walsham, Alexandra. "Introduction: Relics and Remains." *Past and Present* 206, no. 5 (2010): 9–36.

Warren, Donald. *Radio Priest: Charles Coughlin, the Father of Hate Radio*. New York: Simon and Schuster, 1996.

Weinstein, David. *The Forgotten Network: DuMont and the Birth of American Television.* Philadelphia: Temple University Press, 2004.

Weinstein, Donald, and Rudolph M. Bell. *Saints and Society: The Two Worlds of Western Christendom, 1000–1700*. Chicago: University of Chicago Press, 1983.

Williams, David. *Saints Alive: Word, Image, and the Enactment in the Lives of Saints.* Montreal: McGill-Queen's University Press, 2010.

Wilson, Tony. *Watching Television: Hermeneutics, Reception and Popular Culture.* Cambridge: Polity Press, 1993.

Zubrzycki, Geneviève. *Beheading the Saint.* Chicago: University of Chicago Press, 2016.

# Index